T0372715

Post-Truth American Politics

David Ricci has written two books on "political stories," providing tne foundations for post-truth democracy. Yet the present book is arguably the most important yet. The author writes that we need stories to make our way in the world. But many stories, say from identity politics, are necessarily false because they are simplifications of some larger reality. Moreover, not all stories are equally false or equally harmful. Some lead to bad outcomes, so we should counter them with other stories leading to better outcomes. In short, stories are a complex and potent form of political power, deserving attention from scholars, journalists, and activists.

David Ricci teaches Political Science at the Hebrew University in Jerusalem. He has analyzed American liberalism and conservatism in several previous books, including *Politics Without Stories: The Liberal Predicament* (2016).

Post-Truth American Politics

False Stories and Current Crises

David Ricci

Hebrew University of Jerusalem

CAMBRIDGE
UNIVERSITY PRESS

Shaftesbury Road, Cambridge CB2 8EA, United Kingdom

One Liberty Plaza, 20th Floor, New York, NY 10006, USA

477 Williamstown Road, Port Melbourne, VIC 3207, Australia

314–321, 3rd Floor, Plot 3, Splendor Forum, Jasola District Centre,
New Delhi – 110025, India

103 Penang Road, #05–06/07, Visioncrest Commercial, Singapore 238467

Cambridge University Press is part of Cambridge University Press & Assessment,
a department of the University of Cambridge.

We share the University's mission to contribute to society through the pursuit of
education, learning and research at the highest international levels of excellence.

www.cambridge.org
Information on this title: www.cambridge.org/9781009396493

DOI: 10.1017/9781009396479

First published 2023

A catalogue record for this publication is available from the British Library

Library of Congress Cataloging-in-Publication Data
NAMES: Ricci, David M., author.
TITLE: Post-truth American politics : false stories and current crises /
David Ricci, Hebrew University of Jerusalem.
DESCRIPTION: First edition. | New York : Cambridge University Press, 2023. |
Includes bibliographical references and index.
IDENTIFIERS: LCCN 2023010162 | ISBN 9781009396493 (hardback) |
ISBN 9781009396455 (paperback) | ISBN 9781009396479 (ebook)
SUBJECTS: LCSH: United States – Politics and government – 21st century. |
Truthfulness and falsehood – Political aspects – United States. | Mass
media – Political aspects – United States. | Fake news – Political
aspects – United States. | Democracy – United States.
CLASSIFICATION: LCC JK275 .R534 2023 | DDC 320.97309/05–dc23/eng/20230629
LC record available at https://lccn.loc.gov/2023010162

ISBN 978-1-009-39649-3 Hardback
ISBN 978-1-009-39645-5 Paperback

For Gili and Yarden

Contents

Note on cover image

The MAGA on Donald Trump's red hats stands for "Make America Great Again."

It is a national Story which Trump projected in his presidential campaigns, and which inspired his Inaugural Address in 2017. It is false in the sense that it claims America is no longer "great" (whatever "great" means) because someone (unnamed) has caused the country to decline (in an undefined way). Since the guilty party is not named in the story, listeners can fill in the blanks with whoever they dislike.

In short, MAGA is an example of the false stories that help to shape post-truth American politics.

1 GETTING STARTED

Charles Dickens described a muddled society when he wrote about the French Revolution in *A Tale of Two Cities* (1859). As he said, "It was the best of times, it was the worst of times, it was the age of wisdom, it was the time of foolishness, it was the epoch of belief, it was the era of incredulity, it was the season of light, it was the time of darkness, it was the spring of hope, it was the winter of despair."

More than two centuries after that revolution, we are surrounded by Dickensian paradoxes. Among other things, our society contains democracy *and* populism, antibiotics *and* atomic bombs, prosperity *and* poverty, abundant information *and* massive deception, gender progress *and* racial tensions, personal computers *and* cellphone addiction, healthy food *and* epidemic obesity. That is, we enjoy great accomplishments and suffer equally great shortcomings.

Some scholars and pundits have argued that paradoxes like these confound us because our thinking about them is muddled by faulty communications – personal and public – to the point where we live in an age of post-truth. I do not know exactly how to describe that age. But like Dickens said, for every plus, there seems also to be a minus. On the whole, for example, we are safer and happier than earlier generations even while, in some respects, some, or even many, of us are angry or shocked by modernity.[1]

* * * * *

Amid these complicated circumstances, in this book I am writing to explore some political aspects of post-truth America today, where leaders and followers struggle with endless frictions and uncertainties. Of course, every individual has to fend for herself or himself in this brave new world. But we need also to consider, I think, how that world affects us collectively because, for example, the confusion and disarray that Dickens described eventually produced Napoleon and his wars. In which case, we should try to avoid repeating similar outcomes now.

Post-Truth, Politics, and Stories

To that end, let us start our consideration of contemporary politics by defining the term "post-truth" which, as we shall see shortly, is an enormous muddling factor in our society:

> "Post-truth" was the Oxford English Dictionary's word of the year in 2016. It was meant to put a name to a new and alarming trend in political discourse taking hold in the West. Facts seemed to be suddenly deprived of their former importance. Conspiracy theories and "alternative facts" became mainstream everywhere from online chat rooms to the White House press room. Brexit and Trump's win in the 2016 elections ... seem to signal a paradigm shift in British and American politics. The era of truth had given way to one of post-truth. In the frenzy of 2016, it felt like a surreal shock that no one could have seen coming. Liam Will (2021)[2]

---

[1] On the upside, see Steven Pinker, *Enlightenment Now: The Case for Reason, Science, Humanism and Progress* (London: Penguin Books, 2018). On the downside, see Pranab Bardhan, *A World of Insecurity: Democratic Disenchantment in Rich and Poor Countries* (Cambridge, MA: Harvard University Press, 2022).

[2] This passage appeared in *The Yale Review of International Studies* at http://yris.yira.org/comments/5108. It describes Oxford University Press' decision as reported by the BBC at www.bbc.com/news/uk-37995600.

Now, let us add to Will's observation about discourse another, about political stories:

> Policy is rational. Politics is not. It takes a story to move voters, an emotional connection that tells them something about themselves and the world in which they live or, alternatively, the world in which they would like to live. Without a story to tell – without a way to make the issues of an election speak to the values of an electorate – even strong candidates with popular policies can fall flat. And the reverse is also true. A divisive figure with unpopular beliefs can go far if he or she can tell the right kind of story to the right number of people. Jamelle Bouie (2021)[3]

Together, these two passages describe much of what happens in modern democratic politics. We live in a post-truth society, which means that we are not surrounded and supported by familiar, comfortable, and incontrovertible facts. Therefore, as Bouie points out, in that society we increasingly rely on stories, rather than facts, to tell us where we are and how we should proceed.

Accordingly, *Post-Truth American Politics* is dedicated to the proposition that, rather than data and logic, it is stories – which are increasingly promoted by post-truth people – that frame more and more of what we think and say about politics.[4] In which case, we should pay considerable attention to those stories, which powerfully affect our public (and private) lives.

In addition, however, and beyond Bouie's observation that stories drive much of politics, stories in that realm have two important

---

[3] These are the opening sentences of a November 5, 2021, *New York Times* opinion article by Jamelle Bouie, entitled "Why We Have to Wave the Bloody Shirt of Jan. 6." See the article at www.nytimes.com/ 2021/11/05/opinion/democrats-bloody-shirt-jan-6.html.

[4] The relationship between fewer facts and more stories is noted in James Ball, *Post-Truth: How Bullshit Conquered the World* (London: Biteback Publishing, 2017), p. 6: "to tell a lie, you need to care about some form of absolute truth or falsehood, and increasingly public life [in the post-truth world] is run by people who don't care much either way – they care [only] about their narrative." This means they care more that their story will be effective than that it will be true. Culprits include not only politicians but also commercial actors. Thus Google, Microsoft, Meta, and other private sector titans casually lie about why they use cookies: "We value your privacy"; "We use cookies to understand your site usage"; "We use cookies to improve your experience." At the same time, such data pickpockets provide incomprehensible excuses, fashioned by lawyers and other hired guns, to "explain" what they call their "privacy policies." Thus, "Our breakdown and format make it easy for readers to understand and comprehend the different categories of cookies being used, and for what."

characteristics which we should heed. Therefore, I will highlight both of those in later chapters, about crisis points, and about tales which perpetuate those crisis points in American politics today.

The first characteristic is that some political stories are not entirely true. In fact, they are false, even when we might like for them to be true, and I will explain how that works in Chapter 2.

The second characteristic is that, beyond the fact that they are sometimes false, political stories can be dangerous – some because they validate crisis points – as I will show especially in Chapters 5 and 6. From which it follows that we should seriously consider how to deal with them because, as Bouie observes, we are fated to meet political stories, for better or worse, repeatedly in public life.

Preliminaries

These are extremely large matters, and they entail severe practical and ethical dilemmas. They therefore deserve to be approached gradually and carefully. So let us settle some preliminaries in that direction now, starting briefly with one aspect of the Ukraine war because it stands out in political news today.

Global Relations

That some political stories are false we know, but do not always remark, from what we see in news reports about international relations. A recent example is how Russian president Vladimir Putin, as a pretext for aiming the Red Army at Kiev in February 2022, told an obviously false political story, in which the sovereign entity of Ukraine was portrayed as, in effect, a "fake state," created artificially by subterfuge and force in 1991 out of the old Soviet Union. As such, it had no right to exist, said Putin, and it could legitimately be attacked by a Russian army, in a "special military operation" purportedly designed to "protect" Russian-speaking Ukrainian citizens who lived under constant threat, from the Kiev "junta," of "terrorism … neo-Nazism … and genocide."[5]

---

[5] Putin's original story was broadcast on February 21, 2022. See it at http://en.kremlin.ru/events/president/news/67828. When on May 9, 2022, Russia was celebrating its 1945 victory over Nazi Germany, Putin extended the original story to claim that Ukraine, backed

Other diplomatic cases, closer to home, come to mind. Thus, in August 1964, US president Lyndon Johnson proposed, and Congress approved, the Gulf of Tonkin Resolution. That Resolution authorized the president to "take all necessary measures" to repel North Vietnamese aggression such as that which Johnson reported as having taken place against two American destroyers in the Gulf of Tonkin. Later, it became clear that North Vietnamese forces had not attacked those destroyers.

Furthermore, in February 2003, US Secretary of State Colin Powell addressed the United Nations Security Council and insisted that the government of Iraq had "materially breached" United Nations resolutions by producing weapons of mass destruction. The accusation was not true. Nevertheless, in the same speech, Powell asked the Council to authorize military action to punish Iraq for violating those resolutions.

For our purposes, it is worth remembering such performances because they call to mind the great potential power of false political stories: (1) three seemingly authoritative stories, all false; (2) three inspiring calls to close ranks; and (3) three subsequent wars, each appalling.

* * * * *

Powerful and tragic as they are, stories promoted by Putin, Johnson, and Powell, or others like them, are not central to this book, because the realm of international affairs – in which the Ukraine war is being waged – has *always* been full of false stories. That is, such stories have *always* plagued relations between countries, and they (the stories) will continue to do so. Therefore, the nature of participants, means, and ends in the *international realm* together dictate that telling the truth is not a common practice or even a commanding aspiration among nations. So we should expect little of it from their diplomats whose job, as the saying goes (with some exaggeration), is to lie for their countries.

The Domestic Arena

What is significantly new, though, and what urgently demands our attention, is a recent trend in the expression and reception of false

up by Western countries, was preparing to attack the Russian "Motherland" and therefore the war was, for Russia, a matter of legitimate preemptive action. See http://en.kremlin.ru/events/president/transcripts/68366.

political stories. What is new is that, more and more, such stories drive the course of *domestic affairs*. That is, they impinge constantly on how we talk to our friends and neighbors, with whom, by and large, we want to live decently and prosperously.

The point here is that, unlike in the global arena, where action takes place *between* communities which are sometimes hostile or indifferent to one another, truth is a major aspiration in domestic affairs. That is, we hope to achieve it *within* communities, where citizens have some affection for one another and seek to flourish together.

Especially in democratic societies, we know that truth is vital to political health because, without truth, how can democratic citizens think accurately about the condition of their community, and about how they might speak effectively and vote to improve it? In that sense, truth is what economists call a "public good" because, when it exists, it is available to all citizens, and their access to it serves to make all of them better off.[6]

In sum, we know that without access to truth, citizens cannot talk to each other intelligibly, cannot understand each other's interests, and cannot adjust together successfully to real-world conditions.[7] But in many communities, such as in America today – and here is the problem – the truth, or some aspects of it, seems increasingly beyond our grasp in what we now recognize as a post-truth society.

The Post-Truth Society

In that sense – and this is really our subject – false political stories at home are expressions of a post-truth situation within which we

---

[6] Truth as a "public good" (although without using that term) is recommended in the opening sentences of President Franklin D. Roosevelt's First Inaugural Address (1933). As Roosevelt put it, "I am certain that my fellow Americans expect that on my induction into the Presidency I will address them with a candor and a decision which the present situation of our Nation impels. This is preeminently the time to speak the truth, the whole truth, frankly and boldly." See the speech at http://avalon.law.yale.edu/20th_century/froos1.asp.

[7] Timothy Snyder, *On Tyranny: Twenty Lessons from the Twentieth Century* (New York: Crown, 2017), p. 71: "To abandon facts is to abandon freedom. If nothing is true, then no one can criticize power, because there is no basis on which to do so. If nothing is true, then all is spectacle. The biggest wallet pays for the most blinding lights." See also Yochai Benkler, Robert Faris, and Hal Roberts, *Network Propaganda: Manipulation, Disinformation, and Radicalization in American Politics* (New York: Oxford University Press, 2018), p. 5: "Some shared means of defining what facts or beliefs are off the wall and what are plausibly open to reasoned debate is necessary to maintain a democracy."

live together. Therefore, the bottom line here is this. We know that diplomatic stories may dangerously challenge truth and that, therefore, Western premiers, prime ministers, presidents, and chancellors strongly rejected what Putin said in 2022. But we also know that, apart from such stories being told *abroad*, truth is being challenged severely and increasingly *at home*, by conditions which reign within post-truth life in democratic societies.

The Epistemological Crisis

Rudy Giuliani, a presidential lawyer and former mayor of, and US District Attorney in, New York City, has suggested that, actually, objective facts (and consequent truths) simply *do not exist*.

> During an appearance on *CNN's "Cuomo Prime Time"* on Tuesday evening, [Rudy] Giuliani [President Donald Trump's attorney] told CNN's Chris Cuomo that facts are in the eye of the beholder. "If fact [checking] is anything, we've never had anybody with the level of mendacity that he has. Not even close," Cuomo said of Trump. "It's in the eye of the beholder," Giuliani responded. "No, facts are not in the eye of the beholder," Cuomo said. "Yes it is – yes they are. Nowadays they are," Giuliani asserted. Rudy Giuliani (2018)[8]

Giuliani's defense of then-president Donald Trump demonstrated that America is living through a transformation of perceptions and sensations – an epistemological crisis – which is perhaps analogous to the Gutenberg Moment (c.1450). At that time, Johannes Gutenberg's movable-type printing presses began to change the way Europeans related to each other's ideas, circumstances, and achievements by producing affordable and informative books for people who previously had none.

Recently, analogous to the earlier printed books, new instruments of communication have again appeared; previously silent citizens have entered the public conversation; linear thinking may be going

---

[8] At https://edition.cnn.com/2018/08/19/politics/rudy-giuliani-truth-isnt-truth/index.html.

extinct; traditional gatekeepers are often ignored; evidence is constantly challenged; testimonies are doubted; suspicions of bias abound; institutions are increasingly regarded as unreliable; and trust between people who do not agree with one another has almost vanished.[9]

One way of relating to this new situation – a Tower of Babel, really – is to accept, without enthusiasm, the fact that we live in a post-truth world. In that world, science often "works" (as with antibiotics), although sometimes (as in quantum physics) we don't know why.[10] Yet even when it does work, as with Covid-19 vaccines most recently, increasing numbers of people say that it doesn't.

Moreover, whatever we believe about social affairs – via theology, history, journalism, anthropology, literature, economics, psychology, sociology, and more – is relentlessly denied by our adversaries, whoever they are. In charitable moments, we may feel that some of those people sound reasonable, and we may observe that some of them cite respectable sources. But some of them also say they believe in things which may be exactly the opposite of what seems obvious to us, as if, in extreme cases, for them two and two equals five.[11]

[9] On the epistemological crisis, see Eli Pariser, *The Filter Bubble: How the New Personalized Web is Changing What We Read and How We Think* (New York: Penguin, 2012); Tom Nichols, *The Death of Expertise: The Campaign against Established Knowledge and Why it Matters* (New York: Oxford University Press, 2017), *passim*; Michiko Kakutani, *The Death of Truth: Notes on Falsehood in the Age of Trump* (New York: Tim Duggan Books, 2019), esp. pp. 21–42; Andrew Marantz, *Anti-Social: Online Extremists, Techno-Utopians, and the Hijacking of the American Conversation* (New York: Viking, 2019), *passim*; Caitlin O'Connor and James Owen Weatherall, *The Misinformation Age: How False Beliefs Spread* (New Haven: Yale University Press, 2019), esp. pp. 19–45; and Jonathan Rauch, *The Constitution of Knowledge: A Defense of Truth* (Washington, DC: Brookings Institution Press, 2021), *passim*, but esp. pp. 5–9. For a conservative view of the crisis, see Dennis McCallum, *The Death of Truth: Responding to Multiculturalism, the Rejection of Reason, and the new Postmodern Diversity* (Grand Rapids, MI: Bethany House, 1996).
[10] See John Gribbin, *Six Impossible Things: The "Quanta of Solace" and the Mysteries of the Subatomic World* (London: Icon Books, 2019), p. xvi: "Generations of [physics] students have been told, in effect, to 'shut up and calculate' – don't ask what the equations *mean*, just crunch the numbers."
[11] There will always be some differences of opinion on complicated matters and sensibilities. What is particularly worrisome in post-truth times is that propositions which are well demonstrated and therefore should become matters of settled fact are, instead, sometimes deliberately (and successfully) challenged by parties and actors promoting their own interests. See Naomi Oreskes and Erik M. Conway, *Merchants of Doubt: How a Handful of Scientists Obscured the Truth on Issues from Tobacco Smoke to Global Warming* (London: Bloomsbury, 2010).

Put that another way. More than ever, we are puzzled because those who challenge us seem convinced that what *they* (not we) think is patently true, whereas what *we* (not they) think flows from sources as unreliable as "fake news." The opposite, we sometimes admit, also obtains more than it should. That is, we and our friends – who are often silo colleagues and "Like Button" companions – tend to endorse what we believe and discount whatever our opponents claim.

The Muddled Context

Many scholars, pundits, and activists have spoken and written about the post-truth world.[12] Most of them view it anxiously, and so do I. Nevertheless, they have investigated that world thoroughly, and they have speculated about it intensively. And they will continue to do both, most likely finding little or nothing to praise.

This being the case, they don't need me to review here what they already know and have told us, for example, about the decline of rational discourse, about the notion that all claims are subjective, about the belief that no assertion can be divorced from the identity of the one who made it, about the assumption that whoever is not like me is suspect, about the inclination to stoke antipathies, about the suspicion of language itself. Furthermore, they don't need me to add to what they have already discovered.

Accordingly, I will not say much about such matters but will take post-truth as a fixed and powerful force in our modern world.[13] Therefore, in the following chapters, I will assume that post-truth ideas and convictions, many of them depressingly familiar to us all, form the muddled "context" within which modern politics takes place.[14]

[12] Specifically, see Ball, *Post-Truth* (2017); Matthew D'Ancona, *Post Truth: The New War on Truth and How to Fight Back* (London: Ebury, 2017); and Evan Davis, *Post-Truth: Why We have Reached Peak Bullshit and What We Can Do About It* (London: Little, Brown, 2017). In general, see also the books cited in n. 9.
[13] Anne Applebaum, *Twilight of Democracy: The Seductive Lure of Authoritarianism* (New York: Doubleday, 2020), pp. 109–119, succinctly enumerates our discourse shortcomings and explains how they flow from technological innovations such as radio, television, computers, the internet, smartphones, and social media.
[14] I am following here Clifford Geertz, "Thick Description: Toward an Interpretive Theory of Culture," in *The Interpretation of Cultures* (New York: Basic Books, 1973), pp. 3–32, esp. p. 14: "culture is not a power, something to which social events, behaviors, institutions, or processes can be causally attributed; it is a context, something within which they can be intelligibly – that is, thickly – described."

I will occasionally recall some aspects of that context, in order to frame narrative elements of modern political life. However, I will not focus on it – for example, I will not say much about the factor of "fake news"[15] – because, for our purposes, the post-truth context is given. But I will concentrate on how the business of politics unfolds within that context. In that sense, overall post-truth behavior is *not* my target.[16] But modern politics *is*, and that is what I am aiming at, front and center.

Democracy

In recent years, many books have discussed democratic politics. Among those are books which warn us that democracy may break down, which regard government of the people as threatened by, say, inequality, resentment, populism, polarization, "elites," clashing identities, and/or governmental gridlock.[17] Furthermore, there are books which discuss Donald Trump and his additions to, or subtractions from, American public life.[18] Not surprisingly, the two kinds of books sometimes overlap.

---

[15] For example, Serena Giusti and Elisa Piras, *Democracy and Fake News: Information Manipulation and Post-Truth Politics* (New York: Routledge, 2020), and Johan Farkas and Jannick Schou, *Post-Truth, Fake News and Democracy: Mapping the Politics of Falsehood* (New York: Routledge, 2020).

[16] Geertz ("Thick Description") was optimistic in that he still wrote about intelligible descriptions of culture (behavior). Closer to today, Edward Luce, *The Retreat of Western Liberalism* (New York: Atlantic Monthly Press, 2017), p. 179, wrote of our post-truth society that, in it, "There is no such thing as neutral information." Where that is the case, it is not clear how scholars can (in Geertz's phrase) "intelligibly describe" America's behavior in the post-truth context. For example, how can they explain what is happening when tens of millions of Americans, fractured by "silos," isolated in "echo chambers," and devoted to various "identities," vote in national elections?

[17] For example, Yasha Mounk, *The People Vs. Democracy: Why Our Freedom Is in Danger and How to Save It* (Cambridge, MA: Harvard University Press, 2018); Steven Levitsky and Daniel Ziblatt, *How Democracies Die* (New York: Crown, 2018); David Runciman, *How Democracy Ends* (New York: Basic Books, 2018); Barry Eichengreen, *The Populist Temptation: Economic Grievance and Political Reaction in the Modern Era* (New York: Oxford University Press, 2018); Adrian Pabst, *The Demons of Liberal Democracy* (Medford, MA: Polity, 2019); Masha Geesen, *Surviving Autocracy* (New York: Riverhead, 2020); and Applebaum, *Twilight of Democracy* (2020).

[18] For example, Newt Gingrich, *Understanding Trump* (New York: Center Street, 2017); Bob Woodward, *Fear: Trump in the White House* (New York: Simon & Schuster, 2018); Michael Lewis, *The Fifth Risk* (New York: Norton, 2018); David Frum, *Trumpocracy:*

However, more specifically than do the authors in both of those categories, I will comment in this essay on how, within the muddle of our post-truth world, a particular element of non-truth, or untruth, or falsity, or error – that is, a particular kind of flawed story – constitutes for democratic political scholars a special challenge.

To this end, the following chapters focus on political stories *within* a society rather than *between* them. Such stories, which I will define in Chapter 2, continually shape our public life, which includes shared principles, shared understandings, shared institutions, and shared expectations. The problem, which I will explore later, is that all of those stories are, to some extent, not true and may produce unwelcome results. This reality, in my estimation, is so dangerous that I believe all democrats (who are not necessarily Democrats) should reflect at some length on how to deal with it.

To Be Realistic

To encourage such reflection, I will discuss how scholars might proceed. I hope to say something sensible along those lines. I am convinced, however, that, even though some political stories are potent enough to warrant our concerted attention, paying special attention to them because they are false cannot dispel our sense that something about thinking (and living together) in modern society has gone seriously awry.

On that score, no matter how successfully we may deal with stories (as well as facts and data), post-truth as a context, as a backdrop, as the social environment surrounding and shaping our lives and politics, will in some form or another march on. It is driven by implacable technological achievements such as radio, television, computers, the internet, smartphones, the Cloud, internet browsers, digital platforms, and algorithms. These generate the pillars of post-truth life, for

---

The Corruption of the American Republic (New York: Harper, 2018); Victor Davis Hanson, *The Case for Trump* (New York: Basic, 2019); James Poniewozik, *An Audience of One: Donald Trump, Television, and the Fracturing of America* (New York: Liveright, 2019); Carlos Lozada, *What Were We Thinking: A Brief Intellectual History of the Trump Era* (New York: Simon & Schuster, 2020); and Roderick P. Hart, *Trump and Us: What He Says and Why People Listen* (New York: Cambridge University Press, 2020).

example, the massive distractions (and deceptions) of advertisements everywhere, the Wow! land of clickbait journalism, the echo chambers of like-minded information (and disinformation), the endless frictions fostered by social media, and a marketplace for ideas which (as we will see) allows slender needles of reason, logic, and science to get lost in an enormous digital haystack that features every sort of ignorance, selfishness, and prejudice.[19]

Political Stories

On that realistic note, let us return to what Bouie observed:

> It takes a story to move voters, an emotional connection that tells them something about themselves and the world in which they live or, alternatively, the world in which they would like to live. Without a story to tell – without a way to make the issues of an election speak to the values of an electorate – even strong candidates with popular policies can fall flat. And the reverse is also true. A divisive figure with unpopular beliefs can go far if he or she can tell the right kind of story to the right number of people. Jamelle Bouie (2021)

Bouie was right on target. Stories are important to politics, and the wrong kind can seriously damage any society. Therefore, we must, from time to time, consider not just the obvious and practical interests – such as money, status, and dignity – which motivate parties and candidates, or pundits and activists, day and night. Along with Bouie, we must also track the stories which various partisans tell, to unite their affections and move neighbors to action.[20]

I am especially concerned because, for example, when in late 2021 only 21 percent of Republicans said that Joe Biden "probably" or "definitely" won the 2020 US presidential election, "facts" seem to

---

[19] Marantz, *Anti-Social*, sums up what happens when we use the internet's new technology. See p. 7: "To change how we talk is to change who we are."
[20] On the power of stories to foster collective action, see especially Frederick W. Mayer, *Narrative Politics: Stories and Collective Action* (New York: Oxford University Press, 2014).

sway people less than they used to.[21] There is the post-truth factor, to the point where stories – such as that of a "stolen election" – may sway many of us even more than they did in the past.[22]

Accordingly, this book is about large and unifying political stories in an era when facts, as opposed to stories, are somewhat in decline. It is about how none of those stories – about, say, the wisdom of the Founders, or the efficacy of markets, or how all people aspire to freedom, or how zygotes are already small persons, or how the United States began (or did not begin) to take shape with the arrival of slaves in 1619 – are entirely true. It is about how political stories may be powerful and influential nevertheless. And it is about how scholars might deal with the falsity of such stories, which cannot be made true, via what the great German sociologist Max Weber called the "ethics of responsibility."[23]

These matters are hugely important. Just think of Donald Trump's "Make America Great Again!" story in 2016, which suggested that, if he would be elected, America would begin to thrive as it once did but no longer does.[24] Or consider the story told by Bernie Sanders, in the same year, about the "One Percent," about how he worried that a skewed distribution of income and wealth generates fear and poverty just as much as, or maybe even more than, confidence and prosperity.[25] Surely those tales, and variations of them, inspired many of the country's voters in 2016 and later.

---

[21] See www.newsweek.com/just-21-percent-republicans-say-biden-probably-definitely-won-2020-poll-1664390 and www.npr.org/2022/01/05/1070362852/trump-big-lie-election-jan-6-families. For a right-wing pundit's claim that a Trump electoral victory was stolen in that year, see Mollie Hemingway, *Rigged: How the Media, Big Tech, and the Democrats Seized Our Elections* (Washington, DC: Regnery, 2021).

[22] Unfortunately, these figures weren't all that new. In the months before the 2004 election, *after* American soldiers reported *no* evidence of weapons of mass destruction (WMD) in Iraq, a *majority* of Republican voters still believed that Iraq had such weapons or programs to develop them. See the polls cited in Jon Nichols and Robert W. McChesney, *Tragedy & Farce: How the American Media Sell Wars, Spin Elections, and Destroy Democracy* (New York: The New Press, 2005), pp. 168–169.

[23] See Max Weber, "Politics as a Vocation" (1919), in *The Vocation Lectures* (Indianapolis, IL: Hackett, 2004), pp. 83–94.

[24] A powerful version of the MAGA story underlies President Trump's 2017 Inaugural Address. See that at https://trumpwhitehouse.archives.Gov/briefings-statements/the-inaugural-address/.

[25] For the One Percent story, see Bernie Sanders, *The Speech: A Historic Filibuster on Corporate Greed and the Decline of our Middle Class* (Scotts Valley, CA: Create Space Independent Publishing Platform, 2012).

The American Case

In effect, my project is a discussion of (a) how stories are necessary in American public life, but also about (b) how certain stories support two extremely dangerous crises, political and economic, which threaten democracy. Along the way, I will emphasize that political life in America (but not only in America) is not just a series of immediate practical calculations but also a contest based on persistent sentiments inspired by, or expressed in, persuasive stories. That is, especially in the post-truth world, much that takes place in politics is driven by large and shared narratives which not only shape the details of national life in the present but also seem likely to influence what citizens will do in the future.

For example, the current lineup of stories (as I will show in Chapter 6), which seek and admire (economic) "growth" rather than (economic) "distribution" (or redistribution), do not do enough to persuade Americans to deal *today* with global warming and climate change.[26] Therefore, if those stories will not be adjusted somehow, the country will continue *tomorrow*, via industry and commerce, to stimulate endless production and consumption – elements of "growth" – and therefore pollute and degrade the powerful but vulnerable natural environment which sustains all life, including ours, on this Earth.[27]

Classes of Stories

Under the circumstances, this essay will refer occasionally to *all* political stories, which constitute an inclusive category of narrative entities. However, it is not about *everything* in that category but chiefly about a particular, essential, fundamental, and problematic *kind* of political story.

Unfortunately, both popular expressions and academic terms fail to draw the distinctions which are needed here, to show how some kinds of political stories are different from others. Still, they (political

---

[26] David Wallace-Wells makes this point less charitably. As he puts it in *The Uninhabitable Earth: A Story of the Future* (New York: Penguin, 2019), neoliberalism promotes endless innovation, economic growth, and consumer satisfaction via the market economy as if that will surely generate endless progress and prosperity for humankind. In which case, p. 191, "neoliberalism is the god that failed on climate change."

[27] Bill McKibben, *The End of Nature* (New York: Random House, 1989), esp. pp. 47–91.

stories *in toto*) are *not* all alike, and I will address their very significant variance by writing especially about Stories with a capital "S" – which I will describe more fully in Chapter 2.

This point can be illustrated by regarding all political stories together as a class of living things. Thus "stories" and "Stories" belong to a single order (class) of intellectual entities (a *genus*) but are not the same thing. This situation is similar, for instance, to how every sort of canine animal belongs to the *genus* called *Canis*, while dogs and wolves, all of whom are canine animals, belong respectively to smaller *species* within *Canis*, known as *Canis familiaris* and *Canis lupus*.

By comparison, in political studies, all sorts of political tales belong to the *genus* of, say, "stories," or "narratives," whereas what we may call Stories – with a capital "S" – have signature characteristics, play a special role in politics, and are a *species* within that *genus*. Therefore, in biological terms, this book zeroes in on important entities which add up to one particular species (which is composed of relatively few Stories) within a larger genus (which is composed of all and various political stories).

Political Science

Now, if we decide that we should target Stories with a capital "S," we will still have to decide how to study them. On that score, sociologists, anthropologists, economists, media scholars, philosophers, and historians, among others, have written, and will continue to write, about some aspects of politics.[28] It is a fact, however, that most political studies are conducted by political scientists. These are the scholars who investigate politics repeatedly, exploring its typical operations and consequences. Yet if they decide to take up this challenge, they will have to widen somewhat the range of their research projects in our post-truth era.

[28] For example, from economics, see Joseph E. Stiglitz, *The Price of Inequality: How Today's Divided Society Endangers our Future* (New York: Norton, 2012); from sociology, see C. Wright Mills, *The Power Elite* (New York: Oxford University Press, 1956); from philosophy, see Michael Walzer, *Obligations: Essays on Disobedience, War, and Citizenship* (Cambridge, MA: Harvard University Press, 1970); from history, see Gary Wills, *Lincoln at Gettysburg* (New York: Simon & Schuster, 1992); from anthropology, see David Graeber, *Debt: The First 5,000 Years* (London: Melville House, 2011, 2012).

Scope and Methods

The key point here has to do with "scope." Political scientists talk among themselves about "scope and methods," usually concentrating on methods. In so doing, they discuss how to investigate various political subjects, from legislatures to election campaigns, from comparative politics to immigration laws, from foreign affairs to citizenship, from technology to bureaucracy, from ethnicity to civil rights.

Research methods in political science are mostly quantitative, and information about them is plentiful, in books for example, such as *Scope and Methods of Political Science: An Introduction to the Methodology of Political Inquiry* (1985); *Empirical Research and Writing: A Political Science Student's Practical Guide* (2014); *Political Science Research Methods* (2015); *The Craft of Political Research* (2017); *The Fundamentals of Political Science Research* (2018); *Theory and Methods in Political Science* (2018).

In fact, however, those books little discuss the "scope" of political science, which defines the targets of political research. That is, they do not say much about the nature and extent of politics (although they usually look for it in public rather than private affairs). What exactly is politics? Where is it? Who does it? Who doesn't? Who wins? Who loses? Who starts on third base? Who is constantly behind? Is politics just about making "decisions" (that is, doing something), or does it also generate "non-decisions" (that is, doing nothing)?[29]

In other words, what are political studies about? Which domain of human activity do political scholars study? What is the sum total or extent of politics, from which we should take particular subjects to investigate, while using appropriate methods?

Power

Generally speaking, political scientists assume that their research and teaching should deal with an activity called politics, where politics is about "power" like history is about "the past," where economics is

[29] See Peter Bachrach and Morton S. Baratz, "Decisions and Nondecisions: An Analytic Framework," *American Political Science Review* (September, 1963), pp. 632–642.

about "scarcity," and where psychology is about how people "think, feel, and behave." Within this matrix of scholarly understandings, the word power, for many political scientists, defines the target of their discipline.[30]

At the same time, we know that power is a matter that can be difficult to locate and/or measure definitively. For example, in December 2021, Senator Joe Manchin (D-WV) announced that he would not support President Joe Biden's "Build Back Better" social welfare, renewable energy, and climate change proposals. Did that happen because the senator received campaign contributions from fossil fuel companies and their lobbyists? Or did that happen because he personally decided, along with many pro-Trump voters in West Virginia, that Biden's policy proposals were dangerously flawed, for whatever reasons?[31] Who influenced who, if at all? And who can tell *for sure*?

Including Stories

Assuming, then, that the exercise of political power is a complicated and even ambiguous business, my basic proposition is that what I call Stories are one element of that business. Whether or not that element is large or small in relation to other political elements – for example, race, ethnicity, gender, money, or piety – is not the issue now. My point, so far, is simply that Stories which politicians, activists, pundits, think tankers, voters, journalists, and others tell come into play somewhere in the give and take of political action (or inaction).

Yet if that is the case, then, when I am putting political Stories up for consideration, I am suggesting that Stories should fall within the scope of political research and teaching. Therefore, I will propose that because we are already well versed in political research *methods*, it is time to consider an important matter of political *scope*, where

---

[30] Political theorists have discussed power settings and relationships, public and private, personal and institutional, and so on. For example, see Steven Lukes, *Power: A Radical View*, 2nd ed. (New York: Palgrave McMillan, 2004).

[31] In 2020, when Manchin was not running for reelection, Republican candidates for president, governor, and senator won every county in West Virginia. See https://edition.cnn.com/election/2020/results/state/west-virginia.

the intent is not to say that political science should be *entirely* about Stories but that it is a discipline where *considerable* account should be taken of them.

The Following Chapters

The subtitle of this book – "False Stories and Current Crises" – aims at two elements of post-truth politics in America. There are Stories, many inspiring, and there are crisis situations, somewhat validated by Stories, which are so dangerous that we should consider whether we want to continue telling familiar Stories which contribute to perpetuating those situations, or whether we will criticize them (the Stories) and try somehow to replace them with Stories that are more benign.

Accordingly, in Chapter 2, I will explain the concept of Stories and how they are vital in any society. The explanation there will be somewhat abstract, fairly reasonable but also somewhat technical, while citing modern thinkers and scholars such as Neil Postman, Rogers Smith, Arlie Hochschild, Gerard Bouchard, Yuval Harari, Kwame Appiah, Hannah Arendt, and Simon Blackburn. Consequently, some readers might feel that the devotion to Stories is merely an academic matter, to be pursued by people who, working mainly on university campuses, will examine and reexamine it among themselves, defining and redefining its basic terms for one another.

I believe, however, that concern for Stories should not just be expressed by academics but projected by at least some of them outwards, to their students and the public. Therefore, I will follow up the formal analysis in Chapter 2 with a description of very tangible and worrisome matters in Chapters 3 and 4.

Both of those chapters will explain how America is beset by two exceedingly dangerous crises – composed of familiar principles and practices, individuals and institutions – where one entails political imbalance and the other entails economic imbalance. After that, in Chapters 5 and 6, we will see that, regardless of the danger of those imbalances, they are, to a considerable extent, perpetuated by various Stories, which many Americans regard as justifying existing political and economic arrangements, more or less.

In other words, Stories are not merely a hypothetical subject for some academic debates but are present and momentous in the off-campus world, where we all live. Therefore, in Chapters 5 and 6, we will consider, for example, very influential, but not always safe, Stories about exceptional Founders, about the blessings of economic growth, about the worth of traditional virtues, about the righteousness of a Christian nation, about the merits of individual responsibility, about the excellence of limited government, about the productivity of entrepreneurship, about the necessity of family values, about the advantages of free trade, about the efficacy of disruptive innovation, about the bond between capitalism and freedom, and many more.

Guidelines

To the extent that political scholars will decide to include Stories in their professional scope, I will suggest, in Chapters 7–10, several guidelines for how to deal with those Stories. Very briefly, these guidelines are as follows.

The first, of "choosing," flows from Max Weber's recommendation that scholars should exercise an ethic of responsibility toward Stories which already exist (he called them "causes," as we shall see). Accordingly, we should consider what consequences those Stories are likely to produce. Then, if we come to believe that the consequences would be dangerous, we should reject those Stories and side with others we regard as more benign. There is the guideline of "choosing."

The second guideline, of "refraining," relates to the fact that many scholars work as professors in universities. The point is that typical scholarly research and teaching may challenge or even deny the validity of Stories – say, about democracy, tradition, markets, community, families, and patriotism – which inspire and comfort most members of our society. On this score, there is a sense in which we should beware of inadvertently weakening conventions and habits which help to maintain social stability and the pursuit of happiness. Here, the guideline is "refraining."

The third guideline, of "dissembling," is counterintuitive for the academic world, where most scholars take pride in achieving truthfulness, or in getting as close to it as they can. Nevertheless, as I will show more fully in Chapter 2, Stories are *all* false. And if that is so, then when a dangerous Story deserves rejection as untrue, less dangerous Stories will, nevertheless, *also* be untrue. But even if they are *all* untrue, where some of them are more and some of them are less dangerous, Stories hold society together and are therefore *indispensable*.

The bottom line here is that, because people need Stories, political scholars will have to endorse *some* of them (the less dangerous) which we *know* are not true. In which case, the third guideline is that, while choosing this Story or that, we must, oddly enough, knowingly promote something less than the truth. That is, we will say yes, this is so, even though we know that it is not *exactly* so. In other words, the third guideline has to do with "dissembling," if only occasionally.

Parameters

This book does not proceed within the framework of a "theory" about political stories or Stories, and in the "Afterword" I will explain why that is so. I will stay on track, instead, by referring to "terms" which provide useful analytical parameters. These terms, some from here and others deployed later, include false stories, the epistemological crisis, the post-truth context, classes of stories, scope and methods of political research, the Enlightenment, progressivism, conservatism, humanism, Left and Right, disenchantment, government by consent, minority rule, polarization, gridlock, neoliberalism, the liberalism of fear, tyranny, the ethics of responsibility, choosing, refraining, and dissembling.

So let us begin.

2 STORIES

> I mean by "narrative" a story. But not any kind of story. I refer to big stories – stories that are sufficiently profound and complex to offer explanations of the origins and future of a people; stories that construct ideals, prescribe rules of conduct, specify sources of authority, and, in doing all this, provide a sense of continuity and purpose .... What is important about stories is that people cannot live without them.
>
> Neil Postman, *Building a Bridge to the 18th Century* (1999)[32]

We have a long way to go, so let us start by keeping in mind what Postman says about stories. A narrative is a story, he says, and "What is important about stories is that people cannot live without them." That is, large tales, or what Postman called "big stories," are absolutely necessary to public life.

Terminology

What Neil Postman, as a professor of culture and communication, called "narratives," Rogers M. Smith, a professor of political science,

---

[32] Neil Postman, *Building a Bridge to the 18th Century: How the Past Can Improve Our Future* (New York: Vintage, 1999), p. 101.

called "stories of peoplehood." Smith, who in 2019 was president of the American Political Science Association, described those stories as tales which are promoted by force or persuasion, and which make, maintain, and transform the sense of belonging to a political community.[33]

For Tea Partiers and Louisiana small-towners, sociology professor Arlie Russell Hochschild wrote about "deep stories." Such a tale she described as "a *feels-as-if* story .... It removes judgment. It removes fact. It tells us how things feel." And it marks out who are with us and who are against us.[34] After which Gerard Bouchard, sociologist and professor of history, wrote about an encyclopedic array of, in effect, deep stories as "social myths." These are not merely fables or legends, he said, but a kind of "collective representation ... a vehicle of what I would call a message – that is, of values, beliefs, aspirations, goals, ideals, predispositions, or attitudes."[35]

These samples show that scholarly terminology about stories is flexible, as befits talking about objects which cannot be summed up by scientific descriptions as precisely as we can sum up what we mean by a giraffe (which is not a lion) or a moon (which is not a galaxy).[36] The main point, though, is that, when many individuals embrace these stories, they are in fact registering what they feel to be shared sentiments and experiences, which help them to understand the world.[37]

---

[33] Rogers M. Smith, *Stories of Peoplehood: The Politics and Morals of Political Membership* (New York: Cambridge University Press, 2003), pp. 43, 60.

[34] Arlie Russell Hochschild, *Strangers in Their Land: Anger and Mourning on the American Right* (New York: The New Press, 2016), pp. 135–151.

[35] Gerard Bouchard, *Social Myths and Collective Imaginaries* (Toronto: University of Toronto Press, 2017), esp. 23–47.

[36] It is a vocabulary in which small distinctions can multiply endlessly. For example, *ibid.*, p. 39, Bouchard writes that he reviewed "no fewer than 138 definitions of myth proposed mostly by European and North America authors, belonging to various periods."

[37] Thus historian Steve Fraser, *The Age of Acquiescence: The Life and Death of American Resistance to Organized Wealth and Power* (Boston: Little, Brown, 2015), p. 214: "Societies everywhere and at all times depend on tales of justification and purpose as much as they do on the means of tangible survival to hold themselves together. These might be thought of as fables, fictive approximations of the truth, perhaps, but ones that both reflect and help constitute social reality."

Yuval Harari

Top-notch journalists such as George Packer, in his *Last Hope: America in Crisis and Renewal* (2021), offer useful popular writings about the importance of large stories.[38] But it is historian Yuval Noah Harari who recently promoted the most widely read thesis on such stories. In his best-selling *Sapiens: A Brief History of Humankind* (2015), Harari reminds us that "any large-scale human cooperation – whether a modern state, a medieval church, an ancient city or an archaic tribe – is rooted in common myths that exist only in people's collective imagination."[39] That is, people manage to live together, for better or worse, by believing in stories – Harari calls them myths – which are powerful but not true.

Extending this insight into his wide-ranging account of human affairs, Harari observes that different eras, different peoples, different religions, different states, and more, all have their myths and stories which justify living in certain ways and not in others, which recommend dwelling with some neighbors and apart from the rest. Yes, there are practical devices, such as artificial irrigation, iron weapons, chariots, water wheels, stirrups, compasses, telescopes, steam engines, electric lights, refrigeration, telephones, plastics, and computers, which enable communities to endure and some even to prosper. But myths control the disposition of those technical devices, and Harari makes this point very plainly. Without effective myths – that is, without religious, legal, national, financial, and additional myths – Harari says that things would fall apart, or, as William Butler Yeats feared, the center might not hold.[40]

---

[38] George Packer, *Last Hope: America in Crisis and Renewal* (New York: Farrar, Straus, and Giroux, 2021), "Four Americas," pp. 63–139, describes four different narratives which inspire four different sectors in American society today. Thus, p. 65: "instead of analyzing trends and events and numbers, I want to talk about what has happened [in modern America] in terms of narratives. Nations, like individuals, tell stories in order to understand what they are, where they come from, and what they want to be .... But just as no one can live a happy and productive life in nonstop self-criticism, nations require more than just facts – they need stories that convey a moral identity."

[39] Yuval Noah Harari, *Sapiens: A Brief History of Humankind* (London: Penguin, 2015), p. 30.

[40] W. B. Yeats, "The Second Coming" (1921), at www.poetryfoundation.org/poems/43290/the-second-coming.

False Stories

Guided by such thinkers, we may ignore here the technical difficulty of extracting the stories they have in mind – let's call the large ones "Stories" – from written or spoken materials, or of determining where they begin and where they end.[41] For our purposes, the important thing to remember is that, from Postman to Harari, while such tales are politically necessary to inspire and unite the societies in which we live, they are also "false." Or, at any rate, they are "not exactly true."

Now, that is a reality which, in ordinary life, is more complicated than we usually think it is. We assume, roughly speaking, that the world of ideas, the world of knowledge, the world of what works, the world of what we believe, the world of bestsellers, the world summed up in our great libraries, the world as it sounds in poetry readings and theaters, is divided, more or less, between fiction and nonfiction chronicles.[42]

However, with regard to large social affairs, all of these chronicles are somewhat fictitious, and that fact has enormous consequences which affect both public life and scholarship about it.[43]

---

[41] I have explored such difficulties in Ricci, *Politics without Stories: The Liberal Predicament* (Cambridge, UK: Cambridge University Press, 2016), esp. pp. 24–26. Scholars have fashioned no vocabulary that can indicate the kind of stories, according to strength and scale, which I have in mind. The problem flows from the fact that politics is a matter of power. Yet in the scholarly world, even in genre studies (which professors of literature and communications use to talk about stories), the genres, or story types, are classified by, say, *form* (poetry, prose, drama, etc.) and *content* (comedy, tragedy, romance) but not *power*. In fact, indeterminacy on the subject of power is inevitable because, for example, we speak often in metaphors about politics, but who can measure the "power" of one metaphor compared to the "power" of other metaphors? And who can know *why* a particular metaphor moves some people and another does not? The same is true for stories. For example, is the fairytale "Hansel and Gretel" more "powerful" than *Uncle Tom's Cabin*? And if so, why? This uncertainty is a perennial problem for men and women who create advertisements, who are modern storytellers par excellence and who admit, especially concerning "parity items" to be marketed, that they don't know how to predict the success (power to persuade) of any particular advert or jingle, in which case they are artists rather than technicians, craftsmen rather than engineers.

[42] The text above uses the word "chronicles" as a stand-in for every form of written and unwritten communication: for texts and lectures, for documents and conversations, for tomes and tales, for scientific formulas and pod talks, for "life is like this," or "life is like that."

[43] In "Truth and Politics," *The New Yorker* (February 17, 1967) and "Lying in Politics," *The New Yorker* (November 18, 1971), Hannah Arendt claimed, without passing judgement on those occasions, that politicians lie pretty much all of the time. Her assumption was that their sort of work, among people of clashing interests, resources, and opinions, simply requires dissembling. That is *not* what I am referring to in the text above.

For example, some pundits and scholars, who could not abide what Donald Trump *did* when he was President, thought that what Trump *said* was also so outrageous as to almost step, rhetorically, outside the bounds of reality.[44] But to express shock over Trump along those lines is, in a way, to assume that there is, in fact, a reality which other leaders *can* portray (although some of them may choose not to do so).[45]

I am proposing, on the other hand, that our modern situation may not warrant such optimism. That is because, strictly speaking, none of the nation's other leaders, no matter how well-intentioned they might be, are going to express, in the current context of post-truth life, an entirely accurate picture of reality. In this sense, even if Trump did not speak "the truth," neither will they.

On Being False

Let me expand on that last point. In the following chapters, I hope to encourage discussion about what, for some readers, may amount to an unfamiliar thesis about political stories, which is that a particular class of them – Stories with a capital "S" – are not true. To that end, I am deliberately writing about "false" Stories rather than about Stories which are "not exactly true."

The two terms mean much the same thing grammatically. But using the word "false" is more strident; is more provocative; is perhaps to suggest a motivation which deserves to be challenged; is, hopefully, to startle readers somewhat by, well, overstating the case, so that they might be more likely than otherwise to keep the issue in mind. Or even to act on it. Consequently, I will in this essay frequently use the adjective "false."

By doing so, I intend to be more irritating than, for example, Francis Fukuyama who, in his *Liberalism and Its Discontents* (2022),

---

44 For example, see Bruno Macaes, "How Trump Almost Broke the Bounds of Reality," at www.nytimes.com/2020/11/12/opinion/donald-trump-reality.html.

45 Philosophers going back to Aristotle, Plato, and Aquinas, and going forward to Russell, Wittgenstein, and Popper, have debated this point intensively, within the rubric of what they call "the correspondence theory of truth." That theory says that it is possible to make statements which are true because they correspond with an actual state of affairs. On the correspondence theory of truth, see Simon Blackburn, *On Truth* (New York: Oxford University Press, 2018), ch. 1, "Correspondence," pp. 15–24.

mildly observes a glitch on this score, but illustrates it with the term "theory" rather than "story," as follows:

> The problems with neoliberal policies [in the last several decades] were not limited to their immediate economic and political effects; there was a deeper problem with the underlying economic theory itself. This ... should remind us that it, like all theories, oversimplifies our understanding of human behavior. This means that we need to be careful in the practical conclusions we draw from it, since *reality will always be more complex than the theory suggests.*[46]

* * * * *

Still, for the record, I intend "false" to signify no more than "not exactly true." And if I am already noting that, I will also observe that, of course, a great deal of political talk is true and not false. Yes, true.

That is, for most of us, many small stories or specific propositions can be stated accurately and should be regarded as reliable sources of useful information. For example, Caesar really did cross the Rubicon, the British did surrender at Yorktown, Lincoln did speak at Gettysburg, the Allied armies did land at Normandy on June 6, 1944, the Organization of Petroleum Exporting Countries (OPEC) did raise oil prices after the Yom Kippur War, and storm warnings issued by the US National Hurricane Center (NHC) are widely considered dependable.

The problem, in my view, arises when stories or propositions grow, when they relate to very large subjects and a great many facts. At that point, they will become – sometimes imperceptibly and sometimes inadvertently – false, not necessarily by partisan intention but by unavoidable inadequacy. Or, as Fukuyama pointed out, "reality" is more complex than "theory."

Story Qualities

The challenging situation with regard to Stories, then – which are large stories – can be described briefly, in the points which follow, and I will return to that situation later.

[46] Francis Fukuyama, *Liberalism and its Discontents* (New York: Farrar, Straus and Giroux, 2022), p. 31. Emphasis added.

1. Society *needs* political Stories. To put the matter plainly, as Postman did, we cannot do without them. They explain what we should think of a great many otherwise enigmatic facts, and they thereby provide the scaffolding of mutual understandings within which societies stand and prosper.[47] In short, they tell us who we are, and what we should do going forward.

   In a way, if people do not have a workable number of Stories – that is, if they have *no* Stories or *too many* of them – the same people will suffer from anarchy (which means not having enough Stories to hold things together) or governmental dysfunction (which can be caused by having too many Stories to hold things together).[48]

2. Obviously, all Stories are *persuasive*. If they were not, people would not embrace them and act accordingly.[49] But, less obviously, all Stories are also *false*. They are not false because they are in all cases deliberately untrue (due to lying) but because none of them can completely describe a world of countless facts and sentiments. Moreover, in a sense, all are false because there are so many Stories available, based on so many different parameters, each with its own disciples, that a curious observer cannot know for sure which one, if any, is valid.[50]

---

[47] On political stories, see especially Rogers M. Smith, *Political Peoplehood: The Roles of Values, Interests, and Identities* (Chicago: University of Chicago Press, 2015), and Mayer, *Narrative Politics*.

[48] For anarchy today, see Libya. For governmental dysfunction today, see Lebanon. When describing a situation where Stories clash, some scholars write about tribes. Thus Amy Chua, *Political Tribes: Group Instinct and the Fate of Nations* (New York: Penguin, 2018). On commercial advertising contributing to the tribalization of American society, see Joseph Turow, *Breaking Up America: Advertisers and the New Media World* (Chicago: University of Chicago Press, 1997), "Image Tribes," pp. 184–200.

[49] No one knows exactly why some Stories are persuasive. Neil Postman, *Amusing Ourselves to Death: Public Discourse in the Age of Show Business* (New York: Penguin, 1985), p. 17, cites the literary theorist Northrop Frye as suggesting that "Through resonance a particular statement in a particular context acquires a universal significance." In this view, the power to persuade presumably emerges from "resonance." But what is resonance? Postman (pp. 17–18) says that Frye "concludes that metaphor is the generative force [for resonance] – that is, the power of a phrase, a book, a character, or a history to unify and invest with meaning a variety of attitudes or experiences." So "metaphor" generates "resonance" and "resonance" then "empowers" (my term) a Story in our minds. Except that we don't know enough about resonance to predict when it will emerge and how powerful it will be.

[50] This was the quandary which characterized Europe's religious wars in the sixteenth and seventeenth centuries, driven by, among other motivations, commitment to clashing Stories entertained by anxious Catholics and Protestants. The dilemma was addressed by the

3. Then too, many Stories are false because some Story parts may clash with other parts of the same Stories.[51] For example, on the Left, *liberty* and *equality* are two principled aims. The problem there is that when people are free (at liberty), they often strive to make themselves, and their children, unequal to other people, which can lead to dangerous social frictions.[52] So, apparently what a good society needs is *some* liberty and *some* equality.[53]

But how much of each? Who knows? Thus, some philosophers have for millennia advocated a middle way, or "the Golden Mean," or "the vital center."[54] Which is as much as to say that, without knowing in advance what specific resolution they should strive for,

Peace of Westphalia (1648), which began the long process of organizing politics and public life in Europe around the secular concept of sovereignty rather than around religious Stories based on revelation.

[51] Defining this point in academic terms, Bouchard, *Social Myths*, pp. 116, 147, citing Claude Levi-Strauss, writes about "tightly integrated clusters of myths (comparable to mythemes), something like constellations ... [o]r the constitutive units of a complex myth."

[52] That free people strive to achieve inequality, and that others vie to catch up to those who are ahead, is described, in the terminology of social choice theory, by Fred Hirsch, *Social Limits to Growth*, 2nd ed. (New York: Routledge, 1978), esp. pp. 27–54. That people will use their freedom to become unequal to other people, and that they will then work hard to pass on their advantages to their children, see Daniel Golden, *The Price of Admission: How America's Ruling Class Buys its Way into Elite Colleges and Who Gets Left Outside the Gates* (New York: Three Rivers, 2007), and Paul Starr, *Entrenchment: Wealth, Power, and the Constitution of Democratic Societies* (New Haven: Yale University Press, 2019), esp. pp. xi–31. The pigs in George Orwell's *Animal Farm* immortalized this strategy when they finalized the commandment of "All animals are equal, but some animals are more equal than others."

[53] One characteristic of the post-truth society is that its marketplace for ideas is so wide and deep – as we will see in Chapter 8, "Choosing" – that almost any statement can be countered (often respectably) by another, diametrically opposed, statement. Therefore, that liberty and equality are *not* at odds is a thesis of New York University law professor Ronald Dworkin. See his *Is Democracy Possible Here? Principles for a new Political Debate* (Princeton: Princeton University Press, 2006), pp. 9–11, but esp. p. 11: "our two principles [of equality and liberty] might ... be expected to conflict with one another. I do not accept this supposed conflict between equality and liberty."

[54] When classical Greek philosophers advocated a golden mean, it was an appropriate goal for city states struggling to rein in conflicting passions and interests. But when Arthur M. Schlesinger, Jr., *The Vital Center: The Politics of Freedom* (Boston: Houghton Mifflin, 1949), promoted a "vital center" in America after the Second World War, that concept signaled the inability of some liberals to stand for anything in particular. More than seventy years later, Francis Fukuyama updated the vital center when he recommended the Greek notion of "moderation," or "nothing in excess," as a cardinal behavioral principle for liberalism today. See Fukuyama, *Liberalism*, p. 154.

people who want to avoid conflict must always pursue compromises; that is, they must settle for apparently imperfect ends. Which means that they should sometimes aim at ends which they know are not entirely true.

Now, beyond the Left, incompatible Story parts also plague the Right. For example, to extol *tradition*, on the Right, suggests that we should cherish the old and hold on to what we have. If it isn't broken, don't fix it. Yet to idealize *free enterprise*, driven by creative destruction, which the Right also admires, says that we should welcome the new and throw away the old. On that score, rightists assume that innovation is precious for overcoming inertia.

Yes, but might not challenging inertia undermine routine and shrink devotion to valuable principles and historic achievements? Some modern conservatives have used the concept of *fusion* to argue that constant innovation does not really undercut familiar virtues, and that, therefore, these two tales are actually one.[55] That is, they may *fuse* with each other. But the word *fusion*, in this context, means nothing in particular, and putting it into a conversation is like noting two different subjects and then inventing a fuzzy term, such as "the dialectic," to presume between them a connection that is not precise, not stable, and not predictable.[56]

4. Nevertheless, just because Stories, for one reason or another, are *all* false, does not mean that they are *equally* false, as if it makes no difference to society which ones people will entertain. On this score, we can see that *some* persuasive Stories, unlike others, produce – or,

---

[55] See Stephanie Slade, "Liberty and Virtue: Frank Meyer's Fusionism" (2021), at https://oll .libertyfund.org/page/liberty-matters-frank-meyer-fusionism-stephanie-slade#Slade,%20 Freedom%20and%20Virtue%20Lead. What binds tradition and free enterprise together more successfully than "fusion" in conservative thought is explained in Linda Kintz, *Between Jesus and the Market: The Emotions that Matter in Right-Wing America* (Durham, NC: Duke University Press, 1997), *passim*, but esp. pp. 187–236. The tactic Kintz describes is to turn capitalist economic activity into "entrepreneurship," and then to regard "economic growth" as generated by godly creativity on the part of every entrepreneur.

[56] For example, on the Right, Russell Kirk prefers *tradition* whereas Friedrich Hayek prefers *markets*. See Russell Kirk, *The Conservative Mind: From Burke to Elliot*, 4th ed., rev. (Chicago: Regnery, 1953), "I: The Idea of Conservatism," pp. 13–20, as opposed to Friedrich A. Hayek, "Why I am not a Conservative," in Frank S. Meyer, *What is Conservatism?* (New York: Holt, Rinehart, and Winston, 1964), pp. 88–103.

at least, do not prevent – *bad results*, such as war, class conflict, poverty, misogyny, oppression of minorities, and climate change.

5. Therefore, scholarly observers, who are as vulnerable to the outcomes of bad Stories as all citizens are, should not overlook the realm of Stories because they (the Stories) are very difficult to analyze, while being more intricate and ambiguous than giraffes or moons. Yes, Stories are difficult to analyze. But they are also vitally important to each of us and are sometimes dangerous, therefore they deserve our attention.[57]

Kwame Appiah

Right. But a critic might say that all of the above, about Stories, is no more than a collection of abstract propositions which academicians might like to discuss among themselves but which do not necessarily connect to real people and events. Wrong. Philosopher Kwame Appiah, *The Lies That Bind: Rethinking Identity* (2018), does not employ the terms I have been using but reaches similar conclusions. Without speaking of "Stories" but with an eye on the tangible and immense impact of identity politics today, he says that "social identities" rest on shared understandings of who we are and how we should act together.

In fact, however, as he points out, such identities – of ethnicity, nation, gender, race, sect, creed, religion, language, and more – are not based on accurate understandings of their respective cases, of who is in which group and who is not, of what has happened to which people and what has not happened to any of them. Still, those identities – which are "the lies that bind," in Appiah's phrase – are necessary

---

[57] It is a fact of life that there are some things – like stories and Stories – which we deal with frequently but are unable to define precisely. Thus Supreme Court Justice Potter Stewart (in *Jacobellis* v. *Ohio*, 1964) admitted that he did not know how to define "pornography" but said that "I know it when I see it." Thus, also, in the scholarly world, we find the concept of a "paradigm" useful even though Thomas Kuhn, who introduced that term to his colleagues in the philosophy of science, used it in more than twenty different ways in his canonical *The Structure of Scientific Revolutions* (Chicago: University of Chicago Press, 1962). On those ways, see Margaret Masterman, "The Nature of a Paradigm" (orig. 1970), at www.cambridge.org/core/books/abs/criticism-and-the-growth-of-knowledge/nature-of-a-paradigm/012EA1E6BA81DECB838CC6B2801DC678.

forces in our personal and collective lives. As he puts it, "Social identities may be founded in error, but they give us contours, comity, values, [and] a sense of purpose."[58]

What to Do?

The question, then, is this. What should political scientists do about Stories, which fall within the "scope" of politics broadly defined? We study and teach about individuals and institutions, about events and trends, about singular acts and complex processes. But, in a way, many of those things, when political, are held together by Stories. That is, many of these things are shaped by Stories which set parameters for our public lives. Yet, in books and professional journal articles, we engage such Stories infrequently and write little about them.

So there, again, is the question. If Stories are within the scope – are actually an integral part – of modern politics, what should we do about them? If, as scholars, we are professionally committed – and I will say more about this – in modern times, to science and reason, to serving society by pursuing truth and avoiding error, how can we participate constructively in a vitally important realm that is, and will remain, *riddled with errors*?

The matter is far from simple, and we can start to address it by considering the general condition of great political Stories in the Western world to which, roughly speaking, America belongs.

---

[58] Kwame Appiah, *The Lies That Bind: Rethinking Identity* (New York: Liveright, 2018), p. 32. Similar analysis, with examples from European history, is available in Peter Burke, *Myths, Memories, and the Representation of Identities* (Brighton, UK: Edward Everett Root, 2019), *passim*.

3 THE ENLIGHTENMENT

Our concern for America's largest Stories must take into account the European Enlightenment. That is because the country's dominant political Stories arose before the Enlightenment but were transformed by it, or emerged from new ideas which first appeared during that era.

Learned opinions on the Enlightenment are endlessly contested.[59] Most scholars agree, though, that the Enlightenment was an historical era – that is, a time frame – covering, more or less, the seventeenth and eighteenth centuries. In those years, an array of unusually creative Western thinkers, some known as *philosophes*, sought new ways to organize society but did not always agree on what practices and principles were, to that end, enlightened or not.[60]

---

[59] For example, Ernest Cassirer, *The Philosophy of the Enlightenment* (Princeton: Princeton University Press, 1951); Alfred Cobban, *In Search of Humanity: The Role of the Enlightenment in Modern History* (New York: George Braziller, 1960); Henry F. May, *The Enlightenment in America* (New York: Oxford, 1976); Peter Gay, *The Enlightenment: An Interpretation*, 2 vols. (New York: Norton, 1977); Jonathan Israel, *Revolution of the Mind: Radical Enlightenment and the Intellectual Origins of Modern Democracy* (Princeton: Princeton University Press, 2010); Anthony Pagden, *The Enlightenment, And Why It Still Matters* (New York: Random House, 2013); and Vincenzo Ferrone, *The Enlightenment: History of an Idea* (Princeton: Princeton University Press, 2015).

[60] The distinction between the Enlightenment as an era and the Enlightenment as a particular canon or point of view, is discussed in Dorinda Outram, *The Enlightenment* (New York: Cambridge University Press, 1995), pp. 1–13.

The Progressive Enlightenment

From the intellectual turmoil of those times, there emerged what we may call a "progressive element" in the Enlightenment.[61] This stream of thinkers – not so compact or clearly defined that it can be described as a school of thought – used reason and science to criticize and reject, among earlier Stories, those which assigned great power and authority to kings, aristocrats, and churchmen. Thinkers such as René Descartes and John Locke insisted that individuals could go beyond faith and revelation to think for themselves; men such as Voltaire and Denis Diderot were especially angry about pain and ignorance fostered by clerical autocrats; philosophers such as Immanuel Kant insisted that to pursue enlightenment was "to know" beyond what people believed until his time;[62] and rebels such as Thomas Paine, in America, declared that common sense, rather than theology and tradition, can enable ordinary people to improve their circumstances together.[63]

The New Vocabulary

For centuries before the Enlightenment, the dominant framework for organizing European society was strongly Christian, and it justified a major role in public life for ordained clergy and anointed monarchs.[64] As early as the Peace of Westphalia (1648), however, and spurred on

---

[61] I am substituting "progressive" for Jonathan Israel's "radical" Enlightenment because the term "progressive" can be taken to mean much the same thing and is in keeping with political confrontations today. See Israel, *Revolution of the Mind*. See also Philipp Blom, *A Wicked Company: The Forgotten Radicalism of the European Enlightenment* (New York: Basic Books, 2010).

[62] Immanuel Kant, "What is Enlightenment" (1784), in Carl Friedrich (ed.), *The Philosophy of Kant: Immanuel Kant's Moral and Political Writings* (New York: Modern Library, 1949), pp. 132–139. When Kant said that we should want to know more, he was implicitly saying that he wanted to *know* more rather than merely *believe* more. Here is an Enlightenment thinker endorsing science, experience, and common sense as opposed to revelation, authority, and faith.

[63] Paine, *"Common Sense"* (1776), in Howard Fast, *The Selected Work of Tom Paine and Citizen Tom Paine* (New York: Modern Library, 1943, 1945), pp. 3–39.

[64] The philosophical underpinnings for this framework are described in Arthur O. Lovejoy, *The Great Chain of Being*, rev. ed. (orig., 1937; Cambridge, MA: Harvard University Press, 1976). For political implications of the Great Chain, where rulers and subjects were presumably born into divinely ordained stations in life, see Paul Lombardo, "The Great Chain of Being and the Limits to the Machiavellian Cosmos," *Journal of Thought* (Spring, 1982), pp. 37–52.

by a century of massively destructive religious wars, mostly between Catholics and assorted Protestants, a commanding notion of secular, and therefore theologically neutral, "sovereignty" began to emerge.[65]

During the later Enlightenment, this sovereignty, in defiance of old Christian Stories, was eventually assigned by progressives to "the people."[66] That collection of individuals included White men but not yet women and various minorities. Progressive thinkers, such as those who endorsed America's *Declaration of Independence*, also insisted that "the people" had various "rights," including one to "government by consent."[67]

In this view of society and the state, concern for "the people" in many walks of life eventually justified "republicanism" or, less often, "democracy," to the point where secular citizenship, frequent elections, separation of powers, checks and balances, and civil rights came to the fore, as in the American Constitution.

Disenchantment

To rephrase all of this for our purposes, the signature achievement of many Enlightenment thinkers, and especially those in the progressive camp, was that they challenged the great Stories which until then had assigned commanding authority to monarchs, aristocrats, and clergymen in European states. Here is why Max Weber, writing in 1919, and assuming that the Enlightenment gave birth to modern societies, concluded – we will come back to this in a moment – that the hallmark of modern thinking is "disenchantment."[68]

Weber did not mean that everyone living in modern times is disenchanted. But he did think that people who are modern in outlook tend not to believe in large Stories – about ghostly forces and a teleological

---

[65] For example, see sovereignty discussed in Thomas Hobbes, *Leviathan: On the Matter, Forme and Power of a Commonwealth Ecclesiasticall and Civil* (orig., 1651; New York: Oxford University Press, 1960), esp. Part II, chs. 17–18, pp. 109–120.

[66] See Edmund S. Morgan, *Inventing the People: The Rise of Popular Sovereignty in England and America* (New York: Norton, 1988).

[67] As when the Declaration says that "governments are instituted among men, deriving their just powers from the consent of the governed."

[68] On Weber's disenchantment, see n. 78. Ritchie Robertson, *The Enlightenment: The Pursuit of Happiness, 1680–1790* (New York: Harper, 2021), pp. 200–206, argues that Weber was wrong on this point.

order – such as those which propped up what Alexis de Tocqueville called Europe's "Old Regime" of temporal and spiritual powers.[69]

* * * * *

Beyond philosophical writings, the chief factors producing disenchantment about such Stories were the rise of theoretical science, exemplified by Isaac Newton's *Principia Mathematica* (1688), and by the practical work of scientists and engineers who discovered or invented useful products such as lightning rods, vaccinations, steam engines, power looms, and canned food.

We should especially highlight the presence of disenchantment today because it corresponds to the rejection of what once were crucial Western Stories. As Weber pointed out, the *philosophes* discredited great Stories – such as the divine right of kings – which, for centuries, had shaped European society and politics.[70] Indeed, in a way, to discredit such Stories was their major aim, and they pursued it so diligently that some modern thinkers, to whom we will return, have argued that the same *philosophes*, perhaps too forward-looking, were remiss in their quest for disenchantment and should have proposed new Stories that could make up for loss of the old.

Other Roads

The progressive Enlightenment did not stand alone. It had especially to compete with rivals when the French Revolution, widely regarded as an Enlightenment project which overthrew the Old Regime in France, lapsed into Jacobin terror, warred fiercely with the crowned heads of Europe, and midwifed the rise of Napoleon, who had little use for government by "the people."

---

[69] Alexis de Tocqueville, *The Ancien Regime and the Revolution* (orig., 1856; New York: Penguin, 2008).

[70] Modern people, as Weber described them, may not know much about what the progressive Enlightenment challenged, because some powerful pre-Enlightenment Stories have little purchase today. For example, when Jefferson (who was not alone) declared that "the pursuit of happiness" was an inalienable right, he (and others of like mind) were actually denying a very old notion, promoted by Christian theologians such as St. Augustine and his disciples, that this Earth is a "vale of tears" and that happiness can only be attained in Heaven. On this point, see Robertson, *The Enlightenment*, esp. pp. 3–9.

To make a long and complex story short and simple, what happened was that nonprogressive Stories and their champions increasingly appeared, and part of the popularity that some of them acquired was fueled by a conviction that societies and states, in Europe perhaps more than in America, needed social ties – for example, the emotional bonds of nationalism – beyond those provided by the French Revolution's watchwords of "liberty, equality, and fraternity."[71]

In effect, then, while shocked by the French Revolution and its outcome, rival thinkers fashioned new Stories that focused on principles and practices which, they said, progressive thinkers had not emphasized. Over time, the additional Stories proposed that the sovereign power properly belonged not exactly to the people, which was a formless mass, but to some specific and especially worthy part of it. For instance, sovereign power belonged to the "nation," or to the "working class," or to a particular "race," or to a "traditional Order" which some advocates thought should still contain significant elements of monarchy, aristocracy, and theocracy.[72]

Thus, in addition to progressive ideas such as the concept of "natural rights" which Jefferson and his colleagues wrote into the Declaration of Independence,[73] there eventually appeared, mainly in Europe but also, variously, in America, Stories promoting "nationalism," "communism," "fascism," "conservatism," "liberalism," "democratic socialism," and more. The resulting options generated enormous worldly consequences – most of which will not concern us here – and, for scholars, enough material for long and fascinating university courses about modern, largely Western, political philosophy.[74]

---

[71] Thus the nationalist Vichy regime (1940–1944) in France discarded the French Revolution's motto and adopted instead "*Travail, Famille, Patrie*" (Work, Family, Homeland).

[72] On a traditional order, see Joseph de Maistre, *On God and Society: Essay on the Generative Principle of Political Constitutions and other Human Institutions* (orig., 1809; Chicago: Regnery, 1959). For another endorsement of a traditional order, see Louis de Bonald, *On Divorce* (orig., 1801; New Brunswick, NJ: Transaction Books, 1992).

[73] On the natural rights concept, see Carl L. Becker, *The Declaration of Independence: A Study in the History of Political Ideas* (New York: Vintage, 1922, 1942), pp. 24–79.

[74] Some of these political "isms" regarded "the people" as fewer than those whom the Enlightenment regarded as "the people." Such downsizing can continue into modern politics. Thus Jan-Werner Muller, *What is Populism?* (Philadelphia: University of Pennsylvania Press, 2016), p. 21, points out, "This is the core claim of populism [including

In America

In America, most nonprogressive Stories gained little traction against the constitutional arrangements established by the Founders and amended only occasionally ever since. For example, although Americans were patriotic, they accepted many diverse immigrants to citizenship, in which case (for the most part) the country cherished inclusive "republicanism" rather than exclusionary "nationalism."[75] Moreover, while committed to "capitalism," or (later) "free enterprise," or (much later) "neoliberalism," most Americans were never enthusiastic about various forms of "socialism."

In short, by 1945, most Americans had rejected severely Right-wing options, such as fascism and Nazism, and by 1989, when the Soviet Union collapsed, they had decided that severely Left-wing options, such as Marxism and communism, had also failed. Among other opinion leaders, they had Hannah Arendt (political philosopher) and George Orwell (English novelist and pundit) and Senator Joseph McCarthy (populist demagogue) to tell them that totalitarian regimes are terrible, dominated by "Big Brother" – a term which Orwell used in his novel, *1984* – and prone to maintaining secret police and concentration camps.

The Current Standoff

There remained in America, however, two ideological camps which today relate to how the Enlightenment has shaped modern society. These camps include scholars, pundits, advocates, politicians, and activists sometimes loosely known, respectively, as liberals and conservatives, or the Left and the Right. The labels are approximate, of

the Trump phenomenon]: only some of the people are really the people." Or, as Newt Gingrich phrases the same claim in *Understanding Trump* (New York: Center Street, 2017), p. 61: "For decades, members of America's elite – in government, academia, and the media – have steered the country in a direction counter to the will of the American people."

75 Note the absence of nationalism, as opposed to the presence of republicanism, in Richard Wightman Fox and James T. Kloppenberg (eds.), *A Companion to American Thought* (Oxford: Blackwell, 1995). This collection discusses "major concepts and thinkers in the diverse traditions of American thought." Its 300+ entries include articles on democracy, liberalism, republicanism, and citizenship, but it has no article on nationalism.

course, and they do not account for diverse exemplars within both camps, from Adlai Stevenson to Michael Walzer, from Barry Goldwater to Newt Gingrich, from Lyndon Johnson to Bernie Sanders, from *The Nation* magazine to Bill Maher, from George Will to *The American Conservative*. The same labels also do not account for the fact that, as we noted and will see again, within each camp it is quite possible, or even probable, that various people will believe respectively in Stories which, from this angle or that, contradict one another.

A Disparity on Stories

As between the two camps, it is striking that American liberals do not much tell large Stories.[76] Partly that is due to the fact that the Democratic Party, which is the liberals' political vehicle today, seeks mainly to amass votes by representing various sectors in the total population. Consequently, liberal politicians and spokespeople are less inclined to promote Stories of the whole than they are to promote a series of specific policy proposals designed to serve groups such as African Americans, women, union members, LGBTQs, and environmentalists.[77]

Furthermore, partly liberals are weak on Stories because, historically, Democratic intellectuals and activists are likely to be modern in the sense that Weber emphasized disenchantment – that is, a loss of faith in divine intervention, or even celestial interest – as the hallmark of modern people.[78] In the circumstances, those liberals (but not *all*

[76] I have written about this disparity in Ricci, *Politics without Stories: The Liberal Predicament* (Cambridge, UK: Cambridge University Press, 2016). That American liberals don't usually *tell* Stories does not mean that they don't *believe* in American Stories. By definition, as Americans (and not Germans), they do. But they don't *campaign* with (that is, tell) Stories in the same way that conservatives do, and that is the main point of *Politics without Stories*.

[77] On how the two parties are different, see Matt Grossmann and David A. Hopkins, *Asymmetric Politics: Ideological Republicans and Group Interests* (New York: Oxford University Press, 2016).

[78] Weber discusses disenchantment in "Science as a Vocation" (1919), in *The Vocation Lectures* (Indianapolis, IL: Hackett, 2004), pp. 1–31. See esp. pp. 12–13: "It means that in principle ... we are not ruled by mysterious, unpredictable forces, but that, on the contrary, we can in principle control everything by means of calculation. That ... means the disenchantment of the world .... [We] need no longer have recourse to magic in order to control the spirits or pray to them. Instead, technology and calculation achieve our ends."

liberals) are a manifestation of how directly progressive Enlightenment ideas still shape some American outlooks today.[79]

On the other hand, American conservatives *do* tell Stories, and very much so.[80] These are chiefly about the virtues of tradition, the efficacy of natural markets, and the merits of limited government.

Furthermore, while they are telling their Stories, conservatives complain that their adversaries stand for nothing in particular. That is, they insist that, while undermining faith in long-standing Stories which authorized power for monarchs, aristocrats, and clergymen, Enlightenment thinkers who promoted reason and science, and who became liberals, failed to create viable replacements for Europe's old Stories. The result, say conservatives, is that liberal sectors of modern society have no spiritual core, no sense of the intrinsic meaning of life, and no firm standards of virtue and moral commitment.

Humanism

In this two-camp lineup, liberals are "humanists." In academic terms, this means that liberals believe that men and women possess "agency." Thus, going back at least to America's Founders, such as James Madison and Alexander Hamilton, they assume that people can act politically to improve their lives without divine inspiration and aid. Against them, starting with, say, Edmund Burke, most conservatives are traditionalists. They doubt that the masses are competent. They insist that "the people" will fail politically unless they will navigate by traditions which rest on faith and useful habits.

Thus Israel, *Revolution of the Mind*, p. 200, describes the disenchanted eighteenth-century outlook of Paul-Henri Thiery d'Holbach as follows: "Everyone 'who wishes to know something,' states d'Holbach, as things presently stand 'is obliged to educate himself.' To become an enlightened and reasonable person, one must erase from one's mind the entire complex of 'false principles' parents, teachers, and preachers had striven to 'infect' everyone with."

[79] Enlightenment ideas do not affect all American liberals equally. For example, Protestant ministers Reinhold Niebuhr and Martin Luther King, Jr., were not disenchanted, as Weber used that term. But they were both liberals.

[80] I have written about that in Ricci, *Why Conservatives Tell Stories and Liberals Don't: Rhetoric, Faith, and Vision on the American Right* (Boulder, CO: Paradigm, 2011).

Moderation Ebbs

The existence of two camps, on the Right and on the Left, which are now familiar to all Americans, challenges political scholars.[81] What should we think of the face-off? Is one camp right and the other camp wrong? Our academic standards, in favor of empirical research, encourage us to refrain from taking sides in such confrontations. Instead, we usually assume that we should address the public mostly on matters of fact rather than opinion.

However, recent experience has shown that one of these camps especially fosters political extremism, whose impact in America is hard to ignore.[82] On the one hand, Republican Party leaders after the Second World War were bipartisan enough to vote for, say, civil rights and environmental protection. Thus, 80% of Republicans in the House and the Senate voted for the Civil Rights Act of 1964, whereas only 70% of Democrats on the Hill, held back by pro-segregation Southern Democrats, came on board.[83]

---

[81] The two categories of Right and Left have been contested by scholars endlessly. They are often traced back to alternative Stories promoted by Edward Burke, *Reflections on the Revolution in France* (1790), and Thomas Paine, *The Rights of Man* (1791). For example, see Yuval Levin, *The Great Debate: Edmund Burke, Thomas Paine, and the Birth of Right and Left* (New York: Basic Books, 2014). See also Seth David Radwell, *American Schism: How the Two Enlightenments Hold the Secret to Healing Our Nation* (Austin, TX: Greenleaf, 2021), *passim*, which describes how a Moderate Enlightenment (Adams, Hamilton) and a Radical Enlightenment (Jefferson, Franklin) together opposed Counter-Enlightenment (anti-democratic) sentiments in America.

[82] See Levitsky and Ziblatt, *How Democracies Die*, pp. 22–23, which claims that "The Republican Party has been the main driver of the chasm [polarization] between the parties." See also Thomas E. Mann and Norman J. Ornstein, *It's Even Worse Than It Looks: How the American Constitutional System Collided with the New Politics of Extremism* (New York: Basic Books, 2012), *passim*, but esp. p. xiv: "one of the two major parties, the Republican Party, has become an insurgent outlier – ideologically extreme; contemptuous of the inherited social and economic policy regime; scornful of compromise; unpersuaded by conventional understanding of facts, evidence and science; and dismissive of the legitimacy of the political opposition."

[83] Here is a comparison. More than fifty years after bipartisan enactment of the Voting Rights Act of 1965, some Democrats proposed to prevent states from maintaining various later-day barriers to voting within their borders. To that end, on August 24, 2021, the John Lewis Voting Rights Advancement Act was passed by the House of Representatives. The vote was 219–212. All House Democrats voted for it; all House Republicans voted against it. The Act was formally introduced in the Senate by 49 Democratic senators on October 5, 2021. Because (in 2022) there was no filibuster-proof supermajority of 60 senators in favor of it, the proposed Act did not even come to a vote.

Furthermore, a year later, 13 Republican senators joined 57 Democratic senators to support the original Medicare and Medicaid program embodied in the Social Security Amendments of 1965, while 70 Republicans joined 237 Democrats in favor of those amendments in the House of Representatives. Then, in 1969, the National Environmental Protection Act was so widely favored that it passed unanimously in the Senate, "without significant opposition" in the House, and was signed into law by Republican president Richard Nixon on January 1, 1970.[84]

On the other hand, in recent years, many elected Republicans have regretted those earlier bipartisan votes, currently oppose equal rights for women,[85] and deny that humans cause global warming and therefore climate change.[86] Almost fifty years after bipartisan support enabled the enactment of Medicare and Medicaid, Democrats proposed the Patient Protection and Affordable Care Act of 2010, widely known as Obamacare, which aimed at making feasible health insurance for many previously uninsured citizens. By this time, however, polarization had descended on American politics. As a result, the Affordable Care Act was supported by 60 Democratic senators while 39 Republican senators opposed it. Correspondingly, every Republican member of the House of Representatives voted against the same Act.

In short, *moderate* Republicans – who were men and women of compromise and a willingness to settle for half a loaf – are now

---

[84] See www.historylink.org/File/9903.

[85] In March, 1972, the Equal Rights Amendment passed in the House of Representatives by 354 to 23 and in the Senate by 84 to 8. Later, Republicans increasingly withdrew their support from what liberals regard as women's rights. See Tanya Melich, *The Republican War against Women: An Insider's Report from Behind the Lines* (New York: Bantam, 1998).

[86] On denying climate change, see Senator James Inhofe (R-OK), *The Greatest Hoax: How the Global Warming Conspiracy Threatens Your Future* (Washington, DC: WND Books, 2012). Inhofe, pp. 70, 175, finds support for his climate change denial in the Bible because Genesis 8:22 declares that "As long as the earth remains, there will be springtime and harvest, cold and heat, winter and summer, day and night." See also Chris Mooney, *The Republican War on Science* (New York: Basic Books, 2005), pp. 78–103. Republicans and Democrats were not always far apart on science. Thus in 1990, the Clean Air Act was passed in Congress by bipartisan majorities of 401–21 in the House and 89–1 in the Senate. (See https://environmentamerica.org/blogs/environment-america-blog/ame/lessons-bipartisanship-1990-clean-air-act-amendments.) Yet when, in August of 2022, Congress passed the Inflation Reduction Act, which authorized substantial federal outlays for limiting climate change, no Republican in the House or Senate voted in favor of that Act.

almost extinct.[87] Consequently, what had been their party came to lead the current conservative camp, which is dominated by former President Donald Trump and senators such as Mitch McConnell (R-KY), Tom Cotton (R-AZ), Lindsey Graham (R-NC), and Ted Cruz (R-TX), none of whom seems to admire moderation.

Max Weber

In these circumstances, as Weber explained, some scholars should exercise the "ethics of responsibility."[88] Most immediately, because we are living in a dangerous Age of Populism,[89] scholars should refrain from passively assuming that the political alternatives which are available – in this case, the American Right and the American Left – are morally equivalent.[90]

To reject moral equivalence in this situation does not mean that one side is entirely wrong and that the other side is entirely right. It does mean that, as observers and participants, scholars should try to find the best in both camps, the commensurable elements that will most likely lead to progress rather than backsliding, to creativity rather than gridlock. That is where, as we shall see, Weber's prescription can come into play.

---

[87] But see James M. Curry and Frances E. Lee, *The Limits of Party: Congress and Lawmaking in a Polarized Era* (Chicago: University of Chicago Press, 2020), which notes that when Congress actually passes laws, some bipartisanship obtains, therefore polarization is never absolute. That is, some moderation is always present.

[88] Weber, "Politics as a Vocation," esp. pp. 83–94.

[89] On the Age of Populism, see, John B. Judis, *The Populist Explosion: How the Great Recession Transformed American and European Politics* (New York: Columbia Global Reports, 2016); Muller, *What is Populism?*; and Roger Eatwell and Matthew Goodwin, *National Populism: The Revolt against Liberal Democracy* (New York: Penguin, 2018). For a more sympathetic view of populism, see Salena Zito and Bradd Todd, *The Great Revolt: Inside the Populist Coalition Reshaping American Politics* (New York: Crown, 2018).

[90] For example, see the arguments *against* moral equivalence in Jacob S. Hacker and Paul Pierson, *Off Center: The Republican Revolution and the Erosion of American Democracy* (New Haven: Yale University Press, 2006); and Mann and Ornstein, *It's Even Worse Than It Looks*. See also Michiko Kakutani, *The Death of Truth: Notes on Falsehood in the Age of Trump* (New York: Tim Duggan Books, 2019), pp. 73–76. Closer to an argument *in favor of* moral equivalence, see Roderick P. Hart, *Trump and Us: What He Says and Why People Listen* (New York: Cambridge University Press, 2020), p. 231, which claims that it was possible "for perfectly decent people to vote for Trump for perfectly decent reasons."

4 THE POLITICAL CRISIS

So all great political Stories are false, and the Right and the Left in America, which are both heirs to the Enlightenment, but differentially enthusiastic about it, are not working well together. Furthermore, scholars should take an interest in these kinds of things because, while false Stories may shape our lives, they are not all equally false. In which case, along with Weber, we should confront them skeptically, of which I will say more later.

Two Crises

What I have written so far is fairly abstract. Some readers may even regard it as nebulous. To bring them on board, so to speak, it is time to consider concrete "crises" in American public life, where I assign the term *crisis* to an existing situation, not hypothetical but real, which is *extremely dangerous*.

Therefore, in this and the next chapter, I will describe two such crises. That is not many. But it is enough for our purposes.[91]

---

[91] In today's polarized America, thinkers on the Right might not agree that these two situations are crucial and might highlight what they regard as completely different problems in American life. For example, see Dinesh D'Souza, *Hillary's America: The Secret History of the Democratic Party* (Washington, DC: Regnery, 2016), which defines America's biggest problem as a progressive Democratic Party, and Charles R. Kesler, *Crisis of the Two Constitutions: The Rise, Decline, and Recovery of American Greatness* (New York: Encounter Books, 2021), which regards the influence of liberal Pragmatism as America's biggest problem.

A Point on Scope

Most important, these crises are *not* abstract. They are tangible; they are dangerous; they are persistent; they threaten America immediately. And if what drives and perpetuates them is, as we will see, powerful Stories, those Stories should be challenged by scholars.

That is the central lesson. Political conditions may be accompanied by powerful Stories. Where that is the case – and it frequently is – such Stories can be regarded as a matter of "scope" for political research, in the sense of considering, in the totality of modern politics, a factor which political scholars have not much engaged professionally in the past.

* * * * *

Here is the sequence. In this chapter and the next, I will describe two crises, of political and economic imbalance, and after that, in Chapters 6 and 7, we will see how those crises are, to some extent (which cannot be measured precisely), perpetuated by powerful Stories. In other words, during Chapters 4 and 5, I will highlight facts. While doing that, I will put very dangerous circumstances on display. Afterward, in Chapters 6 and 7, I will show how, via various Stories, those circumstances are, for some believers, interpreted favorably, to the point where Weber's warning is very much on target.

The First Iteration

Before the American Civil War, political imbalance emerged because the Founders, with good will toward at least most White men at that time, sought to fashion a federal government that would work well but not become "tyrannical," as they believed King George III had been. To that end, via the Constitution, they deliberately incorporated various mechanisms, such as a national separation of powers, and internal checks and balances, into the new political system.

Moreover, in *The Federalist*, James Madison observed that, in practice, the complicated new institutions authorized by the

Constitution in 1789, composed of many competitive parts, would divide up the nation's supply of "factions," those being various groups of citizens united by shared but narrow interests.[92] Consequently, no single faction in the United States would grow so large as to control large parts of the political system, achieve lasting majority status, and then "tyrannize" other citizens.[93]

An Arena of Factions

We can think of this faction-control system as if all factions – based on, say, location, religion, economic interest, or ethnic origin – would compete within a constitutional structure resembling a large, circular arena. In that arena, factions would seek to dominate this or that part of government, from state legislatures to Congressional committees and more.

Considerable restraint within this circle would be automatic. Madison argued (but not in the terms I am using here) that, on any public policy issue, *one* group of several factions might together achieve a working national majority and political power while, on any other public policy issue, another group of several factions might together achieve a working national majority and political power. But because existing factions, like building blocks, would from time to time shift

---

[92] Madison defined a faction as "a number of citizens ... united and actuated by some common impulse of passion, or of interest, adverse to the rights of other citizens, or to the permanent and aggregate interest of the community." See "The Federalist No. 10," in Alexander Hamilton, John Jay, and James Madison, *The Federalist* (orig., 1788; New York: Modern Library, 1937), p. 54.

[93] I am describing here a post-Second World War understanding of "Federalist No. 10." Until then, the standard view was that early Americans divided approximately into Hamiltonians and Jeffersonians, or Federalists and Anti-Federalists. (On that earlier understanding, see Richard Hofstadter, *The Progressive Historians: Turner, Beard, Parrington* [New York: Vintage, 1970], esp. pp. 167–284 on Charles A. Beard's *An Economic Interpretation of the Constitution* [1913].) The post-Second World War understanding – which de-emphasized class conflict – of American politics as based on multiple and ever-shifting groups, was expressed especially by political scientist Robert A. Dahl, *A Preface to Democratic Theory* (Chicago: University of Chicago Press, 1956), esp. pp. 4–33. For conservatives, that understanding of factions appears, for example, in George F. Will, *The Conservative Sensibility* (New York: Hachette Books, 2019), *passim*. Referring to "Federal No. 10" frequently, Will praised James Madison as the greatest Founder.

sides, now aligning with *these* factional allies and now realigning with *those*, a spirit of compromise (not necessarily comity) would reign.[94]

In other words, *now* (in the circle) I am in the political majority (composed of factions), and *later* I am in the political minority (also composed of factions). Therefore, when I am a winner, I will rule moderately so as not to foster bitterness and stimulate reprisal against myself and my colleagues when I lose.

It was as if, on any one public policy issue (say, on internal improvements such as turnpikes or canals), a line was drawn across the entire circular arena, with some factions on the majority side of that line and some on the minority side. On the next public policy issue (say, on import taxes), another line was drawn, with some of the same but also some different factions in the new majority and the new minority. And so on and so forth. Factions in such a situation would tend to moderation, or at least away from extremism, for being driven by what modern political scientists would later call "cross-cutting" motivations.[95]

Most significantly, as described in this way, constitutional arrangements would not permit a permanent political majority to arise, because issue lines were often shifting and elevating some factions to power while demoting others. Thus, tyranny would not ensue.[96]

Breakdown

For American politics from 1800 to 1860, faction control worked fairly well. Years passed and the national government, led by parties which had branches in the North, the South, and the West, managed to work out partisan compromises to finance and build roads and canals,

---

[94] This sort of analysis was promoted by political scientist David B. Truman, *The Governmental Process: Political Interests and Public Opinion* (New York: Knopf, 1951).

[95] See some complexities of this situation, including "intensity" of convictions within factions, in Dahl, *Preface to Democratic Theory*.

[96] Notwithstanding this success, the nineteenth-century French aristocrat, Alexis de Tocqueville, who little admired popular sentiments, would eventually complain that, in America, *public opinion* could become tyrannical. Alexis de Tocqueville, *Democracy in America*, 2 vols. (orig., 1835, 1840; New York: Vintage, 1945), vol. I, ch. XV, pp. 269–272. Conservative thinkers who praise Burke (who was not a democrat) tend also to praise de Tocqueville, who criticized the force of public opinion (that is, who faulted some expressions of democratic sentiment).

to tax imports, to seize Native American lands, to settle mostly Caucasian pioneers on those lands, to bring new states into the Union, and more. Factional politics was not elegant, but it worked.[97]

Increasingly, however, confrontations wracked the national government. The chief culprit was a set of arrangements flowing from the package of eighteenth-century constitutional compromises whereby slavery was permitted and even protected by the Constitution in return for the agreement of Southern Founders to bring their states into the Union. Within these arrangements, Congressional representation, via the three-fifths rule for over-counting White Southerners, was slanted toward over-representation of Southern states; the two-senator-per-state rule protected the Southern region regardless of how few (White) citizens resided there; and Southern politicians constantly threatened to paralyze the Electoral College and, via the 12th Amendment, throw presidential elections into the House of Representatives, where the pro-slavery South could exercise great power.[98]

Alongside these circumstances, and fueled by moral inclinations and practical calculations, anti-slavery sentiment grew, especially in the North and the West. Sometimes that sentiment was passive. But sometimes, as among abolitionists such as Horace Greely, John Quincy Adams, Frederick Douglass, Harriet Beecher Stowe, Harriet Tubman, and John Brown, it was passionately active.

The result was a democratic crisis, because America's factions, previously somewhat flexible, lined up increasingly on only two opposite sides of what became, in effect, a *permanent* line dividing Americans on the cardinal public policy issue of slavery. Because of this line, for example, the Whig Party, long inspired by Henry Clay, fell apart early in the 1850s, and the Democratic Party, founded by Andrew Jackson and Martin Van Buren, in 1860 split over slavery. Consequently, Northern and Southern wings (factions) of the Democrats ran separate

[97] Sean Wilentz, *The Rise of American Democracy: Jefferson to Lincoln* (New York: Norton, 2005), *passim*.
[98] The Constitution provides, in Amendment XII (1803), that if, in the Electoral College, there will be no majority of votes in favor of any candidates for president and vice president, then those two officers will be elected by the House of Representatives, with each state casting one vote. In such a case, Southern states could form a bloc which could throw its support to the most pro-slavery presidential candidate.

candidates for president and vice president, and the Illinois Republican Abraham Lincoln was elected to the White House.[99]

Impasse

The demographics amounted to this. By 1860, in two conglomerate factions which were, in general, for or against slavery, roughly 22 million Northern and Western Americans confronted approximately 9 million Southern Americans (including perhaps 3.5 million enslaved Black people). And that confrontation, between two fairly cohesive if not totally unified blocs, could not be resolved politically. That is, Northerners and Westerners, who were increasingly opposed to slavery, could not set America free because amending the Constitution to forbid slavery required supermajorities which they could not muster.

It was an immensely dangerous impasse. By 1860, the American majority was stymied, and there was a sense in which national "government by consent" no longer existed in the United States. Nevertheless, even while leaders like Lincoln knew that, according to the Constitution, slavery could not be prohibited throughout the country, many White, Southern activists came to believe that their way of life was going to be quarantined in their region by voters living in the other two regions. Therefore a number of Southern state governments, from Virginia to Texas, declared independence from the Union when Abraham Lincoln was elected president in 1860, after which they began to seize federal assets, such as Fort Sumter in the Charleston harbor.

We should be clear on what happened. Even though Lincoln won in the Electoral College, America's Northern and Western democratic majority – legitimate according to, say, Lockeian and Jeffersonian principles, and in line with a good deal of popular sentiment – was prevented from pursuing what might have been its major policy preference. That

---

[99] On the increasingly bitter polarization over the issue of extending slavery geographically, see Edward E. Baptist, *The Half Has Never been Told: Slavery and the Making of American Capitalism* (New York: Basic Books, 2014, 2016), "Arms: 1850–1861," pp. 343–395, and Steven Hahn, *A Nation without Borders: The United States and Its World in an Age of Civil Wars, 1830–1910* (New York: Penguin, 2016), "Death of a Union," pp. 192–239. When the Northern and Southern Democrats split and nominated separate candidates for president in 1860, Lincoln won a majority (180–123) of electoral votes but only 39.8 percent of the popular votes.

is, the majority could not end slavery, which no longer existed elsewhere in the New World except for Cuba and Brazil. And then, during this volatile stalemate – gridlock is the modern term – the country's minority decided anyway to secede and started a terrible civil war.[100]

Resolution

During and after the war, new circumstances resolved the first iteration of political imbalance. National majority rule finally took hold. But the majority's policy preferences at that time were not realized via democratic persuasion, by debate and bargaining, by bipartisanship and compromise. Instead, they were violently imposed at horrendous cost to both sides.

By rebelling against the Union, the Southern minority temporarily departed and gave up its veto power in that Union. Consequently, the Northern and Western majority which remained in the Union was able to abolish slavery by enacting Amendments XIII, XIV, and XV without freely given Southern consent.[101] Moreover, in the case of *Texas* v. *White* (1869), the Supreme Court by legal fiat put paid to the theory of secession in the name of "states' rights" by declaring that, constitutionally speaking, the United States was "an indestructible union."[102]

* * * * *

The central lesson of all this bears repeating. None of these resolutions could have emerged until the Union exploded. That is, an imbalance in political arrangements that were sanctioned by the Constitution was not reparable by peaceful provisions for amending that document.

---

[100] In his First Inaugural Address (1861), delivered after several Southern states had already seceded, Lincoln described how this gridlock over slavery prevented majority rule: "A majority held in restraint by constitutional checks and limitations," he said, "and always changing easily with deliberate changes of popular opinions and sentiments, is the only true sovereign of a free people. Whoever rejects it does of necessity fly to anarchy or to despotism." See the Address at https://avalon.law.yale.edu/19th_century/lincoln1.asp.

[101] For example, to rejoin the Union, Southern states were required to ratify the new Amendments.

[102] *Texas* v. *White* 74 US 700 (1869).

Instead, when imbalance persistently thwarted the principle of majority rule, it seemed, to many citizens living at that time, that there was no reasonable solution to their circumstances. And they were right.

* * * * *

Nowadays, we are all aware that, despite freeing the slaves, the Civil War did little to repair America's race relations.[103] Northerners during and after the war enacted the 13th, 14th, and 15th Amendments. Thus the formerly enslaved people were freed and granted citizenship. But Republicans soon tired of enforcing Reconstruction with the Union Army and, after the election of 1876, they withdrew federal soldiers from the South and permitted Southern Democrats to enforce an openly brutal Jim Crow system of terrorism, segregation, and peonage.[104] This was eventually followed, well into the twentieth century, by a second, more subtle Jim Crow system, some of it even outside the South, of mass incarceration, economic deprivation, social exclusion, and voting denial.[105]

Race relations are not our subject here.[106] What is clear, however, is that such relations take place today in what may be regarded, for our purposes, as a second version of the political imbalance problem, to which we now turn.

[103] Amendment XV (1870) did not prevent states from setting voting conditions, such as poll taxes and literacy tests, which would eventually disenfranchise most Black people in the South and enable the rise of Jim Crow oppression.

[104] The traditional account of what happened is C. Vann Woodward, *The Strange Career of Jim Crow*, rev. ed. (New York: Oxford University Press, 1957), esp. chs. I–II, pp. 3–95. See also Douglas A. Blackmon, *Slavery By Another Name: The Re-Enslavement of Black Americans from the Civil War to World War II* (New York: Anchor, 2009).

[105] David Cole, *No Equal Justice: Race and Class in the American Criminal Justice System* (New York: The New Press, 1999); and Michelle Alexander, *The New Jim Crow: Mass Incarceration in the Age of Colorblindness*, rev. ed. (New York: The New Press, 2010, 2012).

[106] Richard Cohen, *Making History: The Storytellers Who Shaped the Past* (New York: Simon & Schuster, 2022), ch. 19, "From George W. Williams to Ibram X. Kendi," pp. 524–561, provides a survey of books by historians, sociologists, novelists, and activists who, since the late 1800s, have been talking and writing in order to improve America's understanding of what relations have really obtained between Whites and Blacks.

The Second Iteration

The second iteration of America's political imbalance grew especially after 1945. Before the Second World War, considerable flexibility reigned in public life. Republicans and Democrats both supported and opposed many New Deal measures.[107] That is, each party had liberal and conservative wings. Some Republicans, left over from the Progressive Era, were willing to vote for New Deal social programs such as the National Labor Relations Act (1935). But many Southern Democrats, being Jim Crow zealots, were likely to insist that those measures be watered down, for example, to exclude from FDR's Social Security Act (1935) benefits for many Black Americans who were domestic servants or agricultural laborers.[108]

Then, two large trends began to eliminate outliers. This continued to the point where, today, relations between Democrats and Republicans have polarized almost completely. That situation is usually described as having people of the Left in one party against people of the Right in the other party.[109] For the sake of rhetorical convenience, we shall use those terms even though they are vague and imprecise compared to examples of liberals and conservatives, or the Left and the Right, in particular chapters of Western political history.

Black Migration

The first polarizing trend consisted of Black people moving North and West, to escape Jim Crow brutality and pursue economic opportunity. During the 1920s and afterward, these migrants tended to leave the Republican Party of Abraham Lincoln, which had emancipated them,

---

[107] See Robert D. Putnam, *The Upswing: How America Came Together a Century Ago and How We Can Do It Again* (New York: Simon & Schuster, 2020), pp. 74–79.

[108] On White, Southern, Congressional resistance to making the New Deal color-blind, see Ira Katznelson, *When Affirmative Action was White: An Untold History of Racial Inequality in Twentieth-Century America* (New York: Norton, 2005).

[109] See Thomas B. Edsall, *Building Red America: The New Conservative Coalition and the Drive for Permanent Power* (New York: Basic Books, 2006), and Matthew Levendusky, *The Partisan Sort: How Liberals Became Democrats and Conservatives Became Republicans* (Chicago: University of Chicago Press, 2010).

and to join the Democratic Party which, especially in Northern and Western cities, was relatively friendly to labor unions and social welfare projects.[110]

Consequently, Republican businessmen were likely to become conservatives, energetically promoting pro-market ideas against Franklin Roosevelt's liberal enthusiasm for social insurance, for economic regulation, and for fiscal projects like the Works Progress Administration (WPA, 1933) and the Tennessee Valley Authority (TVA, 1933).[111] After the war, those conservatives helped to generate political pressures which disinclined many Republican officials from continuing in the moderate mold of New York Governor Nelson Rockefeller, Senator Chuck Percy (R-IL), Senator Mark Hatfield (R-OR), Senator Margaret Chase Smith (R-ME), and Senator Leverett Saltonstall (R-MA).

White Migration

The second polarizing trend saw White Southern Democrats move into the Republican Party.[112] As when some businesspeople rejected New Deal economic policies and thereby pushed the Republican Party to the Right, here the reaction was for many segregationists – Whites, of course – to leave the Democratic Party, such as when some of them openly broke away from the 1948 Democratic national convention and created the States Rights Party which in that year nominated Senator Strom Thurmond (D-NC) as its presidential candidate.[113]

Fueled by notions of White supremacy, the movement of Southern voters out of the Democratic Party continued, especially after Senator Barry Goldwater (R-AZ) voted against the national Civil

[110] See Nancy J. Weiss, *Farewell to the Party of Lincoln: Black Politics in the Age of FDR* (Princeton: Princeton University Press, 1983).

[111] See Amity Shlaes, *The Forgotten Man: A New History of the Great Depression* (New York: Harper Perennial, 2008), and Kim Phillip-Fein, *Invisible Hands: The Businessmen's Crusade against the New Deal* (New York: Norton, 2009).

[112] See Joseph Lowndes, *From the New Deal to the New Right: Race and the Southern Origins of Modern Conservatism* (New Haven: Yale University Press, 2008); and Boris Heersink and Jeffery A. Jenkins, *Republican Party Politics and the American South, 1865–1968* (New York: Cambridge University Press, 2020).

[113] Thurmond left the Democrats and joined the Republican Party in 1964.

Rights Act[114] and then, as the Republican presidential nominee, drew considerable Southern support in the 1964 election.[115] The trend continued when Ronald Reagan, former Republican governor of California, opened his presidential campaign in 1980 by assuring White voters at a county fair in Mississippi that he believed in "states' rights" and, if elected, would "restore to the states and local communities those functions which properly belong there."[116]

Polarization

So the two parties moved toward realignment, to the point where one became heavily Right and the other became heavily Left, where the Right is considerably libertarian and the Left is more Keynesian, where the Right is considerably White and the Left is significantly Black. It is as if, like before the Civil War, America's current national factions – drawn to two great conglomerates known as Republicans and Democrats – have again lined up on opposite sides of a single line. This time it is a Right–Left dividing line, where moderation and flexibility have almost disappeared.[117]

[114] Goldwater's views on civil rights appeared within a framework of states' rights as early as 1960 in his *The Conscience of a Conservative* (Shepherdsville, KY: Victor, 1960), p. 37: "It so happens that I am in agreement with the objectives of the Supreme Court as stated in the Brown decision .... I am not prepared, however, to impose that judgment of mine on the people of Mississippi or South Carolina, or to tell them what methods should be adopted and what pace should be kept in striving toward that goal. That is their business, not mine. I believe that the problem of race relations, like all social and cultural problems, is best handled by the people directly concerned .... Any other course enthrones tyrants and dooms freedom." In other words, at the time, Goldwater did not regard "the people of Mississippi or South Carolina" as including all Black citizens of those states, who were mostly prevented from voting by various Jim Crow laws.

[115] In 1964, Goldwater won the popular and electoral vote in five (segregated) Southern states, including Mississippi and South Carolina.

[116] The text of his speech is at https://neshobademocrat.com/stories/ronald-reagans-1980-neshoba-county-fair-speech,49123. In 1980, Reagan won the popular and electoral vote in all eleven states of the Civil War Confederacy.

[117] Today, the feeling of "identity" – more than ideological devotion – has become a powerful motivation, setting America's "Right" and "Left" against each other. In which case, some part of the standoff is less that the Right and Left disagree (ideologically) on policy (say, about national gun control) than that they dislike or even despise each other as different identity groups. This factor can be described as "negative partisanship."

Thus, as we saw, almost fifty years after bipartisan support enabled the enactment of Medicare and Medicaid, Democrats proposed the national Patient Protection and Affordable Care Act of 2010, now widely known as Obamacare, which made possible health care for many previously uninsured Americans. By this time, however, polarization was firmly in place. As a result, the Affordable Care Act was supported by sixty Democratic senators while thirty-nine Republican senators opposed it.

Correspondingly, every Republican member of the House of Representatives voted against the same Act. Moreover, similar polarization infused Congressional votes for a Republican-sponsored Tax Cuts and Jobs Act in December of 2017. On that project, 51 Republican senators voted for the bill while 48 Democratic and Independent senators voted against it. At the same time, in the House of Representatives, not a single Democrat supported the bill and only 13 Republicans out of 240 defected to oppose it.

Constitutional Provisions

In cases like these, when there is a formal Republican majority in the national government blocking or overriding a governmental minority of Democrats, that Republican majority may actually represent only a minority of the national citizenry.[118] This is because the polarization of ideas and aspirations in America intersects with constitutional arrangements which sometimes enable a national minority to elect a governmental majority of senators, or representatives, or even a president, and thereby stymie the will of a national citizens' majority. These arrangements include circumstances, sanctioned by the Constitution, which rest on the two-senators-per-state rule, on gerrymandering in various states, on some states enacting voter suppression laws, and on the Electoral College method for choosing presidents.[119]

[118] In the Senate, due to the filibuster rules – which is an in-house procedural arrangement that does not appear in the Constitution but, in effect, often requires a sixty-vote working majority – forty-one Republican senators today can prevent an elected majority of Democratic senators from enacting legislation. Vice versa is also the case because, as the rules now stand, a minority of forty-one Democratic senators can prevent a majority of Republican senators from legislating.
[119] On gerrymandering within states, which permits minority voter parties to achieve majorities of elected officials (and therefore further gerrymandering), see Laurence

Political Imbalance

We cannot describe America's second political imbalance precisely, because we do not know exactly who belongs today to America's majority and minority voting blocs, which show up most clearly in "blue states" and "red states." To call them Left and Right is rhetorically convenient, as I noted already, but not at all precise.

So let us pause, to see why it is impossible to describe exactly the more than 81 million people who, in 2020, voted for the familiar but lackluster Joe Biden, as opposed to over 74 million people who voted for the also familiar but riveting Donald Trump, an unstable narcissist who, from 2017 to 2020, had shown himself to be patently unfit, by training and temperament, to be the CEO of a nation of 330 million people running history's oldest democracy, the world's most powerful military, and its largest economy.[120]

For example, let us observe that today's vigorous Republican Party is not driven mainly by racism.[121] Yes, Black–White frictions

---

Lessing, "Why the US is a Failed Democratic State," *New York Review of Books* (December 10, 2021), at www.nybooks.com/daily/2021/12/10/why-the-us-is-a-failed-democratic-state/.

[120] On Trump the person, see Justin A. Frank (ed.), *Trump on the Couch: Inside the Mind of the President* (New York: Avery, 2018), and Brandy X. Lee (ed.), *The Dangerous Case of Donald Trump: 37 Psychiatrists and Mental Health Experts Assess a President* (New York: Thomas Dunne Books, 2019). On Trump in office using the "powers" but not fulfilling the "duties" of president, see Joseph M. Bessette, "The Imperial Executive in Constitutional Democracy: Exploring the Powers-Duties Distinction," in Gary Schmitt, Joseph M. Bessette, and Andrew E. Busch (eds.), *The Imperial Presidency and the Constitution* (Lanham, MD: Rowman & Littlefield, 2017), pp. 145–165.

[121] This point is widely contested. On the Right, conservatives may say they favor "colorblind justice," where the underlying proposition is that all Americans, of every race and creed, should be treated equally and without racial prejudice or preference. For example, see Dinesh D'Souza, *The End of Racism: Principles for a Multiracial Society* (New York: Free Press, 1995), esp. pp. 201–287. And Newt Gingrich is against "affirmative action" and "identity politics" as practiced by some minorities. See Newt Gingrich, *Understanding Trump* (New York: Center Street, 2017), esp. pp. 99–117. Nevertheless, some writers and activists maintain that racism is the main force motivating Republicans. For example, see Adam Serwer, *The Cruelty Is the Point: The Past, Present, and Future of Trump's America* (New York: One World, 2021). Some have gone even further, maintaining that systematic racism infects Republicans and Democrats alike, via White behavior which, consciously or unconsciously, oppresses Black citizens. For example, Ta-Nehisi Coates, *Between the World and Me* (New York: Spiegel and Grau, 2015) and Robin Diangelo, *White*

cause some Republicans to close ranks against Democrats. And yes, Black voters, in federal, state, and local elections, sometimes cast as many as 90 percent of their votes for Democratic candidates. But additional conditions and aspirations, which excite various Republicans, *also* underlie polarization today.[122]

A case in point is the deep Republican concern for what is, sometimes, popularly called "culture" – as in the "culture wars" – to a point where Rightists, among them many White evangelicals, assume that they should vote for Republican candidates because they believe that judges appointed by Democrats have spearheaded left-leaning Supreme Court decisions which, say, forbid prayers in public schools, sanction abortions, and permit same-gender marriages.[123]

Furthermore, while polling indicates that race and culture matter very much to American voters, there are technical factors which confound even the most meticulous research into why people, avowedly Left or Right, liberal or conservative, vote as they do. Individual citizens entertain various opinions on this or that aspect of life. But because their voting is a secret act, and because they are not obliged to publicly declare their reasons for doing so, we cannot know for sure, even from extensive (but indirect) research, exactly what drives winning combinations of voters; that is, what personal aspects of sentiment and character unite large numbers of voters who on election day line up together for this or that candidate.[124]

Fragility: Why It's So Hard for White People to Talk about Racism (Boston: Beacon, 2018). That thesis is rejected by, for example, John McWhorter, *Woke Racism: How a New Religion Has Betrayed Black America* (New York: Portfolio/Penguin, 2021).

[122] Alan I. Abramowitz, *The Great Alignment: Race, Party Transformation, and the Rise of Donald Trump* (New Haven: Yale University Press, 2018), esp. pp. 131, 140–141, notes some difficulties of disentangling racial motivations from other voting impulses.

[123] For example, Rus Walton, *One Nation Under God* (Washington, DC: Third Century Publishers, 1975), and Jerry Falwell, *Listen America!* (New York: Doubleday, 1980). Donald Trump received the support of about 80 percent of White Evangelical voters in 2020. See https://divinity.uchicago.edu/sightings/articles/why-white-evangelicals-stuck-trump.

[124] Furthermore, even if voters openly declare their motivations, it is not certain that everyone will tell the truth about such sentiments. (Thus, after President John F. Kennedy was assassinated in November 1963, the number of people who said they voted for him

Red and Blue

Put all this another way. We should not assume that red-state or blue-state citizens are animated by a set of specific factors and outlooks which move them to sort to only one side or the other of the polarization line that has come to animate party politics. That is, they do seem to have sorted, but we don't know exactly why or for how long.[125] Relevant factors abound, but even careful scholarly research cannot say for sure which ones, if any, are decisive from one electoral district or election to another.[126]

What we do know is that there are sometimes tensions between religious and secular Americans, between pro-market and pro-government Americans, between old-fashioned and modern Americans, between mainline and minority Americans, between working women and housewives, between poorer and richer Americans, between isolationist and internationalist Americans, between rural and urban Americans, between less-educated and more-educated Americans, between

in 1960 was larger than the actual number recorded on Election Day in 1960. See www
.cbsnews.com/news/to-tell-the-truth-to-pollsters/.) Pollsters and political consultants are
familiar with this factor, and they conduct "focus groups" as one way of trying to identify real sentiments.

[125] Thus, Andrew Gelman, David Park, Boris Shor, and Jeronimo Cortina, *Red State,
Blue State, Rich State, Poor State: Why Americans Vote the Way They Do* (Princeton: Princeton University Press, 2010), p. 174: "We don't have a simple explanation
for where the polarization comes from." See also David A. Hopkins, *Red Fighting
Blue: How Geography and Electoral Rules Polarize American Politics* (New York:
Cambridge University Press, 2017), pp. 221–222. "The ongoing scholarly dispute
over the degree of political polarization in the contemporary American public offers
two sharply contrasting accounts of the relationship between the policy preferences
of voters and the actions of elected officials .... Each of these perspectives is cogently
argued, effectively supported with ample empirical evidence, and appearing succinct
in its conclusions .... But neither side can fully account for the findings presented
here."

[126] The outcome is clearly influenced by *nurture*. On the other hand, some scholars pro-
pose that leaning Left or Right is chiefly an outcome of *nature*, with psychological fac-
tors (attitudes) driving penchants. For example, Marc J. Hetherington and Jonathan D.
Weiler, *Authoritarianism and Polarization in American Politics* (New York: Cambridge
University Press, 2009); Jonathan Haidt, *The Righteous Mind: Why Good People are
Divided by Politics and Religion* (New York: Pantheon, 2012); and Avi Tuschman, *Our
Political Nature: The Evolutionary Origins of What Divides Us* (New York: Prometheus,
2013).

small towners and suburban Americans, between suburban and center-city Americans, between flyover and coastal Americans, between devout and secular Americans, between traditional and unconventional Americans, and so on, and so forth.[127]

Plus, not all of the sorting involves what scholars might consider to be, say, first-order factors. Thus Republicans tend to favor NASCAR and men's professional golf, whereas Democrats tend to prefer tennis and the WNBA.[128] And rumor has it that Republicans eat more hamburgers and Democrats eat more salads.[129]

Two Tribes

The result, when voting, is a jumble of individual inclinations which somehow add up to a "two-tribe" America, for electoral purposes producing fairly predictable Republican "red states" (mostly in the South, the Midwest, and the Southwest) and fairly predictable Democratic "blue states" (mostly among Northeast and West Coast states),

[127] For example, James Davison Hunter, *Culture Wars: The Struggle to Define America* (New York: Basic Books, 1991); Maurice Isserman and Mchael Kazin, *America Divided: The Civil War of the 1960s*, 2nd ed. (New York: Oxford University Press, 2004); Morris Fiorina, *Culture War? The Myth of a Polarized America*, 2nd ed. (New York: Pearson Education, 2006); Nolan McCarty, Keith T. Poole, and Howard Rosenthal, *Polarized America: The Dance of Ideology and Unequal Riches* (Cambridge: MIT Press, 2006); Hetherington and Weiler, *Authoritarianism and Polarization*; Levendusky, *The Partisan Sort*; Alan I. Abramowitz, *The Disappearing Center: Engaged Citizens, Polarization, and American Democracy* (New Haven: Yale University Press, 2010) and *The Polarized Public: Why American Government is so Dysfunctional* (London: Pearson, 2012); Jeffery J. Mondak, *Personality and the Foundations of Political Behavior* (New York: Cambridge University Press, 2010); Christopher Ellie and James A. Stimson, *Ideology in America* (New York: Cambridge University Press, 2012); Andrew Hartman, *A War for the Soul of America: A History of the Culture War* (Chicago: University of Chicago Press, 2015); Daniel H. Hopkins, *The Increasingly United United States: How and Why American Political Behavior Nationalized* (Chicago: University of Chicago Press, 2018); and Nolan McCarty, *Polarization: What Everybody Needs to Know* (New York: Oxford University Press, 2019).

[128] On red–blue sports preferences, see www.businessinsider.com/politics-sports-you-like-2013-3.

[129] And not just rumor. See Alison Perelman, "Political Appetites: Food as Rhetoric in American Politics," Ph.D. dissertation, Department of Communications, University of Pennsylvania (2013), ch. 1, "Tell Me What You Eat and I Will Tell You Who You Are," pp. 1–39, at https://repository.upenn.edu/cgi/viewcontent.cgi?article=2065&context=edissertations.

with only a few states being so irregular in electoral outcome as to be called purple.[130]

The Second Iteration

Here, then, is the second iteration of political imbalance. The confrontation of two tribes nowadays, somewhat reflecting Left and Right sentiments, and somewhat sorted into red states and blue states, apparently produces, or is produced by, a dividing line, like before the Civil War, which is so fixed that moderation and compromise rarely emerge. Instead, the system generates gridlock, where federal immobility rests on a national citizens' minority which wields entrenched veto powers against a national citizens' majority.

In the circumstances, like before the Civil War, majority rule does not reign, and the larger collection of American factions, represented by the Democratic Party, cannot overcome the smaller collection of American factions, represented by the Republican Party. The forms of democracy remain – that is, free speech, frequent elections, competitive parties, boisterous campaigns, etc. – but the substance of democracy has waned, because the Democratic Party majority often cannot peacefully shape budgets, regulations, taxation, appointments to high public offices, and the long-term missions of both military and civilian agencies.

Gridlock

"Gridlock" is the common term which encompasses polarization and its political consequences.[131] Some of gridlock's major components, whose numbers change from time to time, are these:

---

[130] Steve Kornacki, *The Red and the Blue: The 1990s and the Birth of Political Tribalism* (New York: HarperCollins, 2018), and Amy Chua, *Political Tribes: Group Instinct and the Fate of Nations* (New York: Penguin, 2018). In fact, America does not resemble a *really* tribal society like Afghanistan, and failure to understand that Afghanistan is tribal in fact may have adversely affected America's exit from that country in August 2021.

[131] See James A. Thurber and Antoine Yoshinaka (eds.), *American Gridlock: The Sources, Character, and Impact of Political Polarization* (New York: Cambridge University Press, 2015).

(1) A minority of American citizens now elect a majority of the Senate. This is because most large metropolitan population centers – including New York City, Los Angeles, San Francisco, Chicago, and Philadelphia – are located in relatively few states. The result is that in, say, 2021, there were 50 Democratic senators and 50 Republican senators, yet the Democrats in the Senate represented 41 million more people (voters) than the Republicans.[132] Furthermore, the Senate is governed mainly by its sixty-member cloture rule, enforced by the perennial option of filibustering or threatening to filibuster, which buttresses minority power in that House of the Congress.[133]

(2) Many red-state Representatives are elected in gerrymandered state voting districts which rely on voter suppression laws to disqualify or hamper citizens who are likely to vote for Democratic candidates.[134] The result is that, for example, in 2016, Republican members of Congress received 63,164,365 national votes while Democratic members received 61,750,853 votes. But the disparity in House seats awarded was much larger, so that 241 Republicans were elected against 194 Democrats.[135]

(3) The Electoral College is based on the Constitution's two-senators-per-state provision and mostly on states which choose to

---

[132] On the 41 million popular majority, see www.vox.com/policy-and-politics/2020/1/30/20997046/constitution-electoral-college-senate-popular-vote-trump.

[133] See www.washingtonpost.com/news/politics/wp/2017/04/10/the-senate-may-be-developing-an-electoral-college-issue/. Conservative pundit Rod Dreher refers to this situation casually as "the 60-vote threshold," which turns an outrageous (in my opinion) practice into a bland matter with no context and therefore not worth discussing. See www.theamericanconservative.com/dreher/abortion-our-liberal-democracy/.

On January 19, 2022, fifty Senate Democrats (plus the Democratic Vice President) failed to reach the sixty-vote threshold in order to enact a federal voting rights act. See www.nytimes.com/live/2022/01/19/us/biden-voting-rights-filibuster.

[134] Ari Berman, *Give Us the Ballot: The Modern Struggle for Voting Rights in America* (New York: Picador, 2015); Zachary Roth, *The Great Suppression: Voting Rights, Corporate Cash, and the Conservative Assault on Democracy* (New York: Crown, 2016); and Carol Anderson, *One Person, No Vote: How Voter Suppression is Destroying our Democracy* (New York: Bloomsbury, 2018). See also David Pepper, *Laboratories of Autocracy: A Wake-Up Call From Behind the Lines* (Cincinnati, OH: St. Helena Press, 2021), pp. 1–4, on how, for the 2020 federal election, Hamilton County in red-state Ohio, home to more than 830,000 people, including the city of Cincinnati, had only one drop-off box for mail-in ballots.

[135] See www.brookings.edu/blog/fixgov/2017/02/22/misrepresentation-in-the-house/.

award electoral votes en bloc. That is, in those states, winners take all
the electoral votes rather than permitting electors to cast their votes
according to popular vote percentages. The result is that, in 2000 and
2016, Republican presidential candidates lost the popular national
vote but were elected nevertheless, by an Electoral College which
favors national minority voters.

(4) According to polarized practice, these minority Republican
presidents then nominated, to lifetime Supreme Court jobs, avowedly
conservative judges, so that today the Right has a clear 6–3 majority in that institution.[136] To that end, in an act of exceptional partisanship, a Republican-dominated Senate refused to permit President
Obama to appoint a replacement judge after Justice Antonin Scalia
died in February 2016. The Republicans stalled; they refused to hold a
Senate confirmation hearing on Obama's nominee; and when Donald
Trump entered the White House, he promptly appointed to the Court
Neil Gorsuch, a known conservative.[137] As Senator Mitch McConnell (R-KY), leader of the Senate Republicans at that time said: "One
of my proudest moments was when I looked Barack Obama in the
eye and I said, 'Mr. President, you will not fill the Supreme Court
vacancy.'"[138]

Undercounting

To make things worse, the current political imbalance, which may
someday explode like it did in 1861, may be more unbalanced than
it looks when judged by routine voting statistics. That is because it
is mainly citizens on the Left who fail to vote due to voter suppression laws enacted especially in red states, whereupon those nonvoting
majority citizens do not appear in the final vote counts. And some

[136] For a claim that the Supreme Court is now a Republican institution and therefore
represents the national minority rather than the national majority, see www.salon
.com/2021/08/30/biden-commission-on-supreme-court-isnt-moving-fast-enough--or-
thinking-big-enough/.
[137] For an account of this appointment, see Carl Hulse, *Confirmation Bias: Inside Washington's War over the Supreme Court, from Scalia's Death to Justice Kavanaugh* (New
York: Harper, 2019), *passim*, but esp. pp. 159–181.
[138] McConnell is quoted in Ezra Klein, *Why We're Polarized* (New York: Simon & Schuster,
2020), p. 199.

Democrats-at-heart, who are not suppressed in blue states, are likely anyway to stay home or at work on election day. This is because electoral outcomes in their lopsided states are known in advance, in which case relatively little campaign money is spent to get out the vote and some majority-sentiment citizens may feel that their votes are not needed to push Leftish candidates over the top.[139] If some of those people really do stay home, the number of national majority citizens is understated in national election results.

Tyranny

We may sum up as follows. On the one hand, there have been two iterations of imbalance. The first exploded, wherefore the second may be very dangerous. Of course, to regard it as dangerous does not mean that we can know when, why, or if, for sure, the second imbalance will explode.

Still, even while we can only guess at what lies ahead, we should pay attention to circumstances of political imbalance which seem likely to persist, because they violate a great principle of American democracy, which is the principle of majority rule. And that violation, generating resentment, may someday provoke a political calamity.

On the other hand, to broaden the discussion, we should add to it a very significant analytical term because, where political imbalance obtains, it fosters and enables what Western thinkers have long regarded as "tyranny" of the minority. And this in a society whose Founders, many of them revered to this day, rebelled against tyranny, no more nor less, and sought to insure that it would not plague their country again.

* * * * *

Let us note, then, that, in a way, tyranny is our real target. In which case, what we have not seen so far, but what we will see a little further

---

[139] In the presidential election of 2012, from April 11 until Election Day on November 6, just ten states accounted for 99.6 percent of all advertising spending by the major party campaigns and their allies. For the same election, citizens who lived in California contributed $137 million to the campaigns of Obama and Romney, of which $320 were spent on ads in California! These numbers are from www.fairvote.org/2012chart.

along, is that the current political imbalance – which is tyrannical –
is supported and even validated, to some extent, by certain political
Stories. To the extent that that is so, as we shall see, the crises will be
especially difficult to resolve.

Before reaching those Stories in Chapter 6, though, let us consider America's second crisis, which flows from economic imbalance.

5 THE ECONOMIC CRISIS

As America has had two versions (iterations) of political imbalance, one after the other, two stages also mark the evolution of America's economic imbalance, this time tracking a movement from classic capitalism to neoliberalism.

Stage One

What we may call "classic capitalism" started during what scholars call the Industrial Revolution and gathered strength along with the Enlightenment.[140] That revolution introduced new elements of science and technology into Western society, and those enormously disruptive forces had to be framed somehow within new ownership and administrative arrangements.

Early Economists

According to eighteenth- and nineteenth-century economists such as Adam Smith and David Ricardo, the new arrangements, gradually enacted and continuously unfolding, looked like elements of a new

---

[140] Robert C. Allen, *The Industrial Revolution: A Very Short Introduction* (New York: Oxford University Press, 2017).

society emerging from what was left of European feudalism.[141] This society could be understood as a set of economic relationships which embraced three social "classes" – the owners of land, the owners of labor, and the owners of capital.

Serious thinkers assumed that leaving feudalism behind was preferable to perpetuating it, because effective interactions between these three classes and their resources would improve income and living conditions for many Europeans.[142] Making more of everything seemed, to these thinkers, obviously worth doing at a time when most people had little.

But the same thinkers also understood that the three economic classes which they identified were somewhat in conflict, in the sense that landowners received "rents" for which they usually did not work, while workers received, from their (capitalist) employers, "wages" which did not always reflect the full value of whatever skills and efforts they contributed to generating industrial or commercial output.

For our purposes, then, and along with Smith, Ricardo, and other early economists, we can see that the Industrial Revolution, like the French Revolution, had not just an upside – which we now call "economic growth"[143] – but also a downside. That downside was most famously condemned by Karl Marx, who extended the three-class analysis of earlier thinkers and insisted that the arrangements of classic capitalism were more progressive than feudalism but eventually led to workers suffering "exploitation" at the hands of capitalists who, in Marx's phrase, owned most of the "means of production."[144]

---

[141] The relevant works are Adam Smith, *An Inquiry into the Nature and Causes of the Wealth of Nations* (orig., 1776; New York: Modern Library, 1937), and David Ricardo, *The Principles of Political Economy and Taxation*, 3rd ed. (orig., 1821; London: Dent, 1911).

[142] Thus Smith postulated his famous "invisible hand," which would override the restrictions of guild regulations and encourage the productive "division of labor." Economists regard Smith as the founder of modern economic theory, but the term "invisible hand" appeared in *The Wealth of Nations* only once, in Book IV, ch. 2, p. 423.

[143] Early economists did not use the term "economic growth" but aspired to it. For example, in *The Wealth of Nations*, Book I, chs. I–III, pp. 3–21, Smith explains how government, by fostering the division of labor, can increase the nation's "wealth."

[144] In the vocabulary of modern economists, this downside, if you regard it as that, can be discussed as a matter of unfair or improper "distribution" or the need for "redistribution."

Because White Americans gradually dispossessed tribe after tribe of Native Americans, they had access to enormous areas of cheap farmland. Consequently, most of them were not directly and immediately involved in early stages of the Industrial Revolution. But as that revolution progressed, say in New England cotton mills, some Americans came to express, in an approximate way, the commercial ideas of men like Alexander Hamilton, which were mainly pro-capitalist, as opposed to the more traditional ideas promoted by men like Thomas Jefferson, who praised independent and small farmers.[145]

The Gilded Age

This debate continued after the Civil War, when great private corporations – embodied in the lives and times of men such as Andrew Carnegie, Cornelius Vanderbilt, J. P. Morgan, George Pullman, John D. Rockefeller, J. B. Duke, and Henry Ford – grew increasingly able to concentrate ownership and expand profits. Such corporations, in industry after industry, from railroads to petroleum, from steel to meat packing, from tobacco to telephones, and more, operating in the world's largest domestic marketplace, and profiting from efficiencies of mass production, gained substantial control over large swathes of American economic life.

In this process, Americans created a Gilded Age, which they named after great disparities of wealth and shocking displays of it.[146] What obtained was a harbinger of the huge income and wealth gaps which have recently appeared in today's One Percent Age dominated

---

[145] On these commercial and agrarian ideals, see Richard Hofstadter, *The Age of Reform: From Bryan to F.D.R.* (New York: Vintage, 1960), "The Agrarian Myth and Commercial Realities," pp. 23–59.

[146] Mark Twain published *The Gilded Age: A Tale of Today* in 1873. For an example, see Steve Fraser, *The Age of Acquiescence: The Life and Death of American Resistance to Organized Wealth and Power* (Boston: Little, Brown, 2015), p. 171: "Mrs. [Jacob] Astor herself was … described as a 'walking chandelier' because so many diamonds and pearls were pinned to every available empty space on her body." For a leftover of similarly flamboyant spending, tourists today (as I was in 2008) in Ashville, North Carolina, can visit George Vanderbilt's country estate Biltmore, with its 250-room French Renaissance stone chateau, which was constructed in the early 1890s. The estate now occupies only 8,000 of its original 125,000 rural acres.

by Amazon, Apple, Microsoft, Oracle, Facebook, Google, Citibank, Walmart, Koch Industries, Exxon Mobile, McKinsey, the Blackstone Group, Perdue Farms, Halliburton, Cargill, FedEx, Ford, Bechtel, Staples, Bain Capital, Boeing, Nike, Berkshire Hathaway, and so on.[147]

More technically, in the Gilded Age unbridled economic markets, sanctioned by governmental permissiveness called *"laissez-faire,"* became intolerable to many struggling Americans. The exploitation and poverty which they suffered affected millions of children, women, miners, factory workers, family farmers, and more. This downside of classic capitalism provoked numerous labor strikes, some very violent,[148] and considerable political resistance from populist party activists and progressives in both parties during the late 1800s and early 1900s.[149]

Consequently, politicking to regulate some of classic capitalism's abuses and uncertainties produced the Interstate Commerce Act (1887), the Sherman Antitrust Act (1890), the Pure Food and Drug Administration (1906), the Federal Reserve Act (1913), the Federal Trade Commission (1914), and the Clayton Antitrust Act (1914). Some states and the national government even enacted laws to restrict child labor, limit employee work hours, and empower union organizers, but the Supreme Court, which was not then in a progressive mood, struck down several of those.[150]

---

[147] By 1897, the richest 1 percent of American families (4,000 of them) possessed as much wealth as the other 11.6 million families. As of 2018, the richest three American individuals possess as much wealth as the 50 percent of Americans who have the least wealth. See https://time.com/5122375/american-inequality-gilded-age/.

[148] For example, Almont Lindsey, *The Pullman Strike: The Story of a Unique Experiment and a Great Labor Upheaval* (orig., 1942; Chicago: University of Chicago Press, 1967); William Serrin, *Homestead: The Glory and Tragedy of an American Steel Town* (New York: Vintage, 1993); and Scott Martelle, *Blood Passion: the Ludlow Massacre and Class War in the American West* (Rutgers, NJ: Rutgers University Press, 2008).

[149] On populists and progressives, see Robert Wiebe, *The Search for Order, 1977–1920* (New York: Hill and Wang, 1966); Louis L. Gould, *America in the Progressive Era, 1890–1914* (New York: Routledge, 2001); Michael McGerr, *A Fierce Discontent: The Rise and Fall of the Progressive Movement, 1870–1920* (New York: Oxford University Press, 2005); Charles Postel, *The Populist Vision* (New York: Oxford University Press, 2009); and Jackson Lears, *Rebirth of a Nation: The Making of Modern America, 1877–1920* (New York: Harper Perennial, 2010).

[150] For example, *Lochner* v. *New York* 198 U.S. 45 (1905); *Adair* v. *United States* 208 U.S. 161 (1908); and *Hammer* v. *Dagenhardt* 247 U.S. 251 (1918).

The New Deal

The Roaring Twenties generated considerable material progress in America but also heightened conflicts between labor and capital. Then an overheated stock market collapsed in 1929 and ushered in the Great Depression.[151] The following national election of 1932 brought Franklin Roosevelt to the White House and Democratic majorities to the Congress. As a result, until the Second World War, the New Deal enacted various government regulations to restrain large corporations, to reduce poverty, and to empower some of America's less economically successful people.

These measures included the Glass–Steagall Banking Reform Act (1933), which separated commercial from investment banking and instituted a federal bank deposit insurance program; the Agricultural Adjustment Act (1933), which, by limiting production, helped farmers to achieve stable incomes; the Tennessee Valley Authority Act (1933), which brought electricity to impoverished Appalachian families; the Public Works Administration (1933), which was followed by the Works Progress Administration (1935), and which built roads, bridges, dams, hospitals, airports, and other infrastructure, thereby providing work for the unemployed, who reached 25 percent of the workforce at the Depression's height; the Securities Exchange Act (1934), which reined in stock market abuses; the National Labor Relations Act (1935), which protected workers who wanted to organize, join unions and bargain collectively with their employers; the Social Security Act (1935), which provided unemployment insurance, aid to the disabled, and the beginning of national old age pensions; and the Fair Labor Standards Act (1938), which banned child labor in some industries and created America's first federal minimum wage law, of 25 cents per hour.

The Post-War Surge

America went to war in 1941 within New Deal regulations intended to impose considerable social responsibility on the market-centered

---

[151] An old but still powerful description of what happened to the stock market in those days is John Kenneth Galbraith, *The Great Crash* (New York: Houghton Mifflin, 1955, 1961).

economy of classic capitalism, and while creating effective frameworks of cooperation between government agencies and private employers. In those circumstances, American capitalists, workers, and farmers during the Second World War produced prodigious quantities of weapons and food, and, with extraordinary logistical sophistication, shipped what was necessary overseas to enable Allied soldiers to win the war.[152]

By 1945 in America, factories were booming, full employment reigned, and millions of veterans, from every social class, came home to higher education and then productive work. In these circumstances, from the war's end to the early 1970s, this market economy – a sort of "democratic capitalism" – with a broad array of politically conceived and enforced parameters and restraints generated unprecedented prosperity from domestic sales and foreign trade.[153]

Partly this prosperity depended on much of the industrial world lying in ruins after the Second World War, whereas American factories were untouched and ready to sell everywhere. Partly it was because the American dollar replaced British gold as the standard for international commerce via the Bretton Woods Agreements (1944), the World Bank (1944), and the International Monetary Fund (1944). And partly it was because, spurred by the Cold War, America's national government adopted "military Keynesianism," a sort of perpetual public works program of constant and enormous military spending, which not only kept up general demand for goods and services but also paid for major new infrastructure in freeways, higher education, scientific research, and technology.[154]

---

[152] Today, America is considered the world's leading military power and apparently maintains approximately 6,000 battlefield tanks. In less than four years of the Second World War, American factories produced around 88,000 tanks. On US military production during that war, see Alan L. Gropman, *Mobilizing U.S. Industry in World War II* (1996), esp. pp. 93–106, at www.files.ethz.ch/isn/23588/mcnair50.pdf.
[153] The term "democratic capitalism" appears in Jacob S. Hacker and Paul Pierson, *Winner-Take-All Politics: How Washington Made the Rich Richer – and Turned its Back on the Middle Class* (New York: Simon & Schuster, 2010), pp. 73–91.
[154] On military Keynesianism, see Jeff Faux, *The Servant Economy: Where America's Elite is Sending the Middle Class* (New York: Wiley, 2012), p. 39. See also Linda Weiss, *America Inc.? Innovation and Enterprise in the National Security State* (Ithaca, NY: Cornell University Press, 2014).

The results were impressive. A great many ordinary Americans, helped by union bargaining to achieve high wages and good working conditions, moved out of poverty.[155] Well-paid manufacturing jobs were available; employment in service sectors expanded; home ownership rose; household conveniences such as washing machines, dryers, freezers, and air-conditioners, multiplied;[156] and life became healthier and longer, due to medical progress and the federal enactment of Medicare.

Generally speaking, a great many people did well, on a rising tide that lifted all, or most, boats. Solid increments of affluence went not just to top earners but also to factory workers, clerks, drivers, miners, nurses, salesmen, farmers, and small business people, and especially to the 40 percent of income recipients whose steadily rising incomes placed them in what economists like Thomas Piketty call "the patrimonial middle class."[157]

Stage Two

Unfortunately, the good times did not last long for many of the Americans who had prospered in the Second World War's aftermath. Consequently, when the downside set in and persisted, some scholars came to believe that classic capitalism had evolved, regrettably, into what

---

[155] This is the "great compression" argument, where the wage compression of the 1940s, between different income quintiles, was more or less maintained until the 1970s. See Claudia Goldin and Robert A. Margo, "The Great Compression: The U.S. Wage Structure at Mid-Century," *Quarterly Journal of Economics* (February, 1992), pp. 1–34. The opposite of the great compression is the "great divergence," whereby between roughly 1980 and 2010, American incomes became more unequal. See this in Timothy Noah, *The Great Divergence: America's Growing Inequality Crisis and What We can Do About It* (New York: Bloomsbury, 2012).

[156] On the increasing number of household appliances, see Paul L. Wachtel, *The Poverty of Affluence: A Psychological Portrait of the American Way of Life* (Philadelphia, PA: New Society Publishers, 1989), p. 14. In 1959, when American Vice President Richard Nixon and Soviet Premier Nikita Khrushchev met at an American kitchen exhibition in Moscow, the Vice President praised America's kitchen appliances as an indication of the superiority of America's (anti-Communist) way of life. See https://teachingamerican history.org/document/the-kitchen-debate/.

[157] Thomas Piketty, *Capital in the Twenty-First Century* (Cambridge, MA: Harvard University Press, 2017), pp. 326–329.

they called "neoliberalism," which since the 1970s constituted a second stage of what many Americans call "free enterprise."[158]

By any name, the post-1970s American economy now embraces more than 330 million people; its principles and practices are enormously complex; many trends among them have moved ahead simultaneously; therefore even economists do not all agree on exactly what transpired between 1970 and 2020.[159] By way of illustration, then, let us consider here only some aspects of what happened; that is, ways in which neoliberalism unfolded.[160]

Neoliberalism

After member states of the OPEC raised oil prices four times in 1974, inflation began to reduce purchasing power for many Americans. Among other consequences, guaranteed minimum wages were worth less than before, and housing became more expensive as interest rates rose. Across the board, life became harder for Americans who failed to keep up.

At the same time, "free trade" in global markets permitted countries such as Japan and Germany, with factories newly built after the

---

[158] The term "free enterprise" is popular in America for commending the local alternative to "communism" or "collectivism" or "socialism," or "big government." This sentiment was expressed succinctly by Milton Friedman in the title of his book *Capitalism and Freedom* (Chicago: University of Chicago Press, 1962).

[159] For example, see Justin Fox, *The Myth of the Rational Market: A History of Risk, Reward, and Delusion on Wall Street* (New York: Harper, 2009); Andrew Ross Sorkin, *Too Big to Fail: The Inside Story of how Wall Street and Washington Fought to Save the Financial System and Themselves* (New York: Penguin, 2009, 2010); Bethany McLean and Joe Nocera, *All the Devils Are Here: Unmasking the Men Who Bankrupted the World* (New York: Penguin, 2010); Jeff Madrick, *Age of Greed: The Triumph of Finance and the Decline of America, 1970 to the Present* (New York: Vintage, 2012); Donald Barlett and James B. Steele, *The Betrayal of the American Dream* (New York: Public Affairs, 2012); Neil Barofsky, *Bailout: How Washington Abandoned Main Street While Rescuing Wall Street* (New York: Free Press, 2012); Rana Foroohar, *Makers and Takers: How Wall Street Destroyed Main Street* (New York: Crown, 2016, 2017); and Adam Tooze, *Crashed: How a Decade of Financial Crises Changed the World* (New York: Viking, 2018).

[160] See David Harvey, *A Brief History of Neoliberalism* (New York: Oxford University Press, 2005); Philip Mirowski, *Never Let a Serious Crisis Go to Waste: How Neoliberalism Survived the Financial Meltdown* (New York: Verso, 2013); and Wendy Brown, *Undoing the Demos: Neoliberalism's Stealth Revolution* (New York: Zone Books, 2015).

Second World War, to compete against aging American factories. The result was that American corporations steadily lost local market share in commodities from steel to televisions, from automobiles to tires, from home appliances to machine tools, from textiles to electronics.

The results were painful and obvious. At home, Volkswagens and Hondas increasingly appeared on American roads, and Panasonic and Sony appliances began to replace Westinghouse and RCA machines. Abroad, fewer American products were sold, causing cutbacks in production and employment, whereupon the combination of inflation and industrial slowdown generated the paradoxical discomfort – inflation and economic stagnation together – which economists called "stagflation."

* * * * *

To improve their market positions and increase profits, American corporations began to refashion themselves into new production configurations called modern "supply chains." Some workers were "downsized" because computerization and robotics permitted products to be made with increasingly less labor. Some workers were "outsourced" to local contractors whose workers were not protected by labor unions. Or their jobs were sent to foreign contractors who employed desperately poor people from developing countries. Some full-time and in-house workers were replaced with short-termers, independent contractors, or "temps,"[161] who worked here and there, in conditions which scholars would later describe as "precarious."[162] And those who remained were often prevented by employers from organizing to bargain collectively.[163]

---

[161] Louis Hyman, *Temp: The Real Story of What Happened to Your Salary, Benefits, and Job Security* (New York: Penguin, 2019), and Sarah Kessler, *Gigged: The End of the Job and the Future of Work* (New York: St. Martin's, 2018).

[162] Guy Standing, *The Precariat: The New Dangerous Class* (New York: Bloomsbury, 2016), describes most temporary, but also some full-time, workers as belonging to the "precariat."

[163] For example, Wal-Mart in 2020 was America's largest employer and employed 1.6 million workers. Wal-Mart called many of these workers "associates," and none of them belonged to a labor union. Wal-Mart used the "associate" designation because the Taft–Hartley Act of 1947 says that "associates" can be considered part of an employer's "management" staff and therefore do not have the same rights to organize that "workers" have. Over the years, efforts to unionize Wal-Mart workers ("associates") have been opposed actively by (real) Wal-Mart managers and have failed. On that point, see

Overall, "deindustrialization" set in, as some corporations either collapsed or emerged smaller than before.[164] The damage to many cities and towns, most starkly visible in Detroit, Youngstown, and other Midwest cities which lost thousands of factories, was enormous.[165] Moreover, once-strong, private-sector labor unions – representing craft workers, truck drivers, automobile assemblers, coal miners, garment and textile workers, steel workers, retail clerks, electricians, and more – were so reduced in size and power that they became an increasingly minor power in national politics.[166]

The Financial Sector

As manufacturing in America declined, what grew as a major force – social, economic, and political – in national life was America's "financial sector," comprised of commercial banks, mortgage agencies, insurance companies, venture capital funds, stock market brokers, and

---

www.theatlantic.com/business/archive/2015/06/how-walmart-convinces-its-employees-not-to-unionize/395051/. See also John Dicker, *The United States of Wal-Mart* (New York: Penguin, 2005), pp. 90–103.

[164] Barry Bluestone and Bennett Harrison, *The Deindustrialization of America* (New York: Basic Books, 1984). See also Robert Reich, *Saving Capitalism: For the Many, not the Few* (New York: Vintage, 2006), pp. 206–207: "When Instagram ... was sold to Facebook for about $1 billion in 2012, it had thirteen employees and thirty million customers. Contrast this with Kodak, which had filed for bankruptcy a few months before. In its prime, Kodak had employed 145,000 people."

[165] The *Detroit Free Press* newspaper recently estimated that, of 139 square miles of land in Detroit, as much as 40 square miles is now vacant land, or land occupied by abandoned homes and factories. See www.freep.com/story/money/business/john-gallagher/2019/10/26/detroit-vacant-land/4056467002/. In Janesville, Wisconsin, on December 23, 2008, the General Motors automobile assembly plant closed down. The plant at its peak employed 7,000 unionized workers, and at 4.8 million square feet of floor space was larger than the Pentagon, which has only 3.7 million square feet. (See Amy Goldstein, *Janesville: An American Story* [New York: Simon & Schuster, 2017].)

[166] For example, unions failed to dissuade President Bill Clinton from joining Republicans in Congress to enact in 1994 the North American Free Trade Agreement (NAFTA), which encouraged corporations to move American jobs to Mexico. On the limited political influence of unions lately, the Center for Responsive Politics reports on declared lobbying expenses and lists labor unions as donating about $50 million out of almost $1.8 billion to what the Center calls "Washington's influence community" in 2021. See www.opensecrets.org/federal-lobbying/ranked-sectors?cycle=2021.

more. The growth of this sector was fostered by pro-capitalist sentiments which were powerfully represented on the American Right, led by politicians such as Senator Barry Goldwater (R-AZ), President Ronald Reagan, Congressman Newt Gingrich (R-GA), Congressman Tom DeLay (R-TX), Congressman Trent Lott (R-MS), Senator Rand Paul (R-KY), Senator Mitch McConnell (R-KY), Congressman Kevin McCarthy (R-CA), and activists such as Grover Norquist, Phyllis Schlafly, the Koch brothers, the Bradley Foundation, and the Cato Institute.

These people and institutions never liked the New Deal, which assumed that markets must be constrained here and there by regulations inspired at least partly by principles of social conscience rather than faith in constant economic growth and change. Instead, especially as Republican strength in the national government grew, conservatives changed the rules of democratic capitalism in order to allow for more extensive and profitable private financial activity.

Some of the landmark rule changes included the following. The Supreme Court decision in *Marquette National Bank of Minneapolis v. First of Omaha Service Corporation* (1978) deregulated credit card interest rates, thereby enabling banks to saddle ordinary Americans with large and long-term debts. The Revenue Act of 1978, in its clause 401(k), authorized voluntary, tax-free personal retirement accounts that enabled employers to cancel previous, contractual, and lifetime retirement plans for which their companies were responsible. The Depository Institutions Deregulation and Monetary Control Act of 1980 abolished limits on interest rates for first mortgages and encouraged subprime lending. The Garn–St. Germain Depository Institutions Act of 1982 allowed state banks to issue adjustable-rate and no-deposit mortgage loans, both of which enticed many people into borrowing on terms that they did not understand and could not afford. The Secondary Mortgage Market Enhancement Act of 1984 authorized *securitization* of mortgages and therefore enabled banks to sell mortgages several times over, in what amounted to a Ponzi scheme that exploded in the Crash of 2008. The Riegle-Neal Interstate Banking Act of 1994 permitted headquarter banks to open branches in many states, thereby permitting already big banks, such as Wells Fargo, JP Morgan Chase, Bank of America, and Citigroup, to grow bigger and exercise more market power than previously. The Gramm–Leach–Bliley Act of 1999 repealed that part of the Glass–Steagall Act of 1933 which had prevented conflicts of interest – between client and broker – by forbidding national and state banks to engage in brokerage and insurance together. The Bankruptcy Abuse Prevention and Consumer Protection Act of 2005 made filing for personal bankruptcy difficult – if not impossible – for ordinary Americans trapped by debt in student loans, credit cards, and mortgages.

Personal Outcomes

The move from a former "democratic capitalism" to the present "neoliberalism" generated very different, and sometimes even frightening, degrees of success. In plain English, some people became winners and others became losers.

Economists attributed these disparities to various causes. Some of these were complex, such as automating factories and computerizing offices. One simple trend, though, was that, if and when American jobs were sent to cheap-labor countries, corporations which could continue to outsource, if they chose, could successfully offer, to many workers who remained behind, lower wages than they had earned before. On this score, free trade may have increased various indices of *collective* welfare such as the Gross Domestic Product (GDP). But economic exchanges between countries did not necessarily, within those countries, distribute growing prosperity *personally*, somewhat equally across the board, as in America during 1945–1970.

For example, while new economic processes advanced, the "middle class" shrank.[167] What we call the middle class is difficult to define conclusively. But economists often describe it as roughly the middle quintiles – say 40–50% of American families – which seemed

---

[167] On the Right, see Fred Siegel (ed.), *The Revolt Against the Masses: How Liberalism has Undermined the Middle Class* (New York: Encounter, 2013). On the Left, see Joseph E. Stiglitz, *The Price of Inequality: How Today's Divided Society Endangers our Future* (New York: Norton, 2012). For what the Brookings Institution's scholar Isabel V. Sawhill describes as a "centrist approach," see her *The Forgotten Americans: An Economic Agenda for a Divided Nation* (New Haven: Yale University Press, 2018), p. 6.

to lose ground as, over time, the upper 10% received a great deal more of GDP while the lowest 50% gathered a little but not much more (and sometimes lost ground absolutely).[168] Calculating the size of this trend is complicated (and controversial) but, assuming that the trend exists, approximately speaking, then apart from individual suffering it also creates an enormous social/political hazard because the middle class – outstanding in stability and moderation – is, by historical reckonings, the necessary basis for a democratic society.[169]

Collective Outcomes

Collective outcomes – again, winners and losers – also emerged from great shifts in neoliberal activity. Thus many "communities" suffered enormous social damage when key industries downsized or disappeared completely. This was most noticeable in the Rust Belt where, from 1950 to 2018, population declined in Detroit, Michigan, from 1,849,000 to 672,000; in Cleveland, Ohio, from 914,000 to 383,000; and in Pittsburgh, Pennsylvania, from 676,000 to 301,000. This while Houston, Texas, in the Sun Belt, was growing from 596,000 in 1950 to 2,304,000 in 2020.

Moreover, the financial sector eventually collapsed (temporarily), because over-speculation, in search of quick and easy profits, especially in the realm of high-risk mortgage securities, generated the Crash of 2008. This sector was exactly that part of capitalism most "unleashed" by several decades of dismantling New Deal principles and practices in favor of increasingly market-based decisions and projects. Confronted by the disastrous Crash, Washington budgeted hundreds of billions of federal dollars to prop up banks that were considered "too big to fail," even while millions of homeowners were unable to pay their mortgages and lost their houses.[170]

---

[168] For some relevant figures, see www.cbpp.org/research/poverty-and-inequality/a-guide-to-statistics-on-historical-trends-in-income-inequality.

[169] Drawing on thinkers such as Aristotle and James Madison, Ganesh Sitaraman makes this argument in his *The Crisis of the Middle-Class Constitution: Why Economic Inequality Threatens our Republic* (New York: Knopf, 2017).

[170] On this disparity, see David Ricci, *A Political Science Manifesto for the Age of Populism: Challenging Growth, Markets, Inequality, and Resentment* (New York: Cambridge University Press, 2020), p. 49, and footnotes 176, 177 on pp. 161–162.

And, perhaps worst of all, the practitioners of unceasing economic growth, which ostensibly paved the road enabling what Americans regarded as the pursuit of happiness, paid little or no attention to what most scientists warned against, which was "climate change."[171] Public talk about global warming was surrounded by fuzzy thinking which assumed that "sustainable growth" could combine more goods and services with "environmental protection," all the while denying that there are some environmental red lines which cannot be crossed safely and that there may not be enough time left for capitalist entrepreneurs to invent technological fixes that will stop the warming.[172]

Where Are We Now?

Like political imbalance, the problem of economic imbalance appeared twice. First, when classic capitalism, from the nineteenth century and into the late 1920s, had to be restrained by progressivism and was eventually reined in even further after 1932 by the New Deal and Keynesian interventions. And, second, when neoliberal sentiments after 1970 encouraged repealing much of the New Deal to the point where pro-market practices undermined much of the equality that had characterized Keynesian prosperity and did little to address global warming and climate change, for which everyone is paying now with forest fires,

---

[171] See 15,000 scientists around the world issuing in 2017 a global warning on climate change, at www.cbc.ca/news/science/15000-scientists-warning-to-humanity-1.4395767. The unvarnished facts of climate change appear year after year in reports from the United Nations-sponsored Intergovernmental Panel on Climate Change (IPCC). See them, including the 2022 report, at www.ipcc.ch/2021/08/09/ar6-wg1-20210809-pr/.

[172] See Milton and Rose Friedman, *Free to Choose: A Personal Statement* (New York: Harcourt, 1980), p. 215: "The real problem is not 'eliminating pollution' but trying to establish arrangements that will yield the 'right' amount of pollution: an amount such that the gain from reducing pollution a bit more just balances the sacrifice of the other good things – houses, shoes, coats, and so on – that would have to be given up in order to reduce pollution. If we go farther than that, we sacrifice more than we gain." Or, as Senator Lindsey Graham (R-SC) said, "I don't want to be lectured about what we need to do to destroy our economy in the name of climate change." See www.nytimes.com/2022/07/20/us/politics/climate-change-republicans-delay.html. On the danger of believing that partial progress on this front is sufficient, and on assuming (in the name of moderation) that there is a "middle ground between a livable and unlivable world," see www.vox.com/22709379/moderate-versus-progressive-democrats-climate.

desertification, hurricanes, floods, coral blight, glacier melting, species extinctions, droughts, and additional natural disasters.[173]

In short, this is very much *not* hypothetical stuff, *not* some kind of potential scenario defined by academic chatter. What we can see are two *real* (not hypothetical) crises in America today; two collections of principles and practices with immensely destructive downsides; two enormously important and problematic configurations in America's public life.

Back to Scope

One of these crises is formally political, while the other is formally economic. Both of them, however, will be dealt with, if at all, by national political institutions such as the presidency, the Congress, Washington agencies, and the federal courts. Accordingly, both crises can and should be regarded as falling within the long-standing ambit, or "scope," of political studies.

The problem, for our purposes, is that an effective scholarly response to these crises will be difficult to achieve. That is because, among other reasons, and as we will see now, both the economic and the political imbalances currently in place are supported and validated by powerful Stories, while Stories are not something that political scientists are accustomed to investigating.

---

[173] The failure of mainstream economic theory to facilitate collective action and thereby explain how to stop global warming is discussed in S. M. Amadae, *Prisoners of Reason: Game Theory and Neoliberal Economy* (New York: Cambridge University Press, 2016), pp. 224–244.

6 POLITICAL STORIES

I said earlier that we should look at facts, and we did that in Chapters 4 and 5. Now let us pick up an earlier thread in our analysis. The two crises of political and economic imbalance in America do not just *exist*. So far, and equally important, they also *persist*. Consequently, both imbalances are not only dangerous *today* but likely to continue to threaten public life into the *future*.

The Culprit

But what drives that continuity? A major culprit is Stories. Thus, apart from resting on short-term tactics and material calculations of immediately interested individuals and groups, America's political and economic imbalances are perpetuated by the sort of long-term stories or Stories which Neil Postman highlighted, which give shape and meaning to national life, and which, in this case, encourage some Americans to admire parts of the imbalances and therefore refrain from repairing them.

So let us explore those Stories, starting in this chapter with Stories that relate to political imbalance, and continuing in Chapter 7 with those that relate to economic imbalance.

Elements at Issue

The elements of political imbalance include,[174] but are not limited to, the fact that there will be two senators from each state, regardless of how many people live in those states;[175] the fact that electors will choose the president, while the Electoral College rests on the two-senators-per-state rule;[176] the fact that each state can, for the most part, determine voting conditions for citizens within itself, thereby permitting local parties to legislate gerrymandering and voter suppression practices;[177] and the fact that Senate rules permit filibustering on most matters, so that, in effect, a supermajority of sixty senators is needed to override a veto of as few as forty-one senators in order to conduct much of the Senate's business.[178] Everyone understands that this last requirement constitutes a denial of majority rule, but many Americans think that such a denial is (sometimes) desirable.

[174] A brief description of major elements in the imbalance appears in Adam Jentleson's article at www.theatlantic.com/ideas/archive/2021/04/how-stop-minority-rule-doom-loop/618536/. A fuller version of Jentleson's analysis appears in his *Kill Switch: The Rise of the Modern Senate and the Crippling of American Democracy* (New York: Norton, 2021). See also writings by law professor Sanford Levinson, who focuses on what he regards as difficult-or-impossible-to-fix shortcomings in American constitutional law and procedures. For example, *Our Undemocratic Constitution: Where the Constitution Goes Wrong (And How We the People Can Correct It)* (New York: Oxford University Press, 2008) and *Framed: America's 51 Constitutions and the Crisis of Governance* (New York: Oxford University Press, 2012).
[175] In the Constitution, Article I, Section 3(1).
[176] In the Constitution, Article II, Section 1(2–4) and Amendment XII.
[177] In the Constitution, Article I, Section 2(1). The power of states to set local election rules is limited by Amendments XIV, XV, XIX, XXIV, and XXVI. In 2021, Democrats in the House of Representatives approved a bill to further limit those rules, but the bill failed to overcome Republican resistance and did not achieve approval by a sixty-vote supermajority in the Senate. See www.nytimes.com/2021/08/24/us/politics/house-democrats-voting-rights-bill.html.
[178] On the filibuster, see www.brookings.edu/policy2020/votervital/what-is-the-senate-filibuster-and-what-would-it-take-to-eliminate-it/ and www.brookings. Edu/wp-content/uploads/2021/01/gs_20210122_debating_filibuster_transcript.pdf. Against the filibuster, see Gregory Koger, *Filibustering: A Political History of Obstruction in the House and Senate* (Chicago: University of Chicago Press, 2010), and Jentleson, *Kill Switch*. In favor of the filibuster, see Richard A. Arenberg and Robert B. Dove, *Defending the Filibuster: The Soul of the Senate* (Bloomington, IN: Indiana University Press, 2012).

Analytic Difficulties

Logically speaking, if Postman and others are right that Stories buttress the sensibilities we have about public affairs, then there must be Stories which justify the existing elements of political imbalance because those elements *do* exist (rather than *do not* exist). Unfortunately, however, there is no way to make a definitive list of such Stories, in order to examine them here.

Among other reasons, that is because, not knowing how to measure the power of *any* story (say, *The Handmaid's Tale*), we cannot know when specific stories (say *The Little Engine That Could*), which are numerous, turn into influential Stories (say "the war on terrorism") which are, relatively speaking, few. It is also because, especially in public affairs, we do not know exactly where to find the first or the last parts of any particular Story, or seams where some Stories overlap and merge with others.

Furthermore, we cannot clearly define a national situation as large as political imbalance. For example, where does it begin and where does it end? And what exactly are its parts? And how firmly are those entrenched, in principles, practices, and personnel?

Put that another way. Among things we do not know with regard to the current political imbalance, we do not know precisely how many voters or elected officials favor what amounts to minority rule, and we do not know exactly why such people believe that that sort of rule should obtain in their country. So we can talk about what we think Americans are thinking, but we cannot, for the most part, talk about their thinking precisely, empirically, objectively, scientifically, or, in the last analysis, definitively.[179]

[179] Surveys and public opinion polls provide useful information about people's beliefs and attitudes. But it is also true that when people respond to questionnaires, they may not know what they are talking about. For example, Tom Nichols, "How America Lost Faith in Expertise and Why That's a Giant Problem," *Foreign Affairs* (March–April, 2017), p. 60: "following the Russian invasion of Crimea, *The Washington Post* published the results of a poll that asked Americans about whether the United States should intervene militarily in Ukraine. Only one in six could identify Ukraine on a map; the median response was off by about 1,800 miles. But this lack of knowledge did not stop people from expressing pointed views .... The people who thought Ukraine was located in Latin America or Australia were the most enthusiastic about using military force there." See also Nichols, *The Death of Expertise: The Campaign*

What we can sense, though, is that Stories – some long and some short, some explicit and some implicit, some for and some against, some amateurish and some professional – encourage many people to believe that various parts of the present political imbalance are virtuous and legitimate. In which case they (the parts) are *not* dangerous and need *no* reform.

* * * * *

Keeping these limitations in mind, let us consider, in a common-sense way, some Stories which bear upon and prop up the institutional elements which constitute, in effect, a minority-rule situation in American politics today.

Extraordinary Founders

One Story, certainly very large and powerful, praises the Founders and their work.[180] Every country has its heroes. That Americans revere especially people who wrote the Declaration of Independence and the Constitution is unusual only in that, as opposed to generals, poets, scientists, theologians, sculptors, and other potential heroes, most of America's leading heroes – that is, the Founders – are remembered almost exclusively for their political deeds. Thus, when Americans speak of men such as John Adams, Thomas Jefferson, Benjamin

---

against Established Knowledge and Why it Matters (New York: Oxford University Press, 2017), *passim.*

[180] For example, on the Right, see the 2022 Heritage Foundation article by Samuel Gregg entitled "Why the Founders Matter for American Conservatism" at www.heritage.org/american-founders/report/why-the-american-founding-matters-american-conservatism. This article favors what it calls the Founding Era's ideas "which give America its distinctive identity." These include "the ideas of natural rights and natural law," the "particular political order of American constitutionalism, especially the separation of powers and the distinct idea of federalism," and "the political economy associated with the idea of a commercial republic." A somewhat parallel article on the Left, in 2010, in *The American Prospect*, is entitled "The Progressivism of America's Founding" and appears at www.americanprogress.org/article/the-progressivism-of-americas-founding/. It summarizes progressive admiration for the Founders and highlights "commitments to human liberty, equality and the public good" in "the Declaration of Independence, the U.S. Constitution, and the political thought of Thomas Jefferson and Alexander Hamilton."

Franklin, George Washington, Alexander Hamilton, and James Madison, the focus is on their public life, which is mainly admired.[181]

Stories to this end are sometimes apocryphal, like the Parson Weems tale about Washington serving as a national leader so upright and honest that, even as a child, he admitted that he cut down his father's cherry tree. But often they are a matter of positive impressions about Founders which are conveyed by popular history books, written in every generation by serious scholars such as Joseph Ellis, Gary Wills, Jon Meacham, Doris Kearns Goodwin, Gordon Wood, and David McCullough.[182] And sometimes they appear in professional jargon, as when conservative lawyers insist that courts in the United States should base their decisions on what modern judges like Antonin Scalia, Samuel Alito, and Clarence Thomas have called an "original interpretation" of the Constitution which – who else? – the Founders created.[183]

The bottom line on Founders is clear and available to people who tend to prefer existing political conditions to innovation. Many

[181] That some of the Founders, like Jefferson and Washington, enslaved other people never fit comfortably into this Story, and their brutality is now widely and publicly condemned.

[182] For example, Joseph Ellis, *The Founding Brothers: The Revolutionary Generation* (New York: Vintage, 2002); Gary Wills, *James Madison* (New York: Times Books, 2002); Jon Meacham, *Thomas Jefferson: The Art of Power* (New York: Random House, 2013); Doris Kearns Goodwin, *Team of Rivals: The Political Genius of Abraham Lincoln* (New York: Simon & Schuster, 2006); Gordon Wood, *The Americanization of Benjamin Franklin* (New York: Penguin, 2004); and David McCullough, *John Adams* (New York: Simon & Schuster, 2004).

[183] A full description of what he called "original understanding" appears in Robert H. Bork, *The Tempting of America: The Political Seduction of the Law* (New York: Touchstone, 1990), pp. 143–160. The "original interpretation" concept is completely rejected in Leonard W. Levy, *Original Intent and the Framers' Constitution* (New York: Ivan R. Dee, 2000), esp. pp. 284–321, and also by Erwin Chemerinsky, *Worse Than Nothing: The Dangerous Fallacy of Originalism* (New Haven: Yale University Press, 2022), esp. 186–207. See also Jacob Hacker and Paul Pierson, *American Amnesia: How the War on Government Led Us to Forget What Made America Prosper* (New York: Simon & Schuster, 2016), p. 11, which quotes former political science professor Woodrow Wilson, *Constitutional Government in the United States* (New York: Columbia University Press, 1908), p. 169: "The Constitution was not meant to hold the government back to the time of horses and wagons." On the other hand, recent praise for the same concept appears in (Supreme Court) Justice Neil M. Gorsuch (with Jane Nitze and David Feder), *A Republic: If You Can Keep It* (New York: Crown Forum, 2019), esp. pp. 108–127.

Americans believe that the Founders were remarkably wise, and that what they fashioned should be revised only rarely or not at all. Two senators for every state? Why not? The Founders agreed to that, didn't they? An Electoral College giving extra weight to sparsely populated states? No problem. While intent on creating a mechanism for choosing an effective yet limited federal executive, the Founders must have known what they were doing, right?

And what about the Equal Rights Amendment? Large Senate and House majorities in 1971–1972 passed the ERA.[184] But it was approved afterward by only thirty-five states. Why *not* regard that potential Amendment as justly rejected by "the people," according to the Founders' prudent conclusion that nothing less than three-quarters of the states (which is thirty-eight states today) should be permitted collectively to ratify an Amendment?[185]

Defending Virtue

Additional narratives can be used to regard minority political advantages as commendable if you assume that your minority is *virtuous*. Thus faith in the Founders inspires some large beliefs – Stories, really – about *tradition*, and these powerful beliefs are endorsed by some modern Americans in an intense contest which conservatives regard as a *culture war*. In this struggle, the Right fights to preserve what it calls righteous traditions which it believes that the Left disdains.[186]

---

[184] On October 12, 1971, the House of Representatives voted 354 for, 24 against, and 51 not voting. On March 22, 1972, the Senate voted 84 for, 8 against, and 7 not voting.

[185] Eight out of eleven former Confederate states did not ratify the ERA.

[186] A striking example of presumptive righteousness, while many Southern Whites were moving into the Republican party, appeared in William F. Buckley, Jr., "Why the South Must Prevail," *National Review* (August 24, 1957), pp. 148–149: "... the White community in the South is entitled to take such measures as are necessary to prevail, politically and culturally, in areas in which it does not predominate numerically ... [because] for the time being, it [the White community] is the advanced race ... [and] the claims of civilization supersede those of universal suffrage." See also George Wallace's inaugural speech when, as a Democrat, he took office in 1963 as Governor of Alabama and declared that he was *against* tyranny emanating from Washington and *for* continued segregation in the South. The text of this speech is available at https://digital.archives.alabama.gov/digital/collection/voices/id/2952. On Wallace's life and career, see Dan Carter, *The Politics of Rage: George Wallace, the Origins of the New Conservatism, and the Transformation of American Politics* (New York: Simon & Schuster, 1995).

Scholars usually trace this contest to the 1960s.[187] Because Storied beliefs unite affections and practices in their respective communities, some Americans, starting in the 1960s, were shocked by the rise of a "counterculture." Here were many young people, sometimes inspired by older thinkers and writers such as Paul Goodman,[188] Herbert Marcuse,[189] and Noam Chomsky,[190] who condemned standard American beliefs, who expressed enormous disaffection for common American sentiments, and who scorned long-standing American practices which they considered obsolete, if not wicked.[191]

These were people who openly, and loudly, demonstrated against the national project of an anti-Communist war in Vietnam, ignored local law and order while agitating for civil rights,[192] disrupted campus life by invading and occupying university buildings, rioted violently and destructively in city neighborhoods, used hard drugs and behaved promiscuously, and openly mocked what they called *the system*, by which they meant America's great institutions of government, education, defense, commerce, religion, and family.[193]

Many conservatives felt very strongly that such radicals, by definition on the Left, threatened the quality of mainstream American life. Moreover, as time passed, even more conservative anger mounted

---

[187] One can go even further and trace its start to the nineteenth century, especially to hostility between Protestants and Catholics. See James Davison Hunter, *Culture Wars: The Struggle to Define America* (New York: Basic Books, 1991), pp. 67–106.

[188] Paul Goodman, *Growing Up Absurd: Problems of Youth in the Organized Society* (New York: Vintage, 1960).

[189] Herbert Marcuse, *One-Dimensional Man: Studies in the Ideology of Advanced Industrial Society* (Boston: Beacon, 1964).

[190] Noam Chomsky, *American Power and the New Mandarins* (New York: Pantheon, 1969).

[191] For example, see The Port Huron Statement, a manifesto published by the Students for a Democratic Society (SDS) in 1962, at www2.iath.virginia.edu/sixties/HTML_docs/Resources/Primary/Manifestos/SDS_Port_Huron.html.

[192] Thus Martin Luther King's *cri de coeur*, *Why We Can't Wait* (New York: Signet, 1963, 1964), was written in a jail cell because he was arrested in Birmingham, Alabama during a civil rights demonstration.

[193] Commentary on the 1960s is endless. For example, William L. O'Neill, *Coming Apart: An Informal History of America in the 1960s* (New York: Quadrangle, 1971), and Harold Hayes (ed.), *Smiling Through the Apocalypse: Esquire's History of the Sixties* (New York: Delta, 1971). For a conservative view of the 1960s, see Allen Bloom, *The Closing of the American Mind: How Higher Education Has Failed Democracy and Impoverished the Souls of Today's Students* (New York: Simon & Schuster, 1987). For a liberal view of the 1960s, see Edward P. Morgan, *What Really Happened in the 1960s: How Mass Media Culture Failed American Democracy* (Lawrence: University of Kansas Press, 2010).

over endless countercultural, or at least unconventional, assaults on traditions which the Right cherished.

* * * * *

For example, conservatives were shocked when prayers in public schools were forbidden by the Supreme Court in *Engel* v. *Vitale* (1962) and *School District of Abington Township* v. *Schempp* (1963). Then fears of religious persecution escalated when the Internal Revenue Service (IRS) canceled Bob Jones University's tax-exempt status due to what the IRS considered to be racial discrimination by that religious (Christian, fundamentalist, and evangelical) institution, after which the ruling was upheld by the Supreme Court in *Bob Jones University* v. *the United States* (1983).

Concern for the quality of public education grew apace, as conservatives assumed that the ideas of progressive thinkers like John Dewey, even unto instructing pupils about sex, were gaining ground in America's grade school education. Along the way, some conservatives resolved to protect their children by removing them from public schools and instituting home schooling.[194]

Then came a cluster of issues known as "family values." When the Supreme Court decided, in *Roe* v. *Wade* (1973), that the Constitution permits abortions, many conservative evangelicals, such as the Reverend Jerry Falwell, joined conservative Catholics to oppose abortion, which they considered to be murder. That women would insist on such a right was attributed by conservatives to pernicious feminist ideas and activists, which were seen as responsible for many mothers working outside the home, for raising divorce rates, and for a general neglect of effective family life.[195]

---

[194] On objectionable teachings in public education, see James C. Hefley, *Textbooks on Trial* (Wheaton, IL: Victor Books, 1976), and Mel and Norma Gabler, *What Are They Teaching our Children?* (Wheaton, IL: Victor Books, 1985). Later, and specifically against Dewey, see Samuel Blumenfeld and Alex Newman, *Crimes of the Educators: How Utopians are Using Government Schools to Destroy America's Children* (Nashville, TN: Post Hill Press, 2021), esp. pp. 1–24.

[195] For example, Jerry Falwell, *The New American Family: The Rebirth of the American Dream* (Dallas, TX: Word, 1992).

In these circumstances, Phyllis Shlafly led a successful campaign to prevent full ratification of the ERA, chiefly on the grounds that it would undermine hallowed gender roles and destroy traditional families.[196] And many conservatives, like Anita Bryant, campaigned against enacting gay rights because they were convinced, among other things, that healthy children need to grow up in families which have two strong, but different, parental role models.[197]

Christian Nationalists

Support for traditional families may arise separately among activists on the Right, in line with preferences expressed by worried groups which are not necessarily aligned with one another. For many voters, however, they are linked by shared Stories in the sense that their concerns reflect a deep commitment to overall Christian values, regardless of one's denomination. And those values, in this view, are challenged by modern and secular forces in America today which, as we have seen, may express what Weber called "disenchantment."[198]

It has been clear for some time that many White Christian evangelicals have supported Republican candidates such as Richard Nixon, Ronald Reagan, the Bushes, George Romney, and Donald Trump. Not all evangelicals (who are mostly Protestants), or other Christian Americans (say, Catholics), are in that camp, though, and research suggests that those whom scholars call "Christian nationalists" are especially likely to vote Republican and therefore show up in the red state vs. blue state political lineup which underlies the map of political imbalance.

Christian nationalists are energized by a Story expressed in many versions, for example, that America's Founders were mostly

---

[196] Schlafly lobbied against the ERA via STOP ERA and The Eagle Forum, which were two organizations she founded. By the late 1970s, it became clear that three more late-stage state ratifications would not be forthcoming and therefore the ERA would not enter the Constitution by receiving the collective approval of thirty-eight states. See Donald T. Critchlow, *Phyllis Schlafly and Grassroots Conservatism: A Woman's Crusade* (Princeton: Princeton University Press, 2008).

[197] For example, Anita Bryant, *The Anita Bryant Story: The Survival of our Nation's Families and the Threat of Militant Homosexuality* (Old Tappan, NJ: Revell, 1977).

[198] A contemporary prevalence of disenchantment is the central point in Charles Taylor, *A Secular Age* (Cambridge, MA: Harvard University Press, 2007).

devout Christians, that their successors aspired to maintain "a city on a hill" (that is, a new Jerusalem), that this sort of Christianity sanctifies personal freedom and the quest for salvation more than mutual assistance via the Social Gospel, that America today continues, as the Pledge of Allegiance implies, to enjoy God's favor,[199] and that the Bible plainly defines abortion, homosexuality, and at least some aspects of humanism and feminism, as sinful and depraved.[200]

Worried that *majority preferences* will push aside *minority truths*, Christian nationalists are especially attentive to how the modern Republican Party is willing to fill the Supreme Court with conservative judges so as to give minority *principles* long-term power over majority *inclinations*. Most Christian nationalists do not seem to have regarded Trump as an admirable Christian, likely to be saved. But many of them were willing to disregard his idiosyncrasies – sins even, as with pornography actress Stormy Daniels – on the grounds that, in public life, he was a person who would resist liberal, radical, and leftist impulses in America and would, for sure, appoint pro-piety judges to the Supreme Court.[201]

[199] The phrase "under God" was added in 1954 to the Pledge of Allegiance during the Cold War, as an act of defining American as opposed to Soviet values. See www.presidency.ucsb.edu/documents/statement-the-president-upon-signing-bill-include-the-words-under-god-the-pledge-the-flag.

[200] For advocates of what is loosely called Christian nationalism, see John W. Whitehead, *The Second American Revolution* (Westchester, IL: Crossway Books, 1982); Tim LaHaye, *Faith of our Founding Fathers: A Comprehensive Study of America's Christian Foundations* (Green Forest, AZ: Master Books, 1990); and D. James Kennedy and Jerry Newcombe, *What If America Were a Christian Nation Again?* (Nashville: Thomas Nelson, 2003). For an overview, see Justin Watson, *The Christian Coalition: Dreams of Restoration, Demands for Recognition* (New York: St. Martin's Griffin, 1999).

[201] See Charles R. Kesler, *Crisis of the Two Constitutions: The Rise, Decline, and Recovery of American Greatness* (New York: Encounter Books, 2021), ch. 18, "Thinking about Trump: Morality, Politics, and the Presidency," pp. 383–399. (In 2022, Kesler was still enthusiastic about how good Trump was for the Court. See his "Annus Mirabilis: So far, it's been a very good year [for Court decisions]," *The Claremont Review of Books* (Summer, 2022), at https://claremontreviewofbooks.com/annus-mirabilis/.) See also Arthur Bloom, "For Trumpism, Skeptical of Trump" (June 2, 2020), at www.theamericanconservative.com/for-trumpism-but-skeptical-of-trump/. Bloom says that "Trump's character does not really bother me" because the Democrats are worse. On support for Trump among Christian nationalists, see Andrew L. Whitehead and Samuel L. Perry, *Taking America Back for God: Christian Nationalism in the United States* (New York: Oxford University Press, 2020), esp. pp. 65–87, 156–160. Against Trump, see Ronald J. Sider (ed.), *The Spiritual Danger of Donald Trump: 30 Evangelical Christians on Justice, Truth, and Moral Integrity* (Eugene, OR: Cascade, 2020).

Which he did, by appointing Justice Neil Gorsuch, Justice Brett Kavanaugh, and Justice Amy Barrett.[202]

A "True" Story

To step back from all of this, what links right-wing talk about tradition and culture is a general understanding – a Story, I would say – which appears repeatedly on the Right. It is an understanding which assumes that American society should be characterized by certain true principles and correct practices, that citizens can know what those ideal terms of reference are, and that they are *not* a constantly shifting mixture of partisan propositions and performances; that is, an expression of pluralism or relativism whereby no one knows what permanently desirable things and behavior are.[203]

The Republican, and onetime Speaker of the House, Newt Gingrich (R-GA), for example, projected this Story succinctly when he claimed that: "From the arrival of English-speaking colonists in 1607 until 1965 [the start of the counterculture?], from the Jamestown colony and the Pilgrims, through de Tocqueville's *Democracy in America*, up to Norman Rockwell's paintings of the 1940s and

---

[202] In the spirit of polarization, the Senate confirmed Justice Barrett in 2020 by a 52–48 vote. Not one Democratic Senator voted for her. As of May 2022, public opinion studies showed that a national majority of Americans believed that women have a right to abortion and that *Roe* v. *Wade* should be left standing as valid law. See www.pewresearch .org/religion /2022/05/06/americas-abortion-quandary/. Nevertheless, on June 24, 2022, Trump's three appointees to the Court joined three more Republican justices and overturned *Roe* v. *Wade* (1973) by issuing several concurring opinions in *Dobbs* v. *Jackson Women's Health Organization* (2022). Apparently, the Court sided with what it regarded as virtue. From Washington's conservative Ethics and Public Policy Center, support for striking down *Roe* appears in Ryan Anderson and Alexander DeSanctis, *Tearing Us Apart: How Abortion Harms Everything and Solves Nothing* (Washington, DC: Regnery, 2022).

[203] For example, George F. Will, *The Conservative Sensibility* (New York: Hachette Books, 2019), p. 23: "America was born with an epistemological assertion: The important political truths [that citizens are motivated by a certain 'human nature' and that they possess 'natural rights' which are not created by government] are not merely knowable, they are known. They are self-evident in that they are obvious to any mind not clouded by ignorance or superstition." (That much of the Founding Generation believed in such truths – via what for them seemed to be shared common sense – is explained in Carl L. Becker, *The Declaration of Independence: A Study in the History of Political Ideas* [New York: Vintage, 1922, 1942], pp. 24–79.)

1950s, there was one continuous civilization built around commonly accepted legal and cultural principles."[204]

The Republican, and former Chair of the National Endowment for the Humanities, Lynne Cheney likewise postulated a society based on true and shared principles. For her, American civilization emerges from Western civilization, which has always promoted admirable, but also knowable, means and ends. Therefore, she decried postmodern academic sentiments that she attributed to the philosopher Michel Foucault. "His ideas," she said, "were nothing less [among liberal academics] than an assault on Western civilization. In rejecting an independent reality, an externally verifiable truth, and even reason itself, he was rejecting the foundational principles of the West."[205]

The Republican, and longtime pundit, Patrick Buchanan evoked a similar blend of *tradition* and *culture* when he spoke to the Republican National Convention in 1992. Declaring that the Republican Party stands *against* abortion, feminism, and gay marriage, but that it also stands *for* Judeo-Christian values, voluntary prayer in schools, and original interpretation of the Constitution, Buchanan then declared that this election "is about who we are. It is about what we believe, and what we stand for as Americans. There is a religious war going on in this country. It is a cultural war, as critical to the kind of nation we shall be as the Cold War itself, for this war is for the soul of America."[206]

The Republican, and two-time president, George W. Bush, offered much the same view of America in 2001, in his First Inaugural Address.

---

[204] Gingrich is quoted in Andrew Hartman, *A War for the Soul of America: A History of the Culture War* (Chicago: University of Chicago Press, 2015), p. 6. A typical Gingrich overview of American civilization appears in his "Introduction to Renewing American Civilization," in Jeffrey A. Eisenach and Albert Stephen Hanser (eds.), *Readings in Renewing American Civilization* (New York: McGraw-Hill, 1993), pp. 1–22.

[205] Lynne V. Cheney, *Telling the Truth: Why Our Culture and Our Country Have Stopped Making Sense – and What We Can Do About It* (New York: Simon & Schuster, 1995), p. 91.

[206] See Buchanan's speech at https://voicesofdemocracy.umd.edu/buchanan-culture-war-speech-speech-text/.

We have a place, all of us, in a long story – a story we continue, but whose end we will not see .... It is the American story – a story of flawed and fallible people, united across the generations by grand and enduring ideals .... Our unity, our union, is the serious work of leaders and citizens in every generation. And this is my solemn pledge: I will work to build a single nation of justice and opportunity. I know this is in our reach because we are guided by a power larger than ourselves who creates us equal in His image.[207]

The Republican Trend

Such sources demonstrate not just conservative ideas and aspirations, but that those beliefs, expressed in powerful Stories, moved strongly into the Republican Party, especially while many Southern voters moved there as well.[208] And for two reasons, this ideological development is important for our purposes.

First, the movement of conservative voters into the Republican Party means that people of the Right now dominate elections (and especially primary elections) in *red states*. And what we know about those states – mostly in the South, the Midwest, and the Southwest – is that they elect very few, if any, Republicans of the sort once known as moderate; that is, the people once called Rockefeller Republicans.[209]

The result of this winnowing is that, nowadays, where Republican officials gain access to federal institutions – in the Senate and the House, in the Presidency, in the Judiciary, and in the Treasury Department, the Environmental Protection Agency, the Department of Education, the Department of Homeland Security, and other Washington agencies – they and their followers are a militant minority on much

---

[207] See Bush's speech at https://georgewbush-whitehouse.archives.gov/news/inaugural-address.html.

[208] For a good example, see the Preamble to the 1992 Republican Party Platform at www.presidency.ucsb.edu/documents/republican-party-platform-1992.

[209] See Geoffrey Kabaservice, *Rule and Ruin: The Downfall of Moderation and the Destruction of the Republican Party, From Eisenhower to the Tea Party* (New York: Oxford University Press, 2017).

the same page, convinced by various Stories that their principles and practices are virtuous. In which case, even if they see that they do not constitute a "numerical majority" of citizens, they can regard themselves as Americans who are "morally entitled" to use the legal means they possess to promote values and lifestyles which they believe are intrinsically commendable.

Second, Stories on the Right about tradition and culture suggest that the right sort of people in America are beleaguered, that liberals and Leftists are sure to use every opportunity to mock, challenge, undermine, and scorn the principles and practices that made America great over generations. In scholarly terms, it is as if enemies of the Right reject what may be defined as crucial elements of American *exceptionalism*.[210]

On this score, many Republican voters and politicians – such as the Christian nationalists – in red states want an America that will be more united than it is now, that will be as patriotic as such Republicans believe it used to be, that will be dedicated to long-cherished practices rather than unconventional behavior, and that will advocate time-honored ethical standards rather than the so-called (and perhaps fleeting) values of pluralism, many of them secular, which challenge propriety today.[211]

---

[210] Thus Norman Podhoretz, then editor of *Commentary Magazine*, a favorite outlet for neoconservatives, asked rhetorically if counterculture partisans really wanted to be Americans at all. "Are they not expressing the yearning *not* to be Americans?" Podhoretz is quoted in Hartman, *War for the Soul of America*, p. 50. The same sentiment – like when, during the Cold War, some Americans accused other Americans of being "un-American" – appears frequently on the Right, as in Glenn Ellmers, "Conservatism is not Enough," *The American Mind* (March 24, 2021). Ellmers, a Claremont Institute fellow, declares that "most people living in the United States today – certainly more than half – are not Americans in any meaningful sense of that term. I don't just mean the millions of illegal immigrants .... I'm really referring to the many native-born people – some of whose families have been here since the Mayflower – who may technically be citizens of the United States but are no longer (if they were ever) Americans. They do not believe in, live by, or even like the principles, traditions, and ideals that until recently defined America as a nation and as a people." See Ellmers' essay at https://americanmind.org/salvo/why-the-claremont-institute-is-not-conservative-and-you-shouldnt-be-either/. Partisanship around this point can be thoroughly uncompromising, as in Daniel J. Flynn, *Why the Left Hates America: Exposing the Lies that have Obscured Our Nation's Greatness* (Roseville, CA: Prima Publishing, 2002), ch. 2, "The Roots of Anti-Americanism," pp. 39–78, and ch. 3, "Anti-American Chic," pp. 79–11.

[211] For example, see President Ronald Reagan's "Farewell Address to the Nation," from January 11, 1989, at www.reaganfoundation.org/media/128652/farewell.pdf.

Limited Government

To those ends, a powerful Story of "limited government" comes into play. This Story justifies a widespread American attitude which appears in the saying, sometimes attributed to Henry David Thoreau, that, "The best government is that which governs least."[212]

The Story of limited government goes back at least to the Declaration of Independence, wherein the American colonies rejected subordinate status in the British Empire, and wherein King George III was described as a tyrant because Jefferson and the Continental Congress, in deference to "the opinions of mankind," knew that political thinkers had long condemned the behavior of tyrants. Some years later, the Founders fashioned a Constitution which they intended would divide up governmental authority and powers to the point where tyranny would not arise.

The bottom line here – and this is where an ideal of limited government comes into play – was that government officials should either be given few powers, or that government institutions should be so splintered that they will not frequently exercise even the few powers which they possess.[213]

This anti-tyranny theme has resonated strongly in American thinking since the Founding, and partisans on the Right since at least the New Deal have wielded it repeatedly to complain about government projects advocated by their liberal opponents. In Ronald Reagan's folksy anecdote, the animus against "big government" gained immortality when he described "the nine most terrifying words" in the English language as: "I'm from the government and I'm here to help."[214]

* * * * *

[212] It also appeared in *The Democratic Review*, "An Introductory Statement of the Democratic Principle" (1837), in Joseph L. Blau (ed.), *Social Theories of Jacksonian Democracy: Representative Writings of the Period 1825–1850* (Indianapolis, IN: Liberal Arts Press, 1954), pp. 21–37, but esp. 27.

[213] Gary Wills, *A Necessary Evil: A History of American Distrust of Government* (New York: Touchstone, 1999) claims that this Story is a myth, based on anti-Federalist ideas and rhetoric, whereas the Constitution as written (not by anti-Federalists) in Philadelphia was really designed to create an *efficient*, rather than *limited* government, and politicians of every persuasion since the Founding have used that government's powers when it suited them and criticized their opponents for doing the same.

[214] This phrase appears in Reagan's news conference of August 12, 1986, at www .washingtonpost.com/archive/politics/1986/08/13/transcript-of-president-reagans-news-

Concerning political imbalance, the point here is that, to many on the Right, this dog does not bark. Conservatives worry constantly about how government deals with matters such as school prayers, women's rights, welfare, racial equality, identity politics, and business taxes. However, the fact that minority rule now obtains in Washington simply does not bother conservatives.

They hear no bark because they sense no principled dilemma. They need not address the technical facts of the case because, if the national majority cannot legislate, its inability to do so may be regarded not as a violation of the principle of government by consent but as an affirmation of constitutional restraint on the selfish majority's penchant for tyrannizing the virtuous minority.[215]

Reactionaries

In sum, there exists an overall justification for America's political imbalance. On this score, in the canon of political thought, the American Right is "reactionary." I do not mean that in a pejorative sense, but in the sense of extolling, as during the Enlightenment, some people in the population who resist – in their opinion, rightfully – others whom the Right believes are abandoning old-time principles and destroying circumstances which

conference/bceaa7d7-a544-4c4e-8af1-51f303a00e25/. On limiting the scope of government activity, see also Phyllis Shlafly, *The Conservative Case for Trump* (Washington, DC: Regnery, 2016), p. 130, where Shlafly lists, as government's "primary duties," only two: national defense and social security.

[215] Thus Mollie Hemingway, *Rigged: How the Media, Big Tech, and the Democrats Seized Our Elections* (Washington, DC: Regnery, 2021), pp. 15–16, observes that Al Franken won (unfairly, by court order) a disputed senatorial election in Minnesota and thereby became the sixtieth Democratic senator in 2009. As a result, she says, the Democrats were able "to pass filibuster-proof legislation." Otherwise, "Obamacare probably would not have passed." What this means, I think, is that if the vote for a new national health care law had been 59–41 in the Senate, it would not have been enacted and Hemingway would have said nothing about it. That is, if the Act had failed to pass, she would not have regarded that as a noteworthy violation of the principle of government by consent, because she regards her side in the Senate as virtuous, in which case a filibuster, or the threat of it, against the majority is morally sound. Other thinkers on the Right also tend to regard their side as virtuous and the Left as immoral. For example, see Tammy Bruce, *The Death of Right and Wrong: Exposing the Left's Assault on our Culture and Values* (New York: Crown Forum, 2004). Ann Coulter promotes this view frequently. For example, Coulter, *Treason: Liberal Treachery from the Cold War to the War on Terrorism* (New York: Crown Forum, 2003).

favor it (the Right). This description of conservatism indicates that different conservatives – in America and abroad, now and then, from Edmund Burke to George Will – may strive to preserve principles and circumstances which vary over time. The constancy, though, is that reactionaries in every era seek to protect a ruling sector or commendable group which they believe may be losing power unjustly.[216]

In the American case, William Buckley, Jr. founded the *National Review* and simultaneously announced his rejection of the status quo by declaring that he wanted to stop the world and get off.[217] This for him meant that he wanted not to continue down the road of secular modernity and Keynesian economic policies.[218]

In a similar vein, Supreme Court Justice Antonin Scalia favored an inclination to "stop" when he declared that, "Except as limited by a constitutional prohibition agreed to by the People, the States are free to adopt whatever laws they like."[219] What Scalia meant was that, in the case of *Obergefell* v. *Hodges* (2015), he dissented from the 5–4 majority opinion and would have permitted state governments to forbid same-sex marriages, which many conservatives regarded as thoroughly immoral.[220]

---

[216] On reaction in the history of political thought, with appropriate references to Karl Mannheim, *Ideology and Utopia* (1936), see Corey Robin, *The Reactionary Mind: Conservatism from Edmund Burke to Donald Trump* (New York: Oxford University Press, 2018), pp. 3–37.

[217] See Buckley, "Publisher's Statement" and "Credenda," *National Review* (November 19, 1955), pp. 5–6.

[218] He had already cut loose from what he regarded as mistaken teachings at his alma mater Yale University. See Buckley, *God and Man at Yale: The Superstitions of "Academic Freedom"* (Chicago: Regnery, 1951).

[219] Kevin A. Ring (ed.), *Scalia's Court: A Legacy of Landmark Opinions and Dissents* (Washington, DC: Regnery, 2004, 2016), p. 398. This is more or less the notion that underlies the Court's recent decision in *Dobbs* v. *Jackson Women's Health Organization* (2022), which strikes down the national right to abortion that had been proclaimed in *Roe* v. *Wade* (1973) and leaves a right (or not) to abortion to be decided by each and every state. Thus, in *Dobbs*: "The Constitution does not confer a right to abortion. *Roe* and *Casey* are overruled, and the authority to regulate abortion is returned to the people and their elected representatives." See www.supremecourt.gov/opinions/21pdf/19-1392_6j37.pdf.

[220] Scalia described this principle of *state* freedom as "fundamental" to America's "system of government." I want to think that he – and the justices who overruled *Roe* v. *Wade* (1973) and *Planned Parenthood* v. *Casey* (1992) in *Dobbs* v. *Jackson* (2022) – would have condemned the nation's Southern states when they (actually, their White voters)

More famously, President Ronald Reagan announced that "It's morning again in America."[221] In this view, it was as if, until that morning, left-wing rioters, flag burners, welfare queens, baby-killers, and judicial activists had smothered many American decencies. Reagan also assured his constituents that, as Thomas Paine said, "We have it in our power to begin the world over again."[222] That is, according to Reagan (although not to Paine), we conservatives can turn the clock back to a better time.

From there, it was not surprising when Donald Trump promised voters that, if elected, he would "Make America Great Again!"[223] In this reactionary view, it was as if the nation *had been great* but no longer is. It was as if America *had been exceptional* but eventually lost some of its special qualities because of liberal projects such as the New Deal, feminism, environmental protection, Obamacare, and identity politics.[224]

---

called that principle "states' rights," and used it to (legally) oppress Southern Black Americans after the Civil War in which "the People" (a *national* majority) banned outright slavery in blood and fire.

[221] This phrase was one of Reagan's campaign slogans in 1984.

[222] Reagan quoted Paine repeatedly. For example, see his speech accepting the Republican nomination for president in 1980, https://usa.usembassy.de/etexts/speeches/rhetoric/rraccept.htm.

[223] Sarah Churchwell tracks the history of related phrases that foreshadowed the MAGA story in her *Behold America: The Entangled History of "America First" and "The American Dream"* (New York: Hachette, 2018), *passim*.

[224] In 2016, Trump won the electoral votes of every former Confederate state except Virginia, whose suburbs of Washington, DC, are home to many federal government workers, contractors, lawyers, consultants, and lobbyists who disliked Trump's anti-Washington campaign messages.

7 ECONOMIC STORIES

We can easily move from Stories sanctioning political imbalance to those warranting economic imbalance because the additional pro-status quo Stories often originate in the thinking of pro-market economists. From there, they pass on to America's public conversation, mediated by many spokespeople – politicians, journalists, lobbyists, teachers, pundits, activists, and more – who, for more than a century, and especially since the Russian Revolution (1917–1923), have regarded America as a worthy capitalist society threatened by ideas and policies promoted by deplorable socialist thinkers and states.

Thus, for more than 200 years, mainstream economists in Europe and America have been analyzing capitalism, free enterprise, neoliberalism, rational markets, or those arrangements by any other name.[225] For generations, they have explored this economy, and more often than not they have commended it. To this end, the central bank of Sweden, which is a capitalist institution, created a so-called Nobel Prize in economics,[226] and the liberal economist Robert Heilbroner,

---

[225] For an explanation of mainstream economics and some of its central ideas, see David Ricci, *A Political Science Manifesto for the Age of Populism: Challenging Growth, Markets, Inequality, and Resentment* (New York: Cambridge University Press, 2020), "Mainstream Economics," pp. 29–44.

[226] See Avner Offer and Gabriel Soderberg, *The Nobel Factor: The Prize in Economics, Social Democracy, and the Market Turn* (Princeton: Princeton University Press, 2016), pp. 1–15, 89–106. The prize is officially entitled "The Sveriges Riksbank Prize in Economic Sciences in Memory of Alfred Nobel."

less enthusiastic than the Swedish Riksbank, was on target when he observed that "The best kept secret in [academic] economics is that economics [what they teach] is about capitalism."[227]

Economic Rhetoric

For our purposes, what mainstream economists say and teach about American economic life amounts – implicitly – to telling stories, even Stories, about it. These economists sometimes claim that their work is *scientific*, in that they dispassionately analyze mainly *facts* (or models). No stories there, right?[228]

Well, not exactly, because, as Deirdre McCloskey points out, many analytical terms central to mainstream economics – such as "rational individuals," "marginal utility," "production functions," "imperfect competition," and more – are not factual but actually rhetorical devices.[229] In which case they convey powerful messages, sometimes unspoken, about the meaning and significance of whatever economic activity they purport to describe.

What McCloskey means by economic rhetoric – and this is where pro-capitalism storytelling occurs – is that mainstream economists tend to speak in terms which compare economic acts to familiar things; that is, in terms which suggest that what people do economically is like *this*, which we know about, or is similar to *that*, which we also know about.

For example, mainstream economists teach us that, unregulated by government, what people do for money is, usually, ethically compatible with what other people – such as the butcher, the brewer,

[227] Heilbroner is quoted in Thomas I. Palley, *Plenty of Nothing: The Downsizing of the American Dream and the Case for Structural Keynesianism* (Princeton: Princeton University Press, 1998), p. 15. The relationship between economic analysis and capitalism is discussed in Robert Heilbroner and William Milberg, *The Crisis of Vision in Modern Economic Thought* (New York: Cambridge University Press, 1995), *passim*.

[228] Whether or not mainstream economists believe that their work is "scientific," an example of their thinking which is often regarded as scientific, sort of, is in Milton Friedman, *Essays in Positive Economics* (Chicago: University of Chicago Press, 1953), "The Methodology of Positive Economics," pp. 1–27.

[229] Deirdre McCloskey, *The Rhetoric of Economics*, 2nd ed. (Madison: The University of Wisconsin, 1998), *passim*.

and the baker – also do for money because an "invisible hand" brings all voluntary (and peaceful) economic acts into harmony with others. And they teach us that, if left mainly alone, markets will reach a point of "equilibrium," wherein people will receive income fairly, according to how much they contribute to the sum total of goods and services generated by their society.

Now, technically speaking, this sort of teaching rests on rhetorical figures of speech, for example, on metaphors, such as the "invisible hand," which suggest that a benign Providence watches over us; on analogies, such as the "law of self-interest," as if the behavior of one human being toward another is as invariable as when the law of gravity dictates relationships between celestial bodies; and on similes, such as the "demand curve," which can be plotted on a graph as if, in real life, preferences and purchases fall into a smooth arc pattern.

In McCloskey's view, and in mine, building on rhetoric often equates to storytelling. On that score, mainstream economists offer abstract "models" of economic activity. And then these models, which Avner Offer and Gabriel Soderberg call "imaginary machines," tell what I call a Story, in many interlocking parts, about how "rational individuals" can work through a "free market economy" which fosters "efficiency," maximizes "utility" (happiness), and promotes "prosperity."[230]

Cognitive Capture

For our purposes, such ideas are cardinally important because, via the process of "cognitive capture," many of us – that is, noneconomists – have incorporated those ideas into our thinking, and we use them when we discuss public affairs. Therefore, we talk about the rate of unemployment, derivatives, the bond market, cost–benefit analysis, austerity, credit default swaps, "too big to fail," moral hazards, venture capital, and more. And what that means is that the collected writings of mainstream economists tell us a good deal about how many Americans, who have been taught economics in colleges and universities, and who work in banks, think tanks, government agencies, trade associations,

---

[230] Offer and Soderberg, *The Nobel Factor*, pp. 16–41.

insurance companies, and more, define economic activity and behavior which they regard as normal and even commendable.

Qualifications

In what follows, therefore, I will describe some economic Stories mostly as they have been taught by mainstream economists and widely considered authoritative (via cognitive capture) rather than looking for examples of the same Stories as expressed by, say, the Chamber of Commerce, the *Wall Street Journal*, the Heritage Foundation, the *National Review*, the Business Roundtable, *Forbes Magazine*, Fox Business News, the Republican Party's national or state platforms, and other disciples and exponents. On the Right, mainstream economic Stories are formulated clearly, taught frequently, regarded as persuasive, and therefore are, I think, representative.[231]

Representative, yes, but these pro-market Stories do not coexist smoothly with Stories on the Right which extol tradition and long-time virtues. For example, as we shall see, the notion of "creative destruction" – of ceaseless economic innovation, of constant technological and administrative change – promotes behavior and activity which severely unsettle values and practices that may seem commendable for being traditional.

The problem there, however, is not the way I select Stories, that is, in the particular array of Stories which I choose to write about. Rather, as I pointed out in Chapter 2, within the Right (and within the Left, say, as between the ideals of freedom and equality), Stories in the same camp do not always jibe. That they are sometimes, or always, incompatible or inconsistent with other Stories which may inspire some people in the same camp, is simply a fact of ideological life, not something that I created intentionally or inadvertently, and not to be resolved here.[232]

---

[231] For summaries of many Republican and/or rightist views, including references to economic affairs, readers can consult George H. W. Bush's speech accepting his party's presidential nomination in 1988, and the Texas Republican Party platform of 2016. On the speech, see www.presidency.ucsb.edu/documents/address-accepting-the-presidential-nomination-the-republican-national-convention-new. On the platform, see www.presidency.ucsb.edu/documents/2016-republican-party-platform.

[232] Contradictions are most visible on the Right, and in the Republican Party, because Rightists tend to tell their Stories openly and clearly. Thus commitments to (frequent)

Economic Growth

To begin with, economists are major contributors to one of the most powerful Stories in American life, and that is the Story of "economic growth." Economic growth, they say, can relieve many social problems by boosting the incomes of everyone, even if not equally. It will raise the poor from poverty; it will make everyone healthier and happier. Furthermore, they say, economic growth is politically desirable. It can ease legislative and executive stress everywhere in American government because, by mitigating scarcity, it can free leaders from having to make zero-sum decisions in situations where crucial commodities are so scarce that there are not enough of them to go around.[233]

Conventional Wisdom

Now, where do Americans stand on these two points? Formally, economic growth became a national goal when President Franklin Roosevelt declared to Congress and his Fireside Chat audience in 1938 that "All the energies of Government and business must be directed to increasing the

---

economic *changes* and devotion to (permanent) *tradition* are patently difficult to reconcile. I wrote about this situation in *Why Conservatives Tell Stories and Liberals Don't: Rhetoric, Faith, and Vision on the American Right* (Boulder, CO: Paradigm, 2011), ch. 4, "Enemies," pp. 81–104, where I observed that people on the Right are not so much united by devotion to all their Stories together (for instance, the Reverend Jerry Falwell, a traditionalist, was always wary of marketplace behavior and values) as they are united by their antipathy to shared enemies (liberals), whom they regard as dominating the Democratic Party and various "elite" sectors of American society. Such liberals are enemies of the Right because some people on the Right regard liberals as inclined to use government agencies to violate *traditions* (say, to limit school prayers or to legalize same-sex marriages), and other people on the Right see liberals as inclined to use government agencies to override *the market* (say, by regulating the financial sector or phasing out the use of fossil fuels). This sort of antipathy – who are we *against* rather than what are we *for* – constitutes a sort of negative but shared partisanship.

[233] A powerful argument for why unswerving pursuit of economic growth is a disastrous national policy, may be found in Kate Raworth, *Doughnut Economics: 7 Ways to Think Like a 21st Century Economist* (White River Junction, VT: Chelsea Green Publishing, 2017), *passim*, but esp. ch. 1, "Change the Goal from GDP to the Doughnut," pp. 27–51. On the downsides of growth, see also Robert Skidelsky, *What's Wrong with Economics: A Primer for the Perplexed* (New Haven: Yale University Press, 2020), ch. 3, "Economic Growth," pp. 30–48.

national income."[234] Subsequently, after the goal of growth had become central to economic thinking, John Kenneth Galbraith could observe in 1958 that "On the importance of production [growth] there is no difference between Republicans and Democrats, right and left, white or colored, Catholic or Protestant."[235] In other words, said Galbraith, all Americans, across the board, want their friends and neighbors to produce more. And more. And more. And therefore, for them, the tale of economic growth is a Story, not just a story.[236]

National Wealth

An early element in this Story comes from the Physiocrats in France and Adam Smith in Scotland. These men perceived what they regarded as inefficiency in regulatory arrangements which added up to state-sponsored "mercantilism" in the eighteenth century. From this premise, they recommended that governments should reduce their regulation of economic activities; that is, they should release the energies of their citizens, according to the Physiocrats especially in agriculture, and according to Smith especially in nascent industry and trade. On the way to this end, the Physiocrats introduced into Western thought the concept of *"laissez-faire,"* as a description of how they thought governments should refrain from interfering with, or supervising, the economy.

The point on this score was to stop thinking of economic activity as emerging from feudal arrangements and taxed or otherwise regulated by European rulers in order to increase their own or

---

[234] See https://millercenter.org/the-presidency/presidential-speeches/april-14-1938-fireside-chat-12-recession.

[235] John Kenneth Galbraith, *The Affluent Society* (New York: Mentor, 1958), p. 101, but also pp. 99–113.

[236] Nationwide enthusiasm for economic growth shows up in the commitment of political leaders to raising the Gross National Product (or Gross Domestic Product) because it is widely regarded as an index of wellbeing. On where this index came from, on what it stands for, and on controversies surrounding it, see Diane Coyle, *GDP: A Brief but Affectionate History* (Princeton: Princeton University Press, 2014), and Dirk Philipsen, *The Little Big Number: How GDP Came to Rule the World and What to Do About It* (Princeton: Princeton University Press, 2015). Philipsen starts his book by summing up the passion for GDP as a conviction that "growth is good. The idea ... has become an article of faith: growth gives rise to progress and prosperity; lack of growth leads to depression and misery."

their country's power and honor. Instead, as Smith put it, if we will rely on a natural division of labor which involves the three modern, nonfeudal classes of landowners, capitalists, and laborers, then people's "natural propensity to truck, barter, and exchange one thing for another" will add to the nation's wealth and all will prosper more than in the past.[237]

The bottom line is clear. Neither the Physiocrats nor Smith rejected every sort of governmental supervision of economic affairs. But they did envision what we now call fairly open "markets," in which people of different ranks, resources, and talents would interact in ways beneficial to all – that is, would produce economic growth. And thus capitalism, or capitalism by any other name – including the "free enterprise" which many Americans admire today – was eventually regarded in Western society, first by economists and then by those whom they taught, as a vast improvement over what came before it.[238]

Comparative Advantage

Thinking beyond England early in the nineteenth century, David Ricardo decided that trucking, bartering, and exchanging can be especially productive in international markets according to the axiom of "comparative advantage." This axiom says that any country can benefit from exporting what it can produce most efficiently and importing what its trading partners can produce most efficiently. That is, exploit

---

[237] Adam Smith, *An Inquiry into the Nature and Causes of the Wealth of Nations* (orig., 1776; New York: Modern Library, 1937), p. 13. Anthropologist David Graeber claimed that scholars have discovered no such propensity in what we call primitive societies. In other words, Graeber proposed that Smith assumed a certain kind of natural human behavior much like mainstream economists now assume that people are "rational individuals." Therefore, according to Graeber, we now know that the assumption of rationality is more a piece of rhetoric than fact. See Graeber, *Debt: The First 5,000 Years* (London: Melville House, 2011, 2012), "The Myth of Barter," pp. 22–41.

[238] One could argue, I think, that the West (roughly speaking) produced the Enlightenment, within which the postulate (as formulated by thinkers like the Physiocrats and Adam Smith) that governments should promote economic growth, was one of the West's major cultural achievements. Much of the rest of the world only slowly adopted this concept of governmental mission, and some countries – for example, Afghanistan under the Taliban – still pursue other goals.

your comparative advantage and let your trading partners exploit theirs. Both sides will gain.[239]

After Ricardo, many economists endorsed his insight and their discipline has generally praised modern "globalization" on the grounds that what we now call free trade – which is an international project – lifts all boats to the point where America is better off and hundreds of millions of people worldwide are no longer as poor as they used to be. For example, economist Paul Krugman told his *New York Times* readers that "If you had taken the time to understand the story about England trading cloth for Portuguese wine that we teach every freshman in Econ. 1, [then] ... you know more about the nature of the global economy than the current U.S. Trade Representative [whom Krugman did not admire]."[240] Similarly, pundit Charles Krauthammer, perhaps recalling what he had studied of economics in college, agreed with Krugman by declaring, in *The Washington Post*: "That free trade is advantageous to both sides is the rarest of political propositions – provable, indeed mathematically."[241]

Krauthammer's belief perfectly demonstrated the power of cognitive capture, where laypeople wind up talking the language of economists. Consequently, when he (on the Right) and Krugman (on the Left) extolled *free trade* arrangements, such as those ratified by the North American Free Trade Act (NAFTA) in 1994, they encouraged all Americans to believe that the current economy, seriously unbalanced but strongly engaged via globalization in considerable international trade, is good for the country.[242]

---

[239] Comparative advantage is explained in David Ricardo, *The Principles of Political Economy and Taxation*, 3rd ed. (orig., 1821; London: Dent, 1911), pp. 77–93.

[240] Paul Krugman, *The Accidental Theorist: And Other Dispatches from the Dismal Science* (New York: Norton, 1998), pp. 113–114. See also Ian Fletcher, *Free Trade Doesn't Work: What Should Replace It and Why* (Sheffield, MA: Coalition for a Prosperous America, 2011), p. 3: "Ninety-three percent of American economists [professors?] surveyed [in 2003] support free trade."

[241] See Krauthammer at www.washingtonpost.com/opinions/save-obama-on-trade/2015/05/14/aabaf342-fa65-11e4-9ef4-1bb7ce3b3fb7_story.html.

[242] Economists such as Joseph E. Stiglitz, in *The Price of Inequality: How Today's Divided Society Endangers our Future* (New York: Norton, 2012), esp. pp. 58–64, have written about the economic downsides of globalization. For our purposes, the political philosopher and intellectual historian John Gray, in his *False Dawn: The Delusions of Global*

Profits

The snag in all of this appeared when economists such as Smith, Ricardo, and Marx realized that "profits" were a problem in the three-class economic model. They saw a society in which landowners controlled land and received for it rents; laborers offered labor and received for it wages; capitalists contributed factories, stores, ships, trains, and other commercial instruments and received for them profits.

But what exactly did the profits represent? In other words, what did capitalists, as a burgeoning middle class almost unknown to feudal society, contribute to the mix of productive factors which enabled industrial societies to prosper?

As profits rose in the nineteenth century, that question turned acute. While both capitalists and workers lived off personal efforts, it seemed that, in many cases, equal amounts of effort generated more income for some capitalists than for many workers. Which suggested that something might be morally askew.

Abstinence

Nassau Senior offered an early justification for this situation with reference to "abstinence." In his view, land existed naturally because God created it; labor also existed naturally because God endowed all human beings with the capacity to work; but the commercial facilities run by capitalists come into existence only because some people save a portion of their income and then use that saving to build productive facilities which would not exist if those people had not saved – that is, if they had not abstained from immediate spending, consumption, and pleasure.

The assumption was that not all people have the foresight and willpower to save but that doing so is good for everyone collectively

---

Capitalism (New York: New Press, 1998), is also instructive. Gray regards globalization, which idealizes constant innovation and comparative advantage, as suffering from serious sociological and philosophical shortcomings. Among them is what Gray calls "delocalization," defined as "the uprooting of activities and relationships from local origins and cultures." In other words, although globalization does lift some boats, it also destroys some communal ties which for many generations have helped people, according to Gray, to live meaningful lives. On capitalism's sometimes small concern for community, see n. 262.

because, without abstinence, there will be no commercial facilities and society as a whole will remain poor. So profits represent the "wages of abstinence," a vital productive factor.

Perhaps, but Senior's argument lost much of its force after observers noted that some people earned profits to the point where they lived comfortably – while exercising no abstinence – but managed nevertheless to build additional commercial facilities and profit still further. In other words, as some capitalists prospered, they did not seem to lack any amenities, therefore explanations beyond self-sacrifice had to be found for profits which sometimes far exceeded the income many workers received for the work they did with considerable effort.

Talents

Starting in the mid-1800s, economists began to promote new justifications for high incomes which went chiefly to capitalists but occasionally to unusually successful workers such as doctors, lawyers, brokers, bankers, and managers. The common denominator for these justifications – and here was a new Story line – was that high earners are especially *talented*, that they don't make just ordinary but *unusual* efforts, which are exceptionally productive and therefore deserve compensation to that extent.

Thus Herbert Spencer offered in England an early theory of talent-centered success when he claimed that societies advance by encouraging "survival of the fittest." We need not disentangle the various meanings which have been attributed to this phrase. For our purposes, what is chiefly important is that historians regard Spencer as a Social Darwinist; that is, as having expressed a *social* interpretation of Charles Darwin's *biological* theory of evolution driven by competition within and among species. On that score, Social Darwinists assumed that, in the domestic arena, it is mainly individual achievements which raise productivity and thereby generate prosperity.

William Graham Sumner, for example, assumed that competition was natural and did not worry that it bred unequal results. Millionaires, he said, "are a product of natural selection." They "can meet the requirement of certain work [of accumulating capital] to be done .... They get high wages and live in luxury, but the bargain is a good one for society."[243] There was the crucial point, that inequality was best for the whole. On that ground, Sumner insisted that the successful owe the less successful no more than good will.[244]

The Social Darwinism promoted by such thinkers attracted amateur disciples.[245] Andrew Carnegie, for example, advocated what he called a "gospel of wealth." This gospel assumed that every society needs people who can accumulate great wealth in the sense of productive factors (technology, facilities, arrangements) not found in nature.[246] Accordingly, a person who does so (like Carnegie) is morally entitled to "administer" that wealth, which in Carnegie's life meant not living in poverty but directing his fortune philanthropically. John D. Rockefeller agreed. As he put it one day in a Sunday School talk, "The growth of a large business is merely a survival of the fittest .... This is not an evil tendency in business. It is merely the working-out of a law of nature and a law of God."[247] Like Carnegie, Rockefeller did not claim to live parsimoniously but eventually administered some of his enormous profits philanthropically.

Creative Destruction

Moving into the twentieth century, academic specialists increasingly replaced general-knowledge thinkers such as Herbert Spencer and

---

[243] William Graham Sumner, *The Challenge of Facts and Other Essays* (New Haven: Yale University Press, 1914), "The Concentration of Wealth: Its Economic Justification," p. 90.

[244] Sumner, *What Social Classes Owe to Each Other* (orig., 1883; Caldwell, ID: The Caxton Printers, 1961), p. 34.

[245] A sentiment resembling Social Darwinism is present today in the American Tea Party, many of whose early members felt that they (as taxpayers) owed bankrupt homeowners nothing because before the Crash of 2008 those homeowners borrowed irresponsibly and government agencies should not bail them out for that. On the Tea Party, see Rightists Dick Armey and Matt Kibbe, *Give Us Liberty: A Tea Party Manifesto* (New York: William Morrow, 2010), and scholars Theda Skocpol and Vanessa Williamson, *The Tea Party and the Remaking of Republican Conservatism* (New York: Oxford University Press, 2012).

[246] Andrew Carnegie, "The Gospel of Wealth" (1889), in *The Gospel of Wealth, and Other Timely Essays* (orig., 1900; Cambridge, MA: Harvard University Press, 2062), pp. 14–49.

[247] Quoted in Richard Hofstadter, *Social Darwinism in American Thought* (Boston: Beacon Press, 1955), p. 45.

William Sumner. Thus, as universities grew and multiplied, the discipline of economics was formally organized in 1885 into the American Economic Association (AEA) which by 2022 claimed 20,000 members. From these economists, there emerged increasingly technical arguments which justified a large measure of economic inequality.

One such argument came from the Austrian-American Joseph Schumpeter, who headed the AEA in 1948. Schumpeter explained that modern economies grow and become more productive by a process of "creative destruction." As he put it, "The fundamental impulse that sets and keeps the capitalist engine in motion comes from the new consumers' goods, the new methods of production or transportation, the new markets, the new forms of industrial organization that capitalist enterprise creates."[248] Forward motion, in this view, proceeds when people compete not by generating old products and services ever more efficiently – say, making good but cheaper cars – but by creating new products and services in order to avoid confrontation with the old.

New, new, new. For example, cotton-picking machines replace sharecroppers; reinforced concrete replaces structural steel; plastic bottles replace those made of glass; outsourcing replaces in-house manufacturing; Boeing jet planes replace ocean liners; Big Macs replace local hamburgers; online orders replace brick-and-mortar stores; spellcheckers replace copy-editors; smartphones replace dinner-table conversation; and more.

To set and drive the capitalist machine, said Schumpeter, some people have to go beyond routine forms of work, in which case the aptitudes (or talents) they have for this exceptional kind of work, which Schumpeter called entrepreneurship, "are present in only a small fraction of the population."[249] That is, "entrepreneurs" are unusual people who should receive special compensation.

Ergo, once again, skewed incomes are morally justified on behalf of the greater good. Not that Schumpeter said exactly that. But

---

[248] Joseph A. Schumpeter, *Capitalism, Socialism and Democracy*, 3rd ed. (New York: Harper Torchbooks, 1942, 1947), p. 83.
[249] *Ibid.*, p. 133.

his approach did suggest that, like it or not, growth is based on economic evolution, on creating new things and new ways of delivering the old, if at all. Therefore, if you want growth – and apparently most people do – it looks like you must embrace entrepreneurs and their creative destruction.

Entrepreneurship and Innovation

And that is where we find first George Gilder and then Clayton Christensen. Gilder, a prominent thinker on the Right during the Reagan era, elevated Schumpeter's entrepreneur into an indispensable figure who provides virtuous leadership on the road to economic progress (via economic growth). If poverty remains here and there, said Gilder, it is not the inevitable fate of innocent losers in a power struggle (against, say, ruthless entrepreneurs) but a condition among ineffective people who suffer from small commitment to "work, family, and faith."[250]

Christensen, a Harvard professor of business administration, does not praise capitalism as a moral enterprise but advises students and practitioners to perform creative destruction via what he calls "disruptive innovation."[251] Like Schumpeter, Christensen sets out to describe, although more mildly than Schumpeter, an economic process which simply exists. Then, he proposes a way for businesspeople to deal with that process profitably.

As Christensen says, financial institutions – say investment funds, banks, brokers, venture capitalists, etc. – place bets on future earnings and thereby drive up, or down, the value of companies that grow or fail to grow. In that situation, companies which try to respond

[250] George Gilder, *Wealth and Poverty* (New York: Basic Books, 1981), p. 68. See also Gilder, *The Spirit of Enterprise* (New York: Simon & Schuster, 1984). Gilder was known as a promoter of virtuous entrepreneurship. Less famous but similarly in favor was Michael Novak, of the American Enterprise Institute. See his *Business as a Calling: Work and the Examined Life* (New York: Free Press, 1996).

[251] Clayton Christensen wrote on this theme in *The Innovator's Dilemma: When New Technologies Cause Great Firms to Fail* (Boston: Harvard Business Review Press, 1997, 2000, and 2016). Then he wrote, together with Michael E. Raynor, *The Innovator's Solution: Creating and Sustaining Successful Growth* (Boston: Harvard Business Review Press, 2003).

to the growth imperative must innovate in order to succeed. In the footsteps of Schumpeter, Christensen observes that, if they want to survive, economically ambitious men and women must disrupt present circumstances in the sense that they must refuse to accept current products and arrangements – which benefit other companies – but must create new products and arrangements which will be more profitable to themselves. To this end, Christensen explains how to plan for the "disruption" which he calls "innovation."[252]

Karl Polanyi

Perhaps special qualities of entrepreneurship and innovation do lie behind large incomes as opposed to small. Perhaps, in that sense, economic inequality is a natural state of affairs.[253] But a serious difficulty remained, which was that to praise a process of endless change, of endless innovation, and of endless disruption, was to accept and sanction conditions of perpetual uncertainty and turmoil where, in fact, not every transformation constituted improvement, and not every change equaled progress.[254] Or, as Schumpeter's phrase "creative destruction" indicates, when one "creates" new commodities and services, one also

---

[252] Christensen is an academic. For a similar view from the business world, see Peter Thiel, *Zero to One: Notes on Startups or How to Build the Future* (London: Virgin Books, 2014). As Thiel puts it, "Doing something *different* is what's truly good for society" (p. 166), and permits business to profit maximally.

[253] Thomas Piketty argues at length (1041 pages) that economic inequality is not natural but socially and politically generated. Therefore, he rejects what he calls the "meritocratic ideology" which justifies colossal income disparities, such as in Silicon Valley. See Thomas Piketty, *Capital and Ideology* (Cambridge, MA; Harvard University Press, 2020), *passim*. Piketty argues, from historical data, (1) that economic growth and wellbeing can be generated even when income disparities are small, and (2) that great innovations produce great incomes by being based on public expenditures and policy decisions in research, development, education, health, transportation, communications, legal protections, differential taxation, and more.

[254] Religious conservatives are wary of change, which they believe can lead Americans away from the Ten Commandments. Anti-Communist conservatives are also wary, such as when they scorn Lenin and Stalin for (reputedly) saying that if you want to make an omelet, you must break eggs. Nevertheless, most politicians and publicists on the modern Right usually praise capitalist innovation and entrepreneurship. Many of them are confident that new technology will eventually halt the global warming which technology caused in the first place.

"destroys" the value of old commodities, old services, old locations, old skills, and old facilities.[255]

The economist Karl Polanyi, who was nowhere near his disciplinary mainstream, famously pointed out this potential downside when he observed that nowhere has liberal [post-Enlightenment] philosophy failed so conspicuously as in its understanding of the problem of change .... [As capitalism flourished] elementary truths of political science and statecraft were first discredited, then, forgotten. It should need no elaboration that a process of undirected change ... should be slowed down, if possible, so as to safeguard the welfare of the community.[256]

Rational Individualism

Polanyi's phrase "to safeguard the welfare of the community" can be variously interpreted.[257] For our purposes, it includes taking care

---

[255] For example, many longshoremen lost their jobs when shipping containers were invented and container terminals were constructed. Mainstream economists may assume that workers so displaced will, sooner or later, find adequate new employment, in which case their pain and loss is only temporary. In *Political Science Manifesto*, esp. pp. 107–109, I discussed this issue with reference to the potential creation of driverless cars while, in America today, an estimated 3.5 million people work as drivers.

[256] Karl Polanyi, *The Great Transformation: The Political and Economic Origins of our Time* (orig., 1944; Boston: Beacon, 1957), p. 33. Polanyi extended this passage by saying that "Such household truths of traditional statesmanship, often ... reflecting the teachings of a social philosophy inherited from the ancients, were in the nineteenth century erased from the thoughts of the educated by the corrosive of a crude utilitarianism combined with an uncritical reliance on the alleged self-healing virtues of unconscious growth."

[257] In the early 1940s Polanyi himself did not go very far, but his phrase might now be interpreted to mean that modern people should stop using the language of *economics* to understand social issues and should use the language of *ecology* instead to discuss large dilemmas of modern life. (For economists who are closing in on that conclusion, as they criticize microeconomic reasoning, see https://bostonreview.net/articles/bad-economics/.) For example, in ecological terms, that the human birthrate in many countries (in Europe, in America, in China, and more) has gone down recently can be seen as a blessing, as a trend that is automatically reducing the human footprint on Earth, as a condition that is accidentally positioning us to ratchet down destructive pollution practices (such as burning fossil fuels, deforesting the land, and overfishing the seas). Instead, declining birthrates are widely regarded (by many governments, think tanks, and media reports) in the language of mainstream economics (via cognitive capture),

that incomes will not be so skewed as to generate major unhappiness, injury, and resentment. But these conditions *do* exist in many communities today.[258] Therefore, we should consider that, to some extent, they exist there *not* because *most* Americans specifically endorse the kind of pro-inequality arguments we have noted but because *many* Americans, consciously or not, are looking elsewhere.

For example, mainstream economists say that economic activity is performed by rational individuals who seek utility, and whose interactions in markets are determined by how much marginal utility each

as problematic if not catastrophic, as if not enough "young workers" will be available to pay for the pensions and medical expenses of "unproductive seniors." Beneath this public conversation today, what is actually being discussed is, in economic language, a market-based recipe for taking care of seniors by, say, importing immigrant workers, whereas, in the language of politics, we *could be* talking about how to adjust national tax systems (a matter of "redistribution") to encourage less consumerism (individualism) and more social insurance (community), so that old people would be cared for without destroying the Earth by maintaining high economic production. Neoliberals – including scholars and politicians – do not talk much about redistribution. On some of the reasons why this is so, see Ricci, *Political Science Manifesto*, pp. 124–127. For an example, see Robert Lucas (Nobel Prizewinner in Economics, 1995), "Of the tendencies that are harmful to sound economics, the most seductive, and in my opinion the most poisonous, is to focus on questions of distribution." Lucas is quoted in Offer and Soderberg, *The Nobel Factor*, p. 36. For the Right in general, Larry Kudlow, of Fox Business News, criticizes Americans who favor what he calls "redistribution rather than prosperity."

[258] Many books describe the lives of people who have fallen behind socially and economically in modern America due to globalization, immigration, outsourcing, automation, computerization, new supply chains, and other trends. For example, see Katherine S. Newman, *Declining Fortunes: The Withering of the American Dream* (New York: Basic Books, 1993); Richard C. Longworth, *Caught in the Middle: America's Heartland in the Age of Globalization* (New York: Bloomsbury, 2009); Sasha Abramsky, *The American Way of Poverty: How the Other Half Still Lives* (New York: Nation Books, 2014); Robert D. Putnam, *Our Kids: The American Dream in Crisis* (New York: Simon & Schuster, 2015); J. D. Vance, *Hillbilly Elegy: A Memoir of a Family and Culture in Crisis* (New York: HarperCollins, 2016); Arlie Russell Hochschild, *Strangers in Their Own Land: Anger and Mourning on the American Right* (New York: The New Press, 2016); Amy Goldstein, *Janesville: An American Story* (New York: Simon & Schuster, 2017); Sarah Smarsh, *Heartland: A Memoir of Working Hard and Being Broke in the Richest Country on Earth* (New York: Simon & Schuster, 2018); Louis Hyman, *Temp: How American Work, American Business, and the American Dream Became Temporary* (New York: Viking, 2018); Eliza Griswold, *Amity and Prosperity: One Family and the Fracturing of America* (New York: Farrar, Straus, and Giroux, 2018); and Robert Wuthnow, *The Left Behind: Decline and Rage in Small-Town America*, 2nd ed. (Princeton: Princeton University Press, 2019).

person contributes to other people who want to buy and sell. CEOs of Fortune 500 companies, for example, who are very well paid, presumably contribute a great deal of marginal utility to the work of their companies.[259]

Now if, via cognitive capture, noneconomists (ordinary people) will look at the economy as an assembly of utility seekers, they will no longer see the population as composed of three social classes interacting in ways that may distribute income unevenly and unfairly.[260] They will see, instead, only individuals (not classes) who receive more or less income, in which case there may be various personal explanations – linked to, say, talent or ingenuity – for why *this* person winds up with more and *that* person winds up with less.

Culture and Virtue

Alternatively, regardless of what economists say, one might view public life as a "culture war" which constitutes a contest between virtue and vice. If that is the case, voters may overlook or set aside notions of economic equity to the extent that their main aim is to avoid what they regard as immoral social policies promoted by feminists, minorities, peaceniks, gays, and the like. Journalist Thomas Frank complained about such an outlook in his book *What's the Matter with Kansas?* (2004), and he claimed that conservatives win elections in Kansas because, via cultural talk, they draw voters' attention away from what he saw as a "deranged" local economy.[261]

---

[259] Actually, that is not necessarily true, because they appoint their Boards (of directors), and those Boards (while beholden to their CEOs) set rates of CEO compensation. See Lucien Bebchuk, Jesse Fried, and David Walker, "Managerial Power and Rent Extraction in the Design of Executive Compensation," *University of Chicago Law Review* (Summer, 2002), pp. 751–846. On CEO compensation recently, which in large corporations reaches hundreds of times average workers' compensation, see https://ips-dc.org/report-executive-excess-2022/.

[260] If you believe that postindustrial society is composed of social classes as was industrial society, you might posit today a fourth class, which (beyond land, capital, and labor) supplies information, including technological ideas and intellectual innovations. Thus Daniel Bell, *The Coming of Post-Industrial Society: A Venture in Social Forecasting* (New York: Basic Books, 1976).

[261] Thomas Frank, *What's the Matter with Kansas? How Conservatives Won the Heart of America* (New York: Metropolitan Books, 2004), pp. 1–27, and esp. p. 2. For

Shareholders and Stakeholders

Distraction also underlies the modern notion, promoted energetically by disciples of the Nobel Prizewinner, economist Milton Friedman, that people who manage large corporations are ethically obliged to direct those corporations so as to maximize the worth of "shareholder" equity. It is the shareholders who own the corporation, Friedman noted, therefore its managers, whom the shareholders (formally) employ, should try, within what markets and laws permit, to prioritize the interests of those owners.

This is an argument which assumes that managers can disregard "stakeholder" interests, which might include the interests of clients, consumers, tenants, workers, neighbors, and taxpayers who pay for infrastructure (such as roads and public education, which benefit corporations); that is, who are stakeholders in the local or even national "community." Forget about those other interests, Friedman implies. After all, "communities" do not exist, or barely exist, in the shareholder thesis.[262] Consequently, managers have no

an example, see Reece Peck, *Fox Populism: Branding Conservatism as Working Class* (New York: Cambridge University Press, 2019), *passim*, but esp. pp. 4–5. Peck argues that Fox News promotes "inter-media agenda setting," by which he means that Fox News seeks to shape the public conversation by highlighting inequality but describing it as flowing not from capitalism but from cultural factors such as liberals, elites, immigrants, and identity politics. In this view, prosperity is generated not by workers (laboring at jobs) but by corporations (which presumably create jobs).

[262] Slighting communities – that is, collective interests – is a frequent neoliberal practice, although approval of it is not always expressed openly. See, however, William Simon, Secretary of the Treasury from 1974 to 1977, observe in his *A Time for Truth* (New York: Berkley, 1978), p. 237, that "There is no such thing as the People; it is a collectivist myth. There are only individual citizens with individual wills and individual purposes." Simon made that point after he left politics. Britain's Prime Minister Margaret Thatcher, while still in office, expressed the same neoliberal sentiment more famously when she declared that "there is no such thing as society. There are individual men and women and there are families." See www.theguardian.com/politics/2013/apr/08/margaret-thatcher-quotes. On the painful loss of "community" in Lancaster, Ohio, which was not factored in to the commercial and financial decisions which closed its Anchor Hocking glass factories on the way to deindustrializing that town, see Brian Alexander, *Glass House: The 1% Economy and the Shattering of the All-American Town* (New York: Picador, 2017), *passim*, but esp. p. 294.

collective values to promote beyond those of their corporate shareholders.[263]

Limited Government

We may wrap up our collection of pro-economic status quo Stories with
two "limited government" propositions. Economist John Maynard
Keynes, during the Great Depression, offered a strong pro-intervention
Story when he declared that governments should smooth out some of
what I have called "economic imbalance" and what Frank regarded
as "economic derangement." Mainstream economists responded to
Keynes with a powerful theory of "social choice" which recommends
little or no government activism.

Social Choice Theory

In this limited government proposition, small government is best. Economist and Nobel Prizewinner James Buchanan, for example, used a theory of social choice (based on the mainstream economics assumption
that individuals are rational) to argue that governments are composed
of people who are self-centered, who talk of serving the public interest
but attend only to their own, and who are therefore unwilling or unable
to formulate other-regarding public policies and carry them out.[264]

---

[263] On the one hand, Friedman's shareholder thesis has many disciples among corporate
managers, which makes sense because some of them might increase their companies'
profits by, for example, outsourcing production to low-cost developing countries even
though doing so would destroy the livelihoods of skilled men and women (stakeholders) at home. On the paragon of outsourcing, and of other profitable power plays, see
David Gelles, *The Man Who Broke Capitalism: How Jack Welch Gutted the Heartland
and Crushed the Soul of Corporate America–and How to Undo his Legacy* (New York:
Simon & Schuster, 2022). On the other hand, the shareholder thesis has been widely
discussed and criticized on moral grounds, to the point where some large corporations
have recently decided that, at least rhetorically, they should serve stakeholders as well as
shareholders. On that score, see the Business Roundtable's official statement in 2019 at
https://opportunity.businessroundtable.org/ourcommitment/.

[264] A major work to this effect is James M. Buchanan and Gordon Tullock, *The Calcu-
lus of Consent: Logical Foundations of Constitutional Democracy* (Ann Arbor: University of Michigan Press, 1962). On economist Buchanan's expression of Southern,
conservative, political ideas, see Nancy MacLean, *Democracy in Chains: The Deep*

This view justifies privatizing many traditionally governmental functions, on the grounds that government officials should not pretend that they can improve the economic situation while, according to social choice theory, they cannot even fix themselves or their agencies.[265] So society should hire private entities to attend to public functions and provide services – from hospitals to toll roads, from lotteries to airport operations, from prisons to contract warriors, from libraries to schools – which, according to social choice theory, they can deliver more effectively than government can.[266]

In short, either economic imbalance or derangement do not exist – there are many mainstream arguments to this effect – or, according to economists like Buchanan, neither, if existing, can be repaired by governmental efforts.

Freedom

A second limited government proposition assumes that America is mainly about "freedom" rather than "equality." This is the powerful

History of The Radical Right's Stealth Plan for America (New York: Penguin, 2017), *passim*. MacLean's book is all about Buchanan and his intellectual influence, therefore it is not feasible to offer here page numbers for specific parts of her thesis. But see p. xxxii: "Where Milton Friedman and F. A. Hayek allowed that public officials were earnestly trying to do right by the citizenry, even as they disputed the methods, Buchanan believed that government failed because of bad faith: because activists, voters, and officials alike used talk of the public interest to mask the pursuit of their own personal self-interest at others' expense." For a layman's expression from the Right, of this view of government officials, see William E. Simon, *A Time for Action* (New York: Reader's Digest, 1980), p. 40: "The bureaucrat's first objective ... is preservation of his job .... Whether real world problems get solved or not is of secondary importance .... [In fact,] bureaucrats have a vested interest in not having problems solved. If the problems did not exist (or had not been invented), there would be no reason for the bureaucrat to have a job."

[265] Buchanan was not alone on this point. Neoliberal economist Friedrich Hayek long argued that market-based decisions based on the practical know-how of businessmen are more objective and less discriminatory than public policies fashioned by inexperienced government officials who tend to serve their own interests. On this aspect of Hayek's ideas, see William Davies, *Nervous States: Democracy and the Decline of Reason* (New York: Norton, 2018), pp. 159–170.

[266] Against privatization, see Donald Cohen and Allen Mikaelian, *The Privatization of Everything: How the Plunder of Public Goods Transformed America and How We Can Fight Back* (New York: The New Press, 2021), *passim*, but esp. pp. 181–187 (on student loans), and pp. 214–280 (on drug prices).

Story told by Milton Friedman in his *Capitalism and Freedom* (1962), where he argued that when government, as an institution, forces people to do this or that, those people are not really free. Freedom, Friedman insisted, is a condition – an absence of restraints – which enables one to make voluntary choices, for better or worse.[267] And therefore freedom exists when government permits marketplace capitalism to flourish and its citizens to make their way in it independently and responsibly.[268]

"Capitalism-as-freedom" was surely a signature American Story during the Cold War confrontation with the Soviet Union in the 1960s, 1970s, and 1980s.[269] Furthermore, even though we cannot measure its power precisely, that Story still infuses much of American thinking, as when many Americans talk about, and aspire to, what they call "free enterprise."

Exceptionalism

In fact, the capitalism-as-freedom Story is about American "exceptionalism," in the sense that it is about regarding America as being special (exceptional) and better than other countries.[270] Accordingly, in

[267] The classic modern liberal alternative to Friedman's view is Isaiah Berlin, *Two Concepts of Liberty* (Oxford: Clarendon Press, 1958), in which Berlin speaks of two kinds of freedom: "freedom from" (restraint), which is "negative freedom," and "freedom to" (act), which is "positive freedom."

[268] In *Capitalism and Freedom* (Chicago: University of Chicago Press, 1962), Friedman describes society as if taxes (based on "force") are a violation of freedom no matter what individuals and their communities receive in return – such as national defense, old age pensions, health care, environmental preservation, police protection, public education, transportation infrastructure, scientific research, and more. Thus the Rightest concept of "Tax Day" (which is defined with no reference to benefits received) as the day of the year on which citizens stop working for government and are finally free to work for themselves. Tax Day is estimated now to fall on as late as June 1 by, among many others, William D. Gairdner, *The Great Divide: Why Liberals and Conservatives Will Never, Ever Agree* (New York: Encounter, 2015), pp. 14–15.

[269] Some on the Left now argue that the cardinal American ideal is equality rather than freedom. For an example of this contention, see Danielle Allen, *Our Declaration: A Reading of the Declaration of Independence in Defense of Equality* (Cambridge, MA: Harvard University Press, 2014).

[270] On the concept of exceptionalism, see the "Introduction," in Michael Kazin and Joseph A. McCartin (eds.), *Americanism: New Perspectives on the History of an Ideal* (Chapel Hill: University of North Carolina Press, 2006), pp. 1–21.

2003, the US aerial bombing and ground war against Saddam Hussein's regime in Iraq was named "Operation Iraqi Freedom." This was President George W. Bush's way of suggesting that, unlike typical great powers, America goes to war not to achieve national gain but to help other people become free.[271] The assumption is that they all *want* to be "free" (in a sense understood by Americans such as Milton Friedman).[272]

To that end, after early fighting in the Iraq war stopped, Paul Bremer, who was the Presidential Envoy to Iraq and head of the Coalition Provisional Authority, discharged ranking Baathist Party government employees and disbanded the Iraqi army. He thereby decapitated functional public rule, sent home over 600,000 trained but suddenly impoverished (unemployed) soldiers and police, and encouraged the country's residents – most of whom were Shi'ite Iraqis, Sunni Iraqis, and Sunni Kurds – to begin practicing, via partisan elections and commercial markets, what Bremer regarded as true freedom.[273] Unremitting sectarian quarrels, ethnic frictions, and massive inter-sectoral violence followed and still plague Iraq.[274]

---

[271] Support for the same Story also appears on the Left. For example, in her speech accepting the Democratic nomination for President in 2016, Hillary Clinton declared that America is exceptional among nations on the grounds that "America is great because America is good." See her speech at https://edition.cnn.com/2016/07/28/politics/hillary-clinton-speech-prepared-remarks-transcript/index.html.

[272] On this assumption, see Michael Novak, *The Universal Hunger for Liberty: Why the Clash of Civilizations is Not Inevitable* (New York: Basic Books, 2004). Novak was a long-time conservative think tanker at the American Enterprise Institute in Washington, DC.

[273] See Stephen C. Pelletiere, *Losing Iraq: Insurgency and Politics* (Westport, CN: Praeger Security International, 2007), pp. 56–77, on Bremer's mistake and what misconceptions underlay it.

[274] Fighting continues today, and its costs are tracked by the Watson Institute for International and Public Affairs at Brown University. Local casualty statistics are unreliable but, for 2003–2019, Iraqi civilian war deaths are estimated by the Institute as being between 184,000 and 207,000. See https://watson.brown.edu/costsofwar/costs/human/civilians/iraqi.

8 CHOOSING

In Chapters 4–7, I discussed principles, people, practices, and events to show that the concept of Stories is not just a hypothetical construct but that real Stories help to perpetuate at least two national crises – of political and economic imbalance – which should be resolved to avoid severe damage to America's civic order and prosperity. Those chapters underscored the notion, discussed in Chapters 2–3, that if, in a somewhat abstract way, we can know that Stories are important in politics, then beyond their being of hypothetical interest, their tangible centrality in crisis situations lends urgency to the proposition that when we study politics, we should include Stories.

Post-Truth Life

In these circumstances, where we have seen that some Stories are dangerous, we should recall our overall context of post-truth life. In the post-truth world, checking out Stories is especially warranted because, to some extent, Stories are more troublesome now than they were in the past. It is not that Stories reigned weakly in the past, in which case scholars could leave be the narratives that were there. No, there were powerful Stories then but, when facts had a greater purchase than today on public understandings; that is, when facts seemed more real – say, within the rubric of reason and science promoted in and after the Enlightenment – some Stories, such as those which supported the Old Regime, turned out to be vulnerable. Consequently, progress was made by scholars, among other people, showing how wrong and/or undesirable some of those Stories were.

To put that another way, Stories told by opinion leaders in the past, such as Martin Luther, Napoleon Bonaparte, Thomas Jefferson, Abraham Lincoln, or Woodrow Wilson, were probably as true as those which such leaders use today – that is, not entirely. What is new about the post-truth society, though, is that so many people now know, or at least believe, that modern leaders of many stripes, and many of their institutions, care little for truth but deliberately and routinely promote inaccuracy and/or deception.[275]

An historian could sum up this situation by saying that America's becoming a post-truth society was a matter of degree rather than of making a clear transition to being a society which suffers from more falsehoods than it did in the past. The problem, I think, is that the degree in modern America has become very large. Thus, for example, when Joan Didion collected her essays about what Republican George H. W. Bush, Democrat William Jefferson Clinton, and Republican George W. Bush said to voters from 1988 to 2000, she called the book of collected essays *Political Fictions*, and, in a nonpartisan way, she referred to the material in it as "fables."[276]

So what has happened in the post-truth society, which surrounds us all, is that a certain malaise has set in, a certain weariness and confusion in the public conversation, a certain puzzlement and even pessimism about how to find shared sentiments and enjoy them

---

[275] Matthew D'Ancona, *Post Truth: The New War on Truth and How to Fight Back* (London: Ebury, 2017), pp. 25–31. I am not offering a verifiable hypothesis here, as if various leaders were (or were not) more truthful in the past than they are today. I know of no way to measure that. But see George Orwell, in "Politics and the English Language" (1946), almost eighty years ago expressing mounting attention to untruth when he observed that "political language ... is designed to make lies sound truthful and murder respectable, and to give the appearance of solidity to pure wind." See the article at www.orwellfoundation.com/the-orwell-foundation/orwell/essays-and-other-works/politics-and-the-english-language/.

[276] Joan Didion, *Political Fictions* (New York: Vintage, 2001), p. 9.

together. Accordingly, serious questions arise about how to deal with what I have called false political Stories which, as in the past, are still promoted, are still necessary, and, with considerable power, are still maintained.

In these circumstances, what should muddled modern people do about Stories? Here is where Max Weber, who lived in a time of clashing political Stories, had something constructive, I think, to tell political scholars today.

Back to Weber

Assuming that, as teachers living in a post-truth society, some scholars will want to heed Weber and deal with Stories in their work, let us now address the question of how to do that; that is, how to relate to powerful narratives which shape both action and inaction in the public sphere.[277] Roughly speaking, what I will say on that subject in Chapters 8–11 refers to three guidelines of "choosing," "refraining," and "dissembling." So let us start in this chapter with the practice of choosing, as Weber recommended.

To that end, we have seen that societies are held together by Stories which may be persuasive but false; that America is polarized between, roughly speaking, the Left and the Right; and that, consequently, gridlock immobilizes many activists and elected officials. Furthermore, within this gridlock, we have seen that politics and economics in America are unbalanced to the point of crisis; that minority rule and neoliberalism threaten to explode if their inequities will not be resolved; but that both are sanctioned by powerful Stories which are widely believed even though they are not true.

Consequently, it seems to me reasonable to believe that if we could adjust certain of America's reigning Stories, today's political and economic imbalances might be mitigated, polarization might lose some of its force, majority rule might be restored, and important public issues might be resolved constructively.

---

[277] On doing and not doing in the realm of public affairs, see Peter Bachrach and Morton S. Baratz, "Decisions and Nondecisions: An Analytic Framework," *American Political Science Review* (September, 1963), pp. 632–642.

But how can scholars promote such a virtuous sequence? Not easily, I believe. So let us see where, as political thinkers, along with Weber, we stand at the moment. Then we will consider how to go forward.

However, bear with me. Where we stand is really quite complicated, and there are no easy solutions in sight.

The Search for Truth

Where we stand starts, as usual, with the Enlightenment. Exemplified by thinkers such as Spinoza, Voltaire, Diderot, Condorcet, and Jefferson, the progressive Enlightenment led to nineteenth-century positivism, which aimed at enabling scholars, especially via "science" and "common sense," to understand society and its needs. St. Simon and Comte broke ground for positivism, but its underlying optimism was already expressed by thinkers like Kant, who argued that, in order to achieve enlightenment, people should "dare to know."[278]

Scholars incorporated the new open-mindedness into higher education, especially in Germany where, in 1810, Wilhelm Humboldt at the University of Berlin promoted the concept of an educational center for research and teaching that would both advance knowledge and generate good character. Humboldt's ideas spread into many European schools and, along with the 1876 creation of Johns Hopkins University in Baltimore, took powerful hold in America. On the way, Darwin's *On the Origin of Species* in 1859 sealed the pursuit of knowledge into mainstream thinking, providing a theoretical explanation for how most universities would eventually look at the social and physical worlds.

These typical institutions of modern learning were from the outset inspired by a conviction that scholars should aim at discovering what might be called "truth" via "science." Most importantly, professors no longer sought truth in old-time Stories (such as those of Christianity), because most post-Enlightenment scholars adopted the "scientific method" as their vocational hallmark.[279] In the

---

[278] Immanuel Kant, "What is Enlightenment?" (1784), in Carl Friedrich (ed.), *The Philosophy of Kant*, pp. 132–139.

[279] America's first research university, Johns Hopkins University, founded in 1876, took as its motto, from John 8:32, the phrase *Veritas vos Liberabit*, "the truth will make you free."

circumstances, Weber famously defined scientific research as the signature characteristic of scholarship in his Munich University lecture entitled "Science as a Vocation" (1917).

None of this came as a surprise, because the desirability of systematically pursuing secular truth seemed obvious in the light of one significant discovery or technical triumph after another, from Newton's laws to pendulum clocks, thermometers, steam engines, vaccinations, lightning rods, mechanical looms, anesthetics, canned foods, public sanitation, automobiles, airplanes, electric appliances, and much more.[280]

Choosing

As a participant in the search for reliable knowledge, Weber recommended to scholars what he called "the ethics of responsibility." In a time of vast political upheaval and turmoil, in a Europe devastated by the First World War, while radical groups of the Left and Right competed violently to remake Russia and Central Europe, Weber, carefully and painstakingly, recommended the ethics of responsibility to his colleagues.

Thus, in the lecture entitled "Politics as a Vocation" (1919), Weber noted that politicians tend to espouse what he called "causes," which are about national or universal goals, and what leaders and their followers should do for their community and posterity. The problem there was that one politician might promote worldview X and another politician might promote worldview Y. In other words, said Weber, scholars might "find themselves caught up in a conflict of ultimate worldviews ... [in which case] it falls to us to *choose* between them."[281]

---

[280] Critics of the (progressive) Enlightenment, who suggest that it failed by not creating Stories to replace those which it rejected, may occasionally, but not necessarily intentionally, leave us unaware of some of the Enlightenment's great achievements; that is, some difficulties which it overcame. A very readable reminder of European shortcomings, in place *before* the Enlightenment, is supplied by William Manchester, *A World Lit Only by Fire: The Medieval Mind and the Renaissance: Portrait of an Age* (Boston: Little, Brown, 1995).

[281] On "causes" and worldviews, see Max Weber, "Science as a Vocation" (1919), in *The Vocation Lectures* (Indianapolis, IL: Hackett, 2004), pp. 78–79. Weber contracted the Spanish flu and died in 1920. He therefore did not live to see the rise of either Stalin or Hitler, both of whom Weber would surely have mentioned as purveyors of dangerous causes if he were to update his vocation lectures in later years.

Choose: that was the imperative. Of course, Weber did not use our vocabulary. But what he called a "cause" was, more or less, what we can now call a Story. That is, a cause for Weber more or less matched what Neil Postman said about "narratives," which are

> big stories ... that are sufficiently profound and complex to offer explanations of the origins and future of a people; stories that construct ideals, prescribe rules of conduct, specify sources of authority, and, in doing all this, provide a sense of continuity and purpose ... [stories that explain] where the nation is now, how it got here, and where it should go.[282]

In short, when Weber concluded that scholars should – on behalf of their students, colleagues, friends, neighbors, and other citizens – decide to endorse one worldview rather than another, he was saying, in effect, that Stories are so important to public life that scholars may be vocationally obliged to choose between them. Which is what I have been suggesting, but not yet in detail, throughout this book.

But on what grounds should we choose? For Weber, the question arose in the context of the First World War. He cautiously eyed politicians who believed strongly that the *causes* they promoted were *true*. He observed that their behavior was based on an "ethics of conviction," which sometimes rested on "absolute convictions."[283] That is, he said, they believed intensely in their causes.

The problem there was that, if politicians insist on doing what is good according to how their causes define what is truly good, their actions may generate undesirable "consequences." For example, adversary politicians inspired by conflicting religious convictions (Stories) may precipitate ferocious results like those generated during Europe's religious wars. On that score, Weber quoted Martin Luther, a man of immense charisma and a leader of intense religious faith, who assumed that "A good Christian does what is right and leaves the outcome to God."[284]

---

[282] See p. 21.

[283] Weber, "Politics as a Vocation" (1919), in *The Vocation Lectures* (Indianapolis, IL: Hackett, 2004), p. 83.

[284] *Ibid.*, also p. 83. I cite Weber as a thinker who insisted that public policy should be shaped by our estimate of its consequences rather than by what we might regard, at critical moments, as axioms of belief and conscience. In which case, Luther was, for

Against such fatalism, Weber proposed that scholars must espouse a scientific – that is, objective – ethics of responsibility, the hallmarks of which are to investigate the likely consequences of every political cause (Story) and, then, to teach according to the findings of those investigations.[285]

A Crucial Injunction

The point here is crucial for our analysis. I have suggested that we should notice Stories as an element within the scope of politics. In effect, then, Weber tells us what we should do if we will endorse that inclusion.

We can rephrase that a little. During the post-Enlightenment pursuit of truth in many scientific realms, Weber was looking for a sort of political truth. He did not propose that, while criticizing causes they regard as dangerous, scholars should then fashion wide-ranging "counter-causes," as if one or another of such counter-causes could be true in a very large sense. That is, Weber did not call upon scholars to

Weber, a perfect example of how *not* to set public policy. Other thinkers, before Weber and until today, have promoted the same insight. For example, in the modern field of international relations, so-called "realists" commend what they call "the logic of consequences." See this theme in Michael Mazaar, *Leap of Faith: Hubris, Negligence, and America's Greatest Foreign Policy Tragedy* (New York: Public Affairs, 2019), *passim*, but esp. ch. 2, "The Origins of a Conviction," pp. 19–62. Mazaar's central thesis is that the Bush II administration went to war in Iraq in 2003 on the basis of sentiments (Mazaar, p. 39, calls them "geopolitical zealotry") driven by a desire to do the right thing (what Weber called "conviction"), rather than by a concern for the likely consequences of making war there. See also the "realist" former US Secretary of State Henry Kissinger, struck by what he thought would be a disastrous eventual outcome of the Ukraine war, recommending at Davos in 2022 that Ukraine cede influence (and territory) to Russia, at www.washingtonpost.com/world/2022/05/24/henry-kissinger-ukraine-russia-territory-davos/.

[285] For a modern example, see Catholic activist George Weigel's article entitled "Dobbs and the Vindication of American Democracy" at www.firstthings.com/web-exclusives/2022/06/dobbs-and-the-vindication-of-american-democracy. Weigel powerfully discusses what he regards as the values espoused by "pro-life" thinkers but says nothing about the likely consequences of such a Supreme Court decision in a country where, apparently, 61% of adults believe abortion should be legal in all or most cases and 37% believe it should be illegal in all or most cases. See the poll results at www.pewresearch.org/fact-tank/2022/06/13/about-six-in-ten-americans-say-abortion-should-be-legal-in-all-or-most-cases-2/.

invent what I would call new Stories.[286] But he did declare that political scholars should speak what they regard as the truth about outcomes which existing Stories (he did not call them that) are likely to produce.

To that end, he insisted that those scholars must "choose." In this sense, his great Vocational Lectures expressed a basic principle of the Enlightenment. And that is how we should remember him, gratefully.

The Soft Sciences

Unfortunately, while Weber took his stand on choosing, the concept of a pursuit of truth was starting to run aground. We should note how that happened, so as to prepare ourselves for considering how Weber's ethics of responsibility might still inspire scholarship today, but not easily.

Doubts about the search for truth did not begin in the "hard sciences." Scientists such as physicists and chemists, accompanied by assorted engineers, still churn out discoveries and inventions – from radios to jet planes, from frozen foods to nuclear reactors, from antibiotics to radar, from DDT to the Green Revolution, from transistors to GPS, from Lipitor to Teflon, from Covid-19 vaccines to quantum computers, and more – which are apparently *true* because they *work*. And they *do* work, which is the main thing. The scientists who work on such projects themselves say that philosophical insight is not the aim.[287]

However, in the "soft sciences,"[288] starting at least with Plato and his Cave, there have always been doubts about what people can

---

[286] Sheldon S. Wolin noted that Weber did not formulate a "political theory" even though "the manifest breakdown of German politics and society called out for one." See Wolin, "Max Weber: Legitimation, Method, and the Politics of Theory," *Political Theory* (August, 1981), pp. 401–424.

[287] Thus the 2022 Nobel Prize in physics was awarded to three physicists for their work on quantum mechanics, which the Nobel Committee described as having "ineffable effects." See www.nobelprize.org/prizes/physics/2022/prize-announcement/. The routine indifference of such scientists to philosophical explanations is discussed in Michael Strevens, *The Knowledge Machine: How Irrationality Created Modern Science* (New York: Liveright, 2020), esp. pp. 152–197.

[288] I am using the word "science" here in the European sense to indicate a field of knowledge. Thus the French speak of *sciences politiques* (political sciences). And the so-called Nobel Prize in economics is awarded for excellence in "economic sciences." In this sense, even philosophy is a *science*, albeit "soft" rather than "hard."

or cannot know about themselves and their societies.[289] Such doubts endured and multiplied until, as early as during the first decades of the twentieth century, they became especially aggravating.

For example, in those years, practitioners in fields such as public relations and advertising aimed increasingly at establishing convictions rather than truth, and governments on both sides during the First World War exercised the same deception when they engaged in "propaganda." Afterward, especially as radio messages multiplied, it became harder and harder to know what to believe about powerfully hawked commercial products and how to interpret dramatic political talk by or about candidates for public office.[290]

Consequently, in the 1920s and 1930s, journalists such as Walter Lippmann,[291] philosophers such as John Dewey,[292] political scientists such as Harold Lasswell,[293] and ad men such as Edward Bernays[294] wrote about what this world of modern persuasion all meant. That is, they wrote about who, amateurs or professionals, might be able to grasp the nature of society, and about who, perhaps ostensible "experts," should lead a democratic nation when "the people" are unable to understand entirely what is happening around them.

The situation did not improve after the Second World War, when signs of irrational impulses and misleading policies, social fictions and official deceits, mounted everywhere. For example, sociologists David Riesman, Nathan Glazer, and Reuel Denney wrote about a "lonely crowd" of "other-directed" personalities;[295] psychologist

---

[289] For example, see Friedrich Nietzsche, *On Truth and Lies in a Nonmoral Sense* (Scotts Valley, CA: CreateSpace Independent Publishing Platform, 2015).

[290] On commercial and political propaganda in the 1920s and 1930s, see David Greenberg, *Republic of Spin: An Inside Story of the American Presidency* (New York: Norton, 2016), pp. 129–229. For example, the successful but truth-challenged electoral campaign against California gubernatorial candidate Upton Sinclair in 1934 was an early project of Campaigns, Inc., the newly minted political consulting firm of Clem Whitaker and Leone Baxter. On Campaigns, Inc., see *ibid.*, pp. 214–222.

[291] Walter Lippmann, *Public Opinion* (New York: Harcourt Brace, 1922).

[292] John Dewey, *The Public and Its Problems* (New York: Holt, 1927).

[293] Harold Lasswell, *Propaganda Technique in the World War* (New York: Roger Smith, 1927).

[294] Edward Bernays, *Propaganda* (London: Routledge, 1928).

[295] David Riesman, Nathan Glazer, and Reuel Denney, *The Lonely Crowd: A Study of the Changing American Character* (New Haven: Yale University Press, 1950).

Erich Fromm doubted the sanity of a society which prepared for nuclear combat;[296] social critic Vance Packard exposed duplicitous advertisements in a roaring economy;[297] Martin Luther King, Jr., was murdered because he insisted that White Americans should honor the "self-evident" principles enshrined in the Declaration of Independence;[298] and the Vietnam War made no sense to many people, while Washington's official explanations for why American soldiers were dying there created obvious "credibility gaps."[299]

Nascent Post-Truth

Looking back, we can see that the rise of commercial advertising, public relations, and governmental propaganda were straws in the wind, early manifestations of a cumulative process whereby, eventually, so much untruth was being deliberately peddled that we now speak of "a post-truth world" to describe where we eventually wound up. Early soft-science practitioners lacked the foresight to see that world being born but, driven by thinkers and events such as those we noted, many scholars eventually joined the chorus of doubts.

Their vocational world is too large to sum up here. But a few examples from it can demonstrate misgivings which, to some extent, made Weber's recommendations for objectively confronting "causes" seem almost naive.

Soft Scientists

In the realm of literature and linguistics, for instance, language came to be seen in many cases as a servant of powerful people rather than as a neutral instrument for describing reality. Thus the revelations of "postmodernism," which in its extreme form claimed that all

---

[296] Erich Fromm, *The Sane Society* (New York: Routledge, 1955).
[297] Vance Packard, *The Hidden Persuaders* (New York: Pocketbooks, 1957).
[298] Martin Luther King, Jr., *Why We Can't Wait* (New York: Signet, 1963).
[299] On doubting official explanations and justifications, see Senator William Fulbright, *The Arrogance of Power* (New York: Random House, 1967); Noam Chomsky, *American Power and the New Mandarins* (New York: Pantheon, 1969); and David Halberstam, *The Best and the Brightest* (New York: Random House, 1972).

declarations and writings are merely competing "texts."[300] In the light of that postulate, philosophers such as Jean-François Lyotard went so far as to insist that even scientific works and formulas are not neutral and objective but only texts to be variously interpreted, or opportunities for expressing "incredulity towards metanarratives."[301] Similarly, linguists George Lakoff and Mark Johnson held that empirical objectivity is unattainable because thinking rests on innumerable metaphors which differ from one "conceptual system" to another.[302]

It did not take long for Michel Foucault to add to postmodernism his notion of "regimes of truth," whereby scholars were encouraged to believe that the political principles admired in any particular society might be valid (true), if at all, only for that society.[303] So much for the progressive Enlightenment faith in a universal Story like that in America's Declaration of Independence, which assumed the existence of natural laws and promoted for "all men" (not just those in a particular society) what the Founders called "liberty, equality, and the pursuit of happiness."[304]

In anthropology and sociology, "relativism" became the standard approach. For example, twentieth-century anthropologists such as Franz Boaz and Ruth Benedict studied different Stories told by various peoples, and sociologists such as Robert Merton and Clifford

---

[300] See Stanley Fish, *Is There a Text in This Class? The Authority of Interpretive Communities* (Cambridge, MA: Harvard University Press, 1982).

[301] Jean-François Lyotard, *The Postmodern Condition: A Report on Knowledge* (Minneapolis: University of Minnesota Press, 1984). I assume Lyotard would not have tried to prove that scientific formulae are merely verbal constructs by sitting next to the atomic bomb test in Almagordo, New Mexico on the morning of July 16, 1945.

[302] George Lakoff and Mark Johnson, *Metaphors We Live By* (Chicago: University of Chicago Press, 1980, 2003), especially pp. 185–222.

[303] Michel Foucault, "Truth and Power," in *Power/Knowledge: Selected Interview and Other Writings* (New York: Vintage, 1980), pp. 109–133, but esp. 131.

[304] Therefore, conservative criticism of postmodernism and Foucault is expressed in Lynne V. Cheney, *Telling the Truth: Why Our Culture and Our Country Have Stopped Making Sense - and What We Can Do About It* (New York: Simon & Schuster, 1995), esp. pp. 87–96. By the standards of social science, Cheney's belief in the American Founders' notion of self-evident truths is a parochial view of human practices and aspirations. As Ernest Gellner, "The Stakes in Anthropology," *The American Scholar* (Winter, 1988), pp. 17–30, points out, Thomas Jefferson and his colleagues in 1776 were "affirming something totally absurd—namely, that views which, for 99 percent of mankind, would have been unintelligible, or at best blasphemous, heretical, and subversive, were actually *self-evident*" (p. 22).

Geertz explored what their colleagues call "the social construction of reality," whereby particular groups of people share different understandings of the world around them.[305] It has never been perfectly clear, however, in such studies and many others, how one people can be compared to another *qualitatively*.

Yes, they may "function" (behave) successfully through different "structures" (institutions) and, in that sense, human beings reproduce themselves in a Darwinian world. But who among them, and whose way of life, is superior? For example, what can we say professionally, scientifically, and conclusively, about a pious congregation of English Quakers as compared to a zealous regiment of Nazi storm-troopers?

Relativism is hard to avoid here, because it emerges from a corrosive "sociology of knowledge" wherein what a person – Quaker or Nazi – believes depends on where she or he stands, to the point where objective and neutral truth, in social affairs, may be unavailable to people who believe no more than what they were raised to believe.[306]

Political Science

In political science, a wide variety of research projects now reflects that discipline's inability to identify and promote truth.[307] Its textbooks and colleagues do not entertain a set of core beliefs about scope and methods, and presidents of the American Political Science Association

---

[305] See Peter L. Berger and Thomas Luckmann, *The Social Construction of Reality: A Treatise in the Sociology of Knowledge* (New York: Doubleday Anchor, 1967).

[306] The sociology of knowledge can be extremely corrosive. For example, Bertrand Russell in effect "canceled" philosopher Immanuel Kant when Russell concluded that Kant's moral theories were no more than spruced-up versions of Pietist (Protestant) ideas which Kant had acquired as a child. See Russell, *Unpopular Essays* (New York: Simon & Schuster, 1950), p. 52.

[307] Political scientists do not agree on which, if any, important truths have been discovered by members of their discipline. See, for example, Gary King, Kay Lehman Schlozman, and Norman H. Nie (eds.), *The Future of Political Science: 100 Perspectives* (Cambridge, MA: Harvard University Press, 2009). The editors of this volume asked a hundred political scientists which research questions should be raised in their fields and which earlier findings were especially noteworthy. Each colleague was invited to address these two questions in 1,000 or fewer words. Their answers agreed neither on what should be done nor on what had already been done especially well. The same pluralism showed up in "Significant Works in Political Science: Some Personal Views," *PS: Political Science and Politics* (Spring, 1983), pp. 196–204, where colleagues did not agree on which works to list as most significant.

(APSA) have given up trying to generalize about what the Association's more than 13,000 members do. The APSA now sponsors more than twenty journals, from *Legislative Politics* to *Political Behavior*, from *Ethnic Politics* to *Politics and Religion*, and more. The variety looks fruitful. The drawback is that many of those journals are devoted to specialized subfields whose practitioners may share few if any professional aims with members of other subfields.[308]

In these circumstances, amounting to great diversity about disciplinary principles and practices, the editors for *Perspectives on Politics* announced to their colleagues that, "Given ... the lack of an Archimedean point for understanding [politics] ... our view is that methodological and substantive pluralism of all sorts may be the only way of leading us to a clearer and deeper understanding of politics."[309] They called this intellectual tangle "perspectival political theory." But it might also be called, less optimistically, an academic version of "Rashomon."

The Marketplace of Ideas

Somewhat unexpectedly, the sum total of all this is that the concept of truth became problematic in the "marketplace of ideas," where scholars express their views. On this score, let us recall that, in

---

[308] This variety reflects an official APSA "commitment to diversify the subfields, geographic foci, and methodological approaches represented in the *APSR*." See "APSA Council Announces New Editorial Team for the American Political Science Review," *P.S.: Political Science and Politics* (October, 2019), p. 775.

[309] Daniel O'Neill and Michael Bernhard, "Perspectival Political Theory," *Perspectives on Politics* (December, 2019), p. 954. For political scientists, these two editors expressed the society-wide, post-truth situation perfectly. If there is no accepted way to decide which academic contentions are true (no Archimedean point), then editors should publish many of those contentions and let readers decide what to conclude from them (the contentions *in toto*). For the profession of journalism, the *New York Times* confronts the same dilemma. For many years, that newspaper separated news articles from opinion articles, where news articles were, presumably, about facts, and where opinion articles, intended to provide interpretation, were positioned on the editorial page or opposite it. During the Trump years, the *Times* started putting at least one opinion article on the front page, and to this day it has continued to do so. Now it declares, under that article on its front page, that "*The New York Times publishes opinion from a wide range of perspectives in hopes of promoting constructive debate about consequential questions.*" Which is the same hope that inspired the editors of *Perspectives on Politics* to forgo some editorial judgements. In the world of art museums, a similar unease about what to display, about standards and guidelines, about whose word is final – in fact, a waning of cultural authority – has also set in. See www.thenation.com/article/culture/museum-crisis/.

keeping with the progressive Enlightenment, John Stuart Mill argued, in *On Liberty* (1859), that we should maintain a marketplace for ideas which will help us at least to approach, if not to arrive at, the truth. Among other disciples, Supreme Court Justice Oliver Wendell Holmes, Jr., agreed, in his famous dissent against political censorship in *Abrams v. United States* (1919), that "the best test of truth is the power of thought to get itself accepted in the competition of the market."[310] Thus, too, *On Liberty*'s vision became an inspiration for scholars such as those who founded the American Association of University Professors (AAUP) in 1915 and wrote Mill's ideal into the Association's "Statement of Principles."[311]

In real life, however, the marketplace of ideas which Mill and the AAUP recommended in theory evolved into a complex arena and, in that arena, truth became, in some ways, less rather than more available.[312] This started with the rise of high-powered persuasion, where

[310] Holmes' dissent in *Abrams* is available at www.law.cornell.edu/supremecourt/ text/250/616. The phrase "marketplace of ideas" entered the Court's lexicon when Justice William O. Douglas used it in his concurring opinion in *United States v. Rumely*, 345 U.S. 41, 56 (1953).

[311] For example, in its 1940 Statement of Principles, the AAUP declared that "Freedom in research is fundamental to the advancement of truth." See www.aaup.org/report/1940-statement-principles-academic-freedom-and-tenure. The importance of truth, for democratic citizens in general, underlay the insistence of Winston Smith, in George Orwell's *Nineteen Eighty-Four*, that "Freedom is the freedom to say that two plus two makes four. If that is granted, all else follows" ([London: Penguin Books, 2008], p. 84).

[312] This tension was not widely foreseen. At mid-twentieth century, growing amounts of available information sometimes inspired optimism about how it could be used. For example, James Conant recommended spreading knowledge around more equally (than was customary) in his "Education for a Classless Society" (1940), a Charter Day Address at the University of California, reprinted in *The Atlantic* at www.theatlantic .com/magazine/archive/1940/05/education-for-a-classless-society/305254/. And Vannevar Bush recommended producing more of it in "Science, the Endless Frontier" (1945), a book-length Report to the President, at www.nsf.gov/od/lpa/nsf50/vbush1945.htm. Karl Deutsch, soon to be president of the American Political Science Association, even argued that more information is good for democracy, on the grounds that increasing the number of communications between previously insular people, from one state to another, can help them make more effective policy decisions. See Deutsch, *The Nerves of Government: Models of Political Communication and Control* (Glencoe, IL: Free Press, 1963). For universities, Yale added the "Woodward Report" (1975), which assumed that academic freedom would endlessly generate useful knowledge. For popular consumption, Thomas Friedman later decreed that growth and circulation of information on the internet, in the Lexus society, helps us all to be good neighbors. See Friedman, *The Lexus and the Olive Tree: Understanding Globalization* (New York: Random House, 2000).

misleading advertising, amoral public relations, official propaganda, partisan broadcasting, "puffery," and more, added up to "spin" and thereby undermined Mill's ideal of a fair exchange of ideas from which some will emerge with widespread support.[313]

Mill hoped that this exchange would be full and free without, to mix metaphors, anyone moving the goalposts or putting a thumb on the scales.[314] But in real life, the chances of winning have always tempted ambitious people to meddle in every kind of market. Consequently, on behalf of considerable gains, various modern consultants, advisors, and strategists – from Ivy Lee to Clem Whitaker and Leone Baxter,[315] from Joe McGinnis to Michael Deaver, from Lee Atwater to Karl Rove to David Axelrod – have chiefly and powerfully promoted the interests of their patrons more than neutrality in the marketplace of ideas.[316]

Eventually, Mark Zuckerberg declared, in tune with much of Silicon Valley thinking, that Facebook brings huge amounts of information to everyone so they can make "better decisions." Zuckerberg claims that Facebook is not a "publisher" but only a "platform" that other people use to communicate. Therefore he refuses to take responsibility for the fact that, unlike the *New York Times* – whose motto commits it to publish "all the news that's fit to print" – Facebook passes on, every day, to perhaps 2 billion people, enormous quantities of *"news" that is not fit to print*. On Zuckerberg's views, see the text of "Founder's Letter, 2012," at https://dig.abclocal.go.com/kgo/PDF/LETTER-FROM-MARK-ZUCKERBERG-SEC.pdf.

[313] For example, see Stuart Ewen, *PR! A Social History of Spin* (New York: Basic Books, 1996).

[314] Mill envisioned a marketplace of ideas very different from that which reigns today. For example, John Stuart Mill, *On Liberty* (orig., 1859; New York: Liberal Arts Press, 1956), pp. 64–67, said that "the free expression of all opinions should be permitted on condition that the manner should be temperate, and do not pass the bounds of fair discussion …. The gravest [of offenses] … is to argue sophistically, to suppress facts or arguments, to misstate the elements of the case, or misrepresent the opposite opinion …. The worst offense … which can be committed by a polemic is to stigmatize those who hold the contrary opinion as bad and immoral men." (For an example of what would have horrified Mill, see Ann Coulter, *Godless: The Church of Liberalism* [New York: Three Rivers, 2007]. Actually, *any* of Coulter's books would have horrified Mill.) Among modern philosophers, Jurgen Habermas recommended a similar marketplace for ideas when he praised "the unforced force of the better argument." See Habermas, *Between Facts and Norms: Contributions to a Discourse Theory of Law and Democracy* (Cambridge, MA: MIT Press, 1992), pp. 148–149.

[315] The first famous political consultants were Whitaker and Baxter, who founded Campaigns, Inc., in 1933. See them at www.newyorker.com/magazine/2012/09/24/the-lie-factory.

[316] See Joe McGinnis, *The Selling of the President 1968* (New York: Trident, 1969). After Fox News fired founder Roger Ailes in 2015, the Fox network decided to stop using the motto he had inspired, which was "Fair and Balanced." See www.nytimes.com /2017/06/14/ business/media/fox-news-fair-and-balanced.html. The current motto is "Most Watched, Most Trusted."

Moreover, in due course, the Supreme Court sanctioned unlimited financial interventions in Mill's marketplace of ideas. That was the outcome of decisions such as *Citizens United* v. *Federal Election Commission* (2010), and *McCutcheon* v. *Federal Election Commission* (2014), which, especially during (expensive) election campaigns, permit wealthy activists to play an outsized role in that marketplace.[317]

The Digital Age

Once created, powerful techniques of modern persuasion would go on to infect later-day instruments such as televisions and smartphones. Then these new instruments, projecting inherent agendas, generated difficulties of their own. Television, for example, overwhelmed much of America's print-based culture with exciting pictures, previously confined to magazines and movies. The small screen entered every home, with the result, said Neil Postman – and here was the agenda – of turning every sort of activity and event into entertainment rather than edification, distraction rather than enlightenment.[318]

Like television, computerized information massively affected everyone's thinking. Thus digital cataloguing and storage, word processing, email, spreadsheets, PowerPoint, Zoom, Facebook, Twitter, Instagram, TikTok, and more have become platforms for generating and exchanging enormous quantities of information (and misinformation), with far-reaching results. Obvious results include silo thinking,

---

[317] News reports claimed that Michael Bloomberg spent more than $400 million of his own money to run for the Democratic Party presidential nomination in 2019–2020. He did not succeed, but his well-heeled campaign may have upset the more normal balance of power among and between other candidates. See www.nbcnews.com/politics/meet-the-press/blog/meet-press-blog-latest-news-analysis-data-driving-political-discussion-n988541/ncrd114005 1#blogHeader.

[318] Neil Postman, *Amusing Ourselves to Death: Public Discourse in the Age of Show Business* (New York: Penguin, 1985). For a shocking example, see Deborah L. Jaramillo, *Ugly War, Pretty Package: How CNN and Fox News Made the Invasion of Iraq High Concept* (Bloomington: Indiana University Press, 2009). As an example of "high concept" – a term familiar to communications scholars – Jaramillo explains how these television stations presented the war as an exciting narrative designed to hold viewers' attention and thereby generate a commercial payoff.

lack of context, shallow minds, criticism of experts, short attention spans, multitasking, network effects, elimination of gatekeepers, political polarization, anger, resentment, disinhibition, alternative facts, and fake news.

The Epistemological Crisis

Earlier, I said that I would not add to what scholars, pundits, and activists have already said about post-truth life, that doing so was not my mission, and that I would take the post-truth world, which they have described, as a given presence in my project. A few words here, however, will put some of that world into perspective for our purposes.

Thus, in today's marketplace of ideas, the ad/spin factor (quality), and the data/overload factor (quantity) combine and reinforce each other, while some insistent players – for example, Fox News, CNN, Facebook, Google, Twitter, Instagram, the *National Review*, Huffington Post, the *American Interest*, Breitbart News, the Drudge Report, and Slate Magazine – are constantly trying to persuade us to read or listen to them.[319]

When all that happens, people from every walk of life don't know who to believe, they don't know what is real and what is "spin," they are distracted by "pseudo-events," their trust in individuals and institutions wanes, and "truth" becomes an endlessly contested issue.[320] In other words, much of America's public conversation, more and more, sounds like a dialogue of the deaf.

Consequently, scholars who investigate the condition of truth in modern society sometimes write about an "epistemological crisis," where epistemology is the science (discipline) of how we can "know" or, as Plato and Aristotle would have said, the science of how to distinguish between objective "knowledge" (certain) and subjective

---

[319] See, for example, Tim Wu, *The Attention Merchants: The Epic Scramble to Get Inside our Heads* (New York: Knopf, 2016). See also James G. Webster, *The Marketplace of Attention: How Audiences Take Shape in a Digital Age* (Cambridge, MA: MIT Press, 2014) and Adam Alter, *Irresistible: The Rise of Addictive Technology and the Business of Keeping us Hooked* (New York: Penguin, 2017).

[320] On pseudo-events, see Daniel Boorstin, *The Image: A Guide to Pseudo-Events in America* (New York: Harper Colophon, 1961), esp. pp. 7–44.

"opinion" (maybe biased).[321] In the circumstances, popular word-smiths today speak about dealing with "*bullsh*t*," which is defined, for this purpose, as talk where truth does not matter.[322]

Many people believe, and I agree with them, that an epitome of disregard for truth in America appeared in the messages that Donald Trump posted, and still posts whenever he can, on social media. One cannot exaggerate, I think, the extent of Trump's disdain for accuracy or consistency, to say nothing of his casual fabrications.[323]

But Trump is an odd case, personally truth-challenged, let us say.[324] In fact, all modern people, including scholars, now wonder what happened to truth, especially in public talk, commercial and political. On that score, former President Trump – a poster-boy for the post-truth society – was, and now is, only symptomatic.[325]

---

[321] For example, Yochai Benkler, Robert Faris, and Hal Roberts, *Network Propaganda: Manipulation, Disinformation, and Radicalization in American Politics* (New York: Oxford University Press, 2018), ch. 1, "Epistemic Crisis," pp. 3–38.

[322] When used as an everyday expression, bullsh*t refers to talk where truth does not matter. But in the scholarly world, which draws finer distinctions, the issue is not so simple. For example, see philosopher Harry G. Frankfurt, *On Bullshit* (Princeton: Princeton University Press, 2005), who, after discussing some remarks by the iconic Ludwig Wittgenstein, concludes that "sincerity itself is bullshit" (p. 67).

[323] For the liberal view of Donald Trump's tendency not to tell the truth, see Eric Alterman, *Lying in State: Why Presidents Lie – and Why Trump is Worse* (New York: Basic Books, 2020). See also the *Washington Post*'s Fact Checker team which claims that Trump made 30,573 "false or misleading statements as president," at www.washingtonpost.com/politics/2021/01/24/trumps-false-or-misleading-claims-total-30573-over-four-years/.

[324] For example, see Justin A. Frank (ed.), *Trump on the Couch: Inside the Mind of the President* (New York: Avery, 2018), and Brandy X. Lee (ed.), *The Dangerous Case of Donald Trump: 37 Psychiatrists and Mental Health Experts Assess a President* (New York: Thomas Dunne Books, 2019).

[325] Many scholars scorn Trump for his indifference to truth. But post-truth symptoms show up also in scholarly precincts. For example, in a recent academic book endorsement: "This is the rare edited volume that features real intellectual heft. It not only bids fair to reorient the study of American political life but it also promises to shape the scholarly sensibilities of generations to come." This endorsement is typical of many academic blurbs today. It comes from a professor who is presumably committed, by vocational standards, to considering facts dispassionately; that is, to disseminating knowledge more than opinion. Nevertheless, the blurb is designed, not surprisingly in our time, to sell the book regardless of truth or accuracy. It is an example of commercial hype gone wild, a classic contribution to today's epistemological confusion. After all, it is beyond exaggeration – really fake news – to suggest that a book written today may "shape the scholarly sensibilities of generations to come." Whoever wrote that blurb doesn't know even what will happen a week from now, in that realm, much less in "generations to come."

Conservative Critiques

Ergo, the marketplace of ideas – a three-ring circus, really – is working poorly these days.[326] So we might conclude that, given such a market, perhaps what Weber called for was irreparably naive.

I don't believe that but, before moving on to consider how political scholars might respond in that workplace to Weber's recommendation for choosing, let us note a final aspect of what happens there. It emerges from what historian Robert Fogel described as a "Great Awakening" of religious sentiment (the fourth in American history), that is, a widespread enthusiasm starting in the 1960s, to the point where, among other trends, mainline Protestant churches (which attracted many Lutherans, Methodists, Episcopalians, etc.) lost ground to evangelical and fundamentalist Protestant churches (which attracted many Baptists, Pentecostals, some Calvinists, etc.). This awakening inspired powerful writings which insist that modern scholars should either refrain from rejecting great conservative Stories or, at least, be constantly aware of high social costs which may flow from promoting too much secularism (the progressive Enlightenment) in American society.[327]

Alasdair MacIntyre

In this particular moment, one recent critic of modernism – or manifestations of liberalism by any other name, such as "utilitarianism," or "emotivism," or "materialism" – was Alasdair MacIntyre, a Catholic philosopher. In 1981, MacIntyre argued that various notions of "individualism" in modern society are remiss for abandoning the classical

---

[326] Conservatives such as Robert Bork, Roger Kimball, and Gertrude Himmelfarb have long argued that Mill was too optimistic, that the competitive marketplace for truth is no place to approach the Truth because it, the Truth, may be overwhelmed in that forum by false liberal propositions. I have discussed this conservative criticism of Mill's *On Liberty* in Ricci, *Why Conservatives Tell Stories and Liberals Don't: Rhetoric, Faith, and Vision on the American Right* (Boulder, CO: Paradigm, 2011), pp. 144–156. For a nonpartisan argument that the current marketplace of ideas – where most people get slanted selections of information from internet and social media sources – is unlikely to move us in the direction of truth, see Claudio Lombardi, "The Illusion of a 'Marketplace of Ideas' and the Right to Truth," at https://americanaffairsjournal.org/2019/02/the-illusion-of-a-marketplace-of-ideas-and-the-right-to-truth/.

[327] See a chart of Fogel's four Great Awakenings at https://press.uchicago.edu/Misc/Chicago/256626.html.

concept of human beings as endowed with a divine *telos*, or end, or purpose, distinctive to our species.[328] This concept, underlying Aristotle's
philosophy of final causes and later Christian theology about souls, and
therefore pervasive in Europe in the Middle Ages, assumes that no men
(people) are islands, that they are members of communities, that they
learn the meaning of life from their neighbors, and that those meanings
are defined and transmitted by shared narratives (Stories, in our term),
often biblical (for Westerners), which their members tell each other.

MacIntyre argued that to deny any human *telos*, which he
regarded as a deplorable act, assures that wide-ranging agreement on
moral ends, as a framework for acceptable behavior, cannot be achieved
in our culture.[329] This failure he attributed to various Enlightenment
thinkers and their followers who, as we saw, deliberately rejected the
Old Regime's great Stories – which empowered kings, aristocrats, and
clergymen – as not true.

Charles Taylor

Charles Taylor, also a Catholic philosopher, observed that "secularism," in large degree, has led, unfortunately, to "disenchantment."[330]
In Taylor's view, pre-Enlightenment Christians lived in a thoroughly
enchanted world which, while it was shaped purposefully by God, promoted strong social ties and shared support for human communities.
Furthermore, that European world, while inspired by Christian thinkers such as John Calvin and the French *politiques*, was on its way to
what Taylor defined as "reforming" itself.

The problem there, in Taylor's view, is that instead of pro-
gressing toward a forward-looking Christianity which would have

---

[328] Alasdair MacIntyre, *After Virtue: A Study in Moral Theory* (South Bend, IN: Notre
Dame University, 1981), pp. 52–61.

[329] The liberal philosopher Michael Walzer, in his *Spheres of Justice: A Defense of Pluralism
and Equality* (New York: Basic Books, 1983), argued that moral consensus cannot be
achieved because every society is composed of different spheres of activity, each characterized by its own forms of principle and practice. Thus what is appropriate in military
affairs (morally speaking) is one thing and what is appropriate in religious affairs (morally speaking) may be another.

[330] Charles Taylor, *A Secular Age* (Cambridge, MA: Harvard University Press, 2007),
pp. 25–28.

retained important elements of spiritual strength, many Western thinkers got sidetracked into promoting secularization as if it were a project of reform, where human flourishing became the highest goal and what Taylor called a "naïve acknowledgement of the transcendent"[331] – that is, traditional faith that nature expresses divine standards for a godly life – became impossible for most people committed to secular values.

In Taylor's vocabulary, such people become (a) "buffered selves" who "no longer fear … demons, spirits, [or] magic forces," and/or (b) "disembedded" individuals who autonomously fashion their own opinions and independently achieve their own relations with God.[332] These people, in our modern, secular society, emerge from what Taylor called a time marked by "subtraction stories," whereby the stories (or Stories) that explained the Old Regime were subtracted from the canon of political thought while Enlightenment thinkers assumed that what would come next – reason, science, materialism, individualism, etc. – would successfully fill in for the earlier Stories.[333]

Which, Taylor concluded, simply did not happen. Stories were removed. But what replaced them rests today, he claimed, on spiritual confusion and widespread malaise.

Paul Kahn

Neither MacIntyre nor Taylor recommended installing a transcendent force – for instance, Christianity – in American politics.[334] But law professor Paul Kahn does.[335] In his view, the liberal notion of a social contract between reasoning individuals – the ideal of Locke, Jefferson, Rawls, and so forth – is inadequate for sustaining a real-world state. Such a state, says Kahn, in return for defense of the realm and individual rights which it provides, must occasionally ask its citizens to

---

[331] *Ibid.*, p. 21.

[332] *Ibid.*, pp. 37–41, 156–158.

[333] On subtraction stories, see *ibid.*, pp. 26–29, 267–268.

[334] MacIntyre, *After Virtue*, p. 263, recommended that Americans hoping to save their souls should work together in small communities to promote good works and faith together with neighbors. The same strategy is recommended by Rod Dreher, *The Benedict Option: A Strategy for Christians in a Post-Christian Nation* (New York: Sentinel, 2017).

[335] Paul W. Kahn, *Putting Liberalism in its Place* (Princeton: Princeton University Press, 2005).

"sacrifice" on the state's behalf. Yet that sacrifice, in Kahn's view, can only be motivated by "love," which he believes is a Christian rather than an Enlightenment value.[336]

In other words, according to Kahn, American liberalism succeeds in spite of itself because, for all its denial of pre-Enlightenment values, there have always been in America enough devout, ethically responsible citizens to uphold not just "rights" (certified by the Enlightenment) but also "obligations" (based on pre-Enlightenment ideals).

Kahn's analysis of liberalism on this point resembles that of the twentieth-century German law professor Carl Schmitt, in that when officials of the state exercise "sovereignty" (say, by requiring military service during a war), the power of sovereign commands rests on loyalty which derives from what Kahn calls "the migration of religious conceptions into the order of politics."[337] That is, first "the monarch" was sovereign by divine right; then "the people" were regarded as naturally sovereign; then the "nation-state" came (electorally) to legitimately represent them; and finally "the people" now respond with reverence, consciously or not, to the nation-state as their representative.[338]

Steven Smith

Law professor Steven Smith described the disenchantment of secular discourse in terms similar to those of Kahn.[339] To that end, Smith

[336] *Ibid.*, pp. 1–27.
[337] *Ibid.*, p. 89.
[338] For Kahn on Schmitt, see *ibid.*, pp. 19–20, 234–241. See Schmitt's worldview in Carl Schmitt, *The Concept of the Political* (orig., 1932; Chicago: University of Chicago Press, 1996, 2007). That book describes the principles and practices of what German law professor Schmitt called *states*, which live in constant hostility and sometimes war with other states. But America is *not such a state*, therefore Smith commits a category error when he assumes that it is. In fact, the term *sovereign* – the hallmark of Schmitt's states – does not appear in the Constitution because the Founders did *not* replace the English monarch with an American sovereign. The French who overthrew Louis XVI replaced him with the "sovereign" French nation. But nothing like that happened in America. Instead, the Founders created, by intent, a limited rather than all-powerful (sovereign) government. Schmitt's ideas were helpful to some Germans, and from 1933 to 1945 he was an active and enthusiastic member of the Nazi Party.
[339] Steven D. Smith, *The Disenchantment of Secular Discourse* (Cambridge, MA: Harvard University Press, 2010).

observed that modern Americans may formally – after the Enlightenment and according to liberalism – assume that their laws and institutions are informed by reason and science even though, at critical moments, they are not. In those moments, such as in a judicial controversy over the legality of doctor-assisted suicide, moral calculations must be made by judges. Those men and women claim that they only "interpret" the law. But, in fact, they "smuggle" into their judicial decisions moral values still derived from transcendental beliefs which the Enlightenment banished.[340]

In Smith's view, America should replace this sort of smuggling with open discussion of moral calculations by easing the separation of church and state, by encouraging citizens to express their religious opinions in public.[341] We need not fear, he argues, that pious Americans will say, for example, that "The nation should ban abortions .... because this is the will of God." Smith insists, instead, that "even devout religious believers who are at all thoughtful hardly ever say that sort of thing, exactly."[342]

A Warning

More critiques of American liberal thinking, for its presumed moral failures, are available.[343] But the four I have cited are sufficient to raise a point we should bear in mind, which is this:

Weber proposed that modern scholars have a vocational obligation to examine political "causes." However, conservatives have fired shots across the liberal bow on this matter.[344] Basically they warn that, unless soft scientists can suggest social, economic, and political

---

[340] On "smuggling" in this sense, see *ibid.*, pp. 34–38.

[341] *Ibid.*, pp. 107–150.

[342] *Ibid.*, p. 220.

[343] For example, Patrick J. Deneen, *Why Liberalism Failed* (New Haven: Yale University Press, 2018).

[344] For a very readable version of the conservative views discussed in the text above, see Timothy P. Carney, *Alienated America: Why Some Places Thrive While Others Collapse* (New York: Harper, 2020), *passim*, which claims that communities in America which cling to long-standing values, traditional families, and religious faith are doing well nowadays. Carney is a fellow at the American Enterprise Institute (AEI) and a political columnist at the *Washington Examiner*.

arrangements which will provide spiritual inspiration in some drab corners of modern life,[345] they should, more or less, leave conservative principles and practices – those being causes, or Stories – alone.

That is, according to MacIntyre and his compatriots, if pro-Weber scholars will decide to choose between Stories, they should, for the most part, refrain from criticizing Stories on the Right. I disagree, on which, more in a moment.

[345] In *The Disenchantment of Secular Discourse*, Smith says that liberal discourse in such corners is "shallow, empty, and pointless" (p. 219) or, in another formulation, "thin, unsatisfying, and often unseemly" (p. 212).

9 THE ETHICS OF RESPONSIBILITY

In this chapter, let us continue to explore "choosing" within the framework of an "ethics of responsibility." Earlier I proposed, as have other observers, that some small stories which people tell become large and powerful Stories which give shape to our lives and the societies in which we live. It is a fact, however, that all Stories are false. That is not because they entail deliberate lies (while some of them do, many of them don't) but because they cannot be entirely true when the reality we live in is too complex to be summed up accurately in every respect.

It is also a fact, however, and this is so regardless of what intentions may underlie them, that all Stories are not *equally* false.[346] Some of them may be more fanciful than others; and some of them can lead a society into error or grief. In which case we should judge Story X as preferable to Story Y, or vice versa. There is the prescription for choosing.

All of those suppositions seem reasonable to me and worth taking into account in scholarly work. But, how can we do that?

---

[346] I don't want to be misunderstood here. As I said earlier, Stories are not necessarily false because they are deliberately untrue; that is, they are not necessarily based on conscious manipulations designed to deceive. In fact, people who tell false Stories are not always lying. Rather, the problem is that falsity will be there in *all* cases because *no* stories about complicated human affairs can sum up events by taking into account *every* point of detail, *every* sort of potential, *every* angle of view, *every* relevant factor, *every* sentiment in play, and more. In this sense, *all* Stories are incomplete; therefore, if only by missing some information, *all* Stories are false.

Growing Doubts

On the question of how, progressive Enlightenment thinkers decided that Stories (they did not use that term) can be addressed by science and reason, as opposed to faith. Therefore, they did that and rejected long-standing Stories which had justified the European Old Regime based upon monarchs, aristocracy, and clergymen. They then introduced the quest for scientific and reasonable knowledge into the West's great institutions of higher learning, with impressive results. That is why Weber postulated science as a vocation for scholars, and why he recommended that scholars should apply an ethic of responsibility to political causes, which was his term for some Stories.

The problem, as I noted, was that doubts about the concept of truth were growing even when Weber made his recommendation, and they grew even more as the twentieth century unfolded. Heirs to the progressive Enlightenment were increasingly offended by the mendacity but also by the power of advertising (in the private sector) and propaganda (in the public sector).[347] Eventually, challenged by postmodernism, many scholars even came to suspect that whatever we think we know, from fiction *and* nonfiction, is inevitably infected – as with ads and public relations talk – with bias and subjectivity.

Nevertheless, with regard to the specific problem of political programs ("causes," or Stories) which irked Weber, we have seen that in America there are two existing situations – of political and economic imbalance – which are extremely dangerous but also, to some extent, justified by Stories. That is, here are two cases where, although all Stories are false, continual belief in some of them – if we judge them by their likely consequences – may increase the chances that American political life will, perhaps soon, explode from social tensions.

Thinking about this national condition suggests that we should return to Weber, who insisted that scholars should sometimes make

---

[347] What we call public relations has long been a post-truth factor. Examples would include repairing or embellishing corporate images, like the switch from Esso to Exxon and Facebook to Meta. See www.somo.nl/wp-content/uploads/2021/12/Parcel-Delivery-on-a-Warming-Planet_Final.pdf. Many books which I read come to me from Amazon, on airplanes that contribute hugely to air pollution and global warming, in boxes marked (via public relations advice, now called "consulting") with the environmentally friendly message that "This box is now made with less material."

very large ethical choices about Stories. However – and here is a sober thought – additional thinking about Stories may stop us from moving at all. Maybe some Stories are so powerful, especially in today's marketplace of ideas – which is endlessly flooded with information and misinformation, and where a great many points of view, right or wrong, are fully and relentlessly funded – that it is pointless even to try to adjust or overturn America's existing Stories.

Specifically, we might conclude that the rightist factional conglomerate in America, including many conservatives and Republicans, which more or less supports political and economic imbalance, may today be so unswervingly committed to the dangerous Stories we have seen in Chapters 6 and 7 that, when voting under conditions of unyielding polarization, "government by consent" cannot be restored and "global warming" cannot be halted. So why try?

A Dream Country

Actually, why *not* try? To despair along these lines would be to ignore a great Enlightenment lesson. The *philosophes* – such as Voltaire, Montesquieu, Rousseau, Diderot, and Condorcet – confronted enormously persuasive Stories. Those Stories were massively promoted by temporal and spiritual authorities. And the same Stories were tenaciously believed by many, if not most, ordinary people.

Nevertheless, if the *philosophes* and other Enlightenment thinkers – like Hobbes, Locke, Spinoza, Smith, Leibnitz, Hume, Hegel, and Kant – had regarded contemporary opinion and the status quo as unbeatable, and if they had doubted the power of their own rhetorical resources, where would we be today?

In other words, if you approve, roughly speaking, of the Enlightenment, the lesson is clear. In common parlance, you must keep your eye on the ball. You must not lose heart; you must press on against all odds; you must, as the Pragmatic philosopher Richard Rorty insisted, wake up every day to "a dream country" and try to realize it.[348] Anything less, he thought, would be to betray our common humanity.

[348] Richard Rorty, *Achieving our Country: Leftist Thought in Twentieth Century America* (Cambridge, MA: Harvard University Press, 1998), p. 101.

The Liberal Retreat

Well, yes, but ... the problem is that many political scholars are, more or less, liberals, at a time when many liberals – as conservatives rightfully say about them – are modern people of little or no faith, are modern people who are not really sure, in the largest sense, that they understand what America is today, where it should go tomorrow, and therefore what sort of advice they should give.

I have discussed some of the historical reasons for this retreat in *Politics without Stories* (2016), so I will only footnote now some of what I said there.[349] Historian George Marsden describes the same loss of faith in *The Twilight of the American Enlightenment: The 1950s and the Crisis of Liberal Belief* (2014). Marsden especially explains how, today, social gospel Protestantism, which was a pillar of the progressive Enlightenment in America, no longer inspires liberals as it did when mainline Protestants were more influential than evangelicals, before mostly liberal ministers, such as Reinhold Niebuhr and Martin Luther King, Jr., were replaced in presidential affections by more conservative ministers such as Billy Graham and Jerry Falwell.[350]

Furthermore, in *After Utopia: The Decline of Political Faith* (1957), Judith Shklar, who as a child fled to the New World from

[349] Ricci, *Politics Without Stories: The Liberal Predicament* (Cambridge, UK: Cambridge University Press, 2016), ch. 9, "The Great Retreat," pp. 155–185. Those reasons ranged from terrifying nuclear war scenarios to pessimistic social science findings, and from the disruptions of globalization, automation, and deindustrialization to the puzzles of postmodern relativism. For example, Jonathan Schell, *The Fate of the Earth* (New York: Avon, 1982), pp. 52–54, predicted that if one 20-megaton Soviet bomb were dropped on New York City, it would kill up to 20 million people, or 10 percent of all Americans. Similarly, Ground Zero, *Nuclear War: What's in it for You?* (New York: Pocket Books, 1982), pp. 129–130, estimated that a Soviet nuclear second strike, of 6,000 warheads, on America would kill 140 million Americans instantly or within several weeks. This estimate did not count the wounded, stranded, homeless, starving, and poisoned, from a population, at that time, of 231 million. Thus the aphorism of those days, now perhaps forgotten, that, after the war, the living would envy the dead.

[350] George M. Marsden, *The Twilight of the American Enlightenment: The 1950s and the Crisis of Liberal Belief* (New York: Basic Books, 2014), esp. pp. 97–125. On the theological differences between, roughly speaking, mainliners and evangelicals, see Christopher Evans, *Liberalism without Illusions: Renewing an American Christian Tradition* (Waco, TX: Baylor University Press, 2010), esp. pp. 99–115.

Nazi imperialism in the Old, wrote about how wars and horrific political events in the twentieth century left many liberals dazed and off-balance.[351] Later, their inability to maintain optimism drove Alan Wolfe to conclude that "The challenge facing liberalism in the future is … to get liberals to once again believe in liberalism. Once upon a time they did, and it was in those days that they made great [public policy] gains" such as, for Wolfe, the New Deal and the Great Society.[352] Adam Gopnik similarly insists on maintaining liberal faith. Like Shklar, he envisions liberalism as set against cruelty, in a world that maintains a great deal of cruelty. As he put it, "Liberalism is realistic about the huge task of remaking worlds. But it is *romantic* about the possibilities of making marginally happier endings for as many as possible within this one."[353]

A Way Out

There is, I think, a sensible way out of this maze. It does not require a new insight or a leap back into previous faith. It does require, though, highlighting particular aspects of intellectual history and then aiming to pursue, within them, realistic goals rather than searching for something which may be unattainable.

Humanism

We can start by recalling that the Founders were "humanists." That means that, in their day and age, they focused not on God's needs, which were important if not always clear, but on humanity's needs, which were, to the Founders, obvious and urgent.[354] The latter, they

---

[351] Judith Shklar, *After Utopia* (Princeton: Princeton University Press).

[352] Alan Wolfe, *The Future of Liberalism* (New York: Vintage Books, 2010, 2011), p. 287.

[353] See Adam Gopnik, *A Thousand Small Sanities: The Moral Adventure of Liberalism* (New York: Basic Books, 2019), p. 19 (emphasis added). Black Americans, such as Senator Cory Booker (D-NJ), are likely to recall lines from Langston Hughes' poem "Let America Be America Again" (1936): "O, yes, say it plain, America was never America to me, And yet I swear this oath – America will be!" See the full poem at https://poets.org/poem/let-america-be-america-again.

[354] As Alexander Pope made this point, "Know thyself then, presume not God to scan; the proper study of man is man." See his "An Essay on Man: Epistle II" (1711), at www.poetryfoundation.org/poems/44900/an-essay-on-man-epistle-ii.

thought, especially in the realm of governmental affairs, could be dealt with by ordinary people, inspired by common sense and free to fashion new institutions based on experience.

Thomas Paine led the way in "Common Sense" (1776):

> In the following pages, I offer nothing more than simple facts, plain arguments, and common sense: and have no other preliminaries to settle with the reader, than that he will divest himself of prejudice and prepossession, and suffer his reason and his feelings to determine for themselves ... [in which case] when a man seriously reflects on the precariousness of human affairs, he will become convinced, that it is infinitely wiser and safer, to form a constitution of our own in a cool deliberate manner, while we have it in our power, than to trust such an interesting event to time and chance.[355]

In Federalist Paper #14, which he wrote to recommend ratifying the Constitution, James Madison proudly expressed the same belief:

> Is it not the glory of the people of America, that, whilst they have paid a decent regard to the opinions of former times and other nations, they have not suffered a blind veneration for antiquity, for custom, or for names, to overrule the suggestions of their own good sense, the knowledge of their own situation, and the lessons of their own experience?[356]

In Federalist Paper #1, Alexander Hamilton agreed:

> It has frequently been remarked that it seems to have been reserved to the people of this country, by their conduct and example, to decide the important question, whether societies of men are really capable or not of establishing good government from reflection and choice.[357]

---

[355] Thomas Paine, "Common Sense" (1776), in Howard Fast, *The Selected Work of Tom Paine and Citizen Tom Paine* (New York: Modern Library, 1943, 1945), pp. 18, 30.
[356] Alexander Hamilton, John Jay, and James Madison, *The Federalist* (orig., 1788; New York: Modern Library, 1937), p. 85.
[357] *Ibid.*, p. 3.

Edmund Burke

Much of this, of course, was anathema to many thinkers who inspired the Right in American life. Their mentor on this score has long been Edmund Burke, an English Member of Parliament who was horrified when Leftists overthrew the French monarchy in 1789 and executed Louis XVI. In response to that example of political creativity, Burke set the gold standard for a militant sort of conservatism when he declared that, "We know that *we* [Burke's emphasis] have made no discoveries, and we think that no discoveries are to be made, in morality, nor many in the great principles of government, nor in the ideas of liberty, which were understood long before we were born."[358]

As for the humanistic notion that ordinary people in every generation are entitled to fashion for themselves new political institutions, Burke insisted that "if we had possessed it [the right to elect our kings] before [as during the Glorious Revolution in 1688], the English nation did at that time most solemnly renounce and abdicate it, for themselves and for all their posterity forever."[359]

Experience

What really happened was that the Founders, whether or not they were devout, acted as though their spiritual faith had little or nothing to do with the work they took upon themselves, which was to create a framework for public life in the United States of America.[360] After all, we should remember that, concerning faith, the Founders knew not only that people often disagree, but that they sometimes disagree violently. That was the lesson taught, not long ago for Jefferson, Adams, Madison,

[358] Edward Burke, *Reflections on the Revolution in France* ([1790] New York: Liberal Arts Press, 1955), p. 97.
[359] *Ibid.*, p. 22.
[360] This is like Machiavelli, in *The Prince*, disregarding Christianity as a yardstick for statecraft. In general, Enlightenment thinkers were against *superstition*, which they thought came mostly from organized churches, and in favor of *religion* as a belief in God and commitment to His values of decent behavior, which those thinkers assumed could be served best if science and reason would help us to understand nature and society, and therefore how they might be organized for the pursuit of happiness. See Ritchie Robertson, *The Enlightenment: The Pursuit of Happiness, 1680–1790* (New York: Harper, 2021), pp. 82–84.

Washington, and the rest, by Europe's appalling Wars of Religion.[361] It followed, for the Founders, that their work must be guided not by *faith* (which varies across sects) but by *experience* (across various ages).

To that end the Founders combed through useful examples of government and statesmanship from many eras and locations in Western history. That is, they used history flexibly and pragmatically – on Pragmatism, more in a moment – not like Burke who (it seemed to Paine) used history with the intention of justifying an Old Regime government in which a minority of citizens, including men like Burke, enjoyed unequal powers and undeserved benefits.

Looking at the Founders in this way can be faulted because some of the Founders were Deists and most of them believed in a transcendent order of Creation. Well, yes, they were Deists and, yes, they believed in the timeless existence of natural rights. But the notion of Deism was mostly a vague description of agnosticism, which permitted one to say, politely, that faith *is* (even for me) an important business although, at the moment, don't ask me about that because I am dealing with something *else* important. Furthermore, to believe in natural rights and champion them was, in a way, just as vague, because using the vocabulary of natural rights helped the Founders to promote crucial, common-sense, republican, and, sometimes, even democratic notions which they had already embraced but didn't know how to justify otherwise.[362]

---

[361] Depending on which source is cited, the following figures are available. During the Thirty Years War (1618–1648), roughly 20% of all Europeans died, among them perhaps 30% of the groups we know today as Germans. During the Second World War, Soviet Union deaths amounted to roughly 15% of the total population. In the same war, German deaths amounted to roughly 10% of total population. In other words, the Thirty Years War, which was a reference point for eighteenth-century statesmen, was worse than even the Second World War, which so quickly followed the massive losses of the First World War.

[362] Natural rights thinking also, but less admirably, gave the Founders and their heirs excuses to oppress native Americans, who believed, for example, that owning parts of the natural world, and turning those parts into private property (à la John Locke) was an absurd notion. American Indian beliefs, and behavior, were overridden, ideologically speaking, by men such as William Henry Harrison, who asked: "Is one of the fairest portions of the globe to remain in the state of nature, the haunt of a few wretched savages, when it seems destined by the Creator to give support to a large population,

Pragmatism

On both grounds, for our purposes, what really animated the Founders was their incipient "pragmatism," although they did not use that term, because Pragmatism as a philosophy had not yet been invented. But then it *was* invented, after the Civil War, in a sense because some later-day thinkers in the progressive Enlightenment, to which the Founders had belonged, decided that old-time Stories were false.

In fact, the American philosophical school of Pragmatism after the Civil War challenged and rejected old Stories. Thus Pragmatists such as Charles Peirce, William James, and John Dewey argued that what many people regard as large and absolute truths – say, via philosophy or theology – may be believable but cannot be confirmed.[363] Therefore, like scientists, the Pragmatists searched for small and specific understandings that "worked," for tangible research that would produce useful results, or, in the language of philosopher Karl Popper later, for "hypotheses" that might be "tentatively true."[364]

By Dewey's time, this sort of practical reasoning – an extension of Enlightenment reason or common sense – helped many Americans deal with, among other things, exciting Stories which were promoted with considerable success by demagogues such as Hitler and Stalin. These Stories could not be disproved philosophically, but they clearly produced terrible consequences such as dictatorship and war.[365] Eventually, intellectuals hoping to avoid the dangers inherent in such Stories, and committed to practical politics that would steadily generate prosperity, would in the 1950s produce the "end of ideology" era.[366]

and to be the seat of civilization, of science, and true religion?" (1809). Harrison (who eventually served as America's ninth president) is quoted in Joyce Appleby, Lynn Hunt, and Margaret Jacob, *Telling the Truth about History* (New York: Norton, 1994), p. 114.

[363] Charles Peirce, "*The Fixation of Belief*" (1877), at www.bocc.ubi.pt/pag/peirce-charles-fixation-belief.pdf.

[364] Karl Popper, *The Logic of Scientific Discovery*, 2nd ed. (orig., 1934; New York: Routledge, 2002).

[365] On the difficulties of disproving Nazism and Stalinism philosophically, during the 1920s and 1930s, see Edward C. Purcell, Jr., *The Crisis of Democratic Theory: Scientific Naturalism and the Problem of Value* (Lexington: University Press of Kentucky, 1973), esp. pp. 117–138.

[366] Daniel Bell, *The End of Ideology: On the Exhaustion of Political Ideas in the Fifties* (New York: Free Press, 1962). See also Chaim I. Waxman (ed.), *The End of Ideology*

They aimed, or so they said, to ignore Stories – such as those support-
ing fascism and communism – and pursue reasonable, practical, and
incremental changes adding up to progress.

Forward to Weber

In other words, American Pragmatists, deliberately and openly,
refused to search for large-scale truth, as in "Truth."[367] Instead, they
judged so-called truths, when embodied in philosophy (Kant, Hegel)
or Stories (Nazism, communism), as dangerous to their main objective, which was to avoid absolute convictions and simply figure out
how to make things work better than they do now. While using a
different vocabulary, years earlier, that was where the Founders had
stood.

It was also, we should note, where Max Weber stood. Weber
did not propose that he would offer a new "cause" to replace any old
cause that might not be working well. On the contrary, he admitted
that, while science can tell us many things, it cannot tell us the meaning of life or, as Weber quoted Tolstoy, it cannot tell us "how to
live."[368] All that Weber wanted, then, was to investigate the earthly
consequences of this or that existing cause, after which he would be
able to compare the consequences flowing from one cause or another
and then say which was more or less helpful.

So here was the bottom line: Weber recommended making true
(accurate) observations, but he was not searching for large "truths."

Debate (New York: Touchstone, 1969), and M. Rejai (ed.), *Decline of Ideology?*
(Chicago: Aldine Atherton, 1971). At mid-century, Seymour Martin Lipset described
democratic politics after ideology as focused on small but tangible issues such as the
price of milk or a marginal increase in workers' wages. He attributed this "change in
Western political life" to the fact that "the fundamental problems of the industrial revolution have been solved." See Lipset, *Political Man: The Social Bases of Politics* (New
York: Doubleday, 1960), p. 406. The discounting of ideological conflict was repeated
by Francis Fukuyama in his "The End of History," *The National Interest* (Summer,
1989), pp. 3–18.

[367] On Pragmatism in general, see Louis Menander, *The Metaphysical Club: A Story of Ideas
in America* (New York: Farrar, Straus, and Giroux, 2002), and Richard J. Bernstein, *The
Pragmatic Turn* (Cambridge, MA: Polity, 2010).

[368] Max Weber, *The Vocation Lectures* (Indianapolis, IL: Hackett, 2004), p. 17.

He did not frame his position as if he were a disciple of the Pragmatists. But he did distinguish, in a pragmatic way, between accurate observations and, say, the Truth.

Judith Shklar

That emphasis on accurate observations brings us to Harvard's Judith Shklar, the last political thinker we should consider in this lineup. Like Weber, she was pragmatic but did not describe herself formally as a Pragmatist.

To appreciate Shklar, let us again backtrack. The Right entertains powerful Stories of markets, tradition, innovation,[369] small government,[370] patriotism,[371] and more, while the Left is more comfortable advocating a series of projects for achieving social justice within the rubric of what is sometimes called "identity politics."

---

[369] For example, Matt Ridley, *How Innovation Works: And Why It Flourishes in Freedom* (New York: Harper, 2020).

[370] On the virtues of small government, see Texas governor Rick Perry, *Fed Up: Our Fight to Save America from Washington* (Boston: Little, Brown, 2010). Some scholars might say that, in the twentieth and twenty-first centuries, in the United States as a national entity, rather than as a collection of fifty separate states, a considerable measure of government intervention and coordination, regulation and services, in the nation's coast-to-coast and market-based economy, is a *practical* necessity based on historical trends. That is, the need for well-organized and generously funded transportation, education, housing, health care, internal migration, commerce, and so on, is more a concrete imperative of national wellbeing than a liberal preference flowing from abstract ideological sentiments. For this thesis, see John Kenneth Galbraith, *The Good Society: The Humane Agenda* (Boston: Houghton Mifflin, 1996), pp. 14–22. See also Jacob Hacker and Paul Pierson, *American Amnesia: How the War on Government Led Us to Forget What Made America Prosper* (New York: Simon & Schuster, 2016), *passim*. Hacker and Pierson claim that "It takes government – a lot of government – for advanced societies to flourish" (p. 1). They then contend that, for more than a century of growing national prosperity, American government has backed education, health, science, infrastructure, social insurance, and other services, to the point where "the mixed economy [of capitalism and government working together] may well be the greatest invention in history" (p. 7).

[371] For example, enthusiasm for patriotism is central to Yoram Hazony, *The Virtue of Nationalism* (New York: Basic Books, 2018). Hazony belongs to the circle of conservative scholars who oppose Enlightenment progressives. For example, he sees John Locke as too liberal, too rational, and not national enough. Hazony's book can be interpreted as lending implicit support to Donald Trump's enthusiasm for a world of competing nation-states and little international cooperation.

Of course, the Right believes that its Stories are *true*.[372] They are wrong, I think, because all Stories are *false*.[373] But the fact that the Left seems short on Stories, in a post-truth time when America is flooded with confusing information (and disinformation), generates a certain unease – even among liberals – that, if things are not somehow linked by Stories, they may fall apart.[374]

Then conservatives come along, focused on meaning and significance, and perhaps on salvation, who charge that liberals are remiss for failing to replace the West's great Stories with new Stories that can provide modern people with firm loyalties and a clear understanding of what is and is not important in life.

---

[372] For example, Lynne V. Cheney, *Telling the Truth: Why Our Culture and Our Country Have Stopped Making Sense – and What We Can Do About It* (New York: Simon & Schuster, 1995), esp. pp. 192–206. See also the credo of *First Things First*, a journal of religious public philosophy: "FIRST THINGS remains committed to speaking the capital-T Truth" (at www.firstthings.com/). A larger point can be made here. In his canonical conservative treatise, *Ideas Have Consequences* (Chicago: University of Chicago Press, 1948), which has inspired several generations of conservative thinkers and activists, Richard M. Weaver declared that ideas matter. Of course (esp. pp. 3–4), he meant *true* ideas. In fact, however, many of the ideas that matter are *not* true, which is *not* what Weaver had in mind.

[373] Some devout conservatives argue that faith – about God and God's will – proves the truth of their Stories. That is, all Stories, including religious Stories, might seem, in abstract, logical, and theoretical ways, to be false. But if we think of religious Stories as validated by faith, we can then overlook some other counts against them. For example, see Simon Blackburn, *On Truth* (New York: Oxford University Press, 2018), esp. ch. 10, "Religion and Truth," pp. 109–121. Blackburn proposes that if religion "welds numbers of people into a social whole, a congregation ... [t]hen it may well be adaptive for social animals such as ourselves to exempt its doctrines from the critical attention that our reasoning powers order us to bestow on beliefs in other areas." This argument can justify meaningful life parameters for many people. What it does not justify, I think, is accusing one's opponents of bad faith, to the point of lying. That is done by Rod Dreher, *Live Not by Lies: A Manual for Christian Dissidents* (New York: Sentinel, 2020). Dreher regards progressive thinkers and activists as promoting a "soft" totalitarianism as bad as the "hard" totalitarianism of the former Soviet Union. In his words, "The secular liberal ideal of freedom so popular in the West, and among many in ... [the] postmodern generation, is a lie" (p. 210). (See also Glenn Beck, *Liars: How Progressives Exploit Our Fears for Power and Control* [New York: Threshold, 2016].) On the other hand, William Deresiewicz, on the Left, says that "religion is a lie." See his essay on "Disenchantment and Dogma," in *Salmagundi* (Fall, 2021 – Winter, 2022) at https://salmagundi.skidmore.edu/articles/360-disenchantment-and-dogma. Again, that really isn't necessary. Better to say "false," which I think is what Deresiewicz really has in mind.

[374] For example, see Jurgen Habermas et al., *An Awareness of What Is Missing: Faith and Reason in a Post-Secular Age* (Cambridge, MA: Polity, 2010), pp. 15–23.

An Escape

In the context of this challenge, what Judith Shklar offered was an escape from what I have called the liberal retreat – from what Marsden called the twilight of the American Enlightenment – when she suggested that liberals are not really obliged, as some conservatives insist, to replace the Old Regime with a new set of Stories.[375] In her view, heirs of the progressive Enlightenment should instead follow the lead of earlier liberals and simply oppose manifestations of "tyranny" as, for example, Thomas Jefferson did when, in the Declaration of Independence, he condemned George III as a tyrant.[376]

In effect, what Shklar recommended was similar to, or even a later-day version of, Thomas Paine's ideal of "common sense." In every generation, we see some things that should not be. There is the application of *common sense*. On those things, reasonable people often agree. There are the *accurate observations*, the standard of experience rather than faith. Following which, they should work together to repair those undesirable things. There is the recipe for *responsible teachings*.

To this end, Shklar observed that, over time, tyranny comes in many forms, from slavery to witch trials, from the Star Chamber to *lettres de cachet*, from child labor to misogyny, from apartheid to military occupations, and more.[377] In these changing circumstances, every generation of liberals, from John Locke to Isaiah Berlin, will have its own targets.

The message was, stick to criticizing those obvious targets, such as the downsides of political imbalance or the costs of neoliberalism

---

[375] Judith N. Shklar, "The Liberalism of Fear," in Nancy Rosenblum (ed.), *Liberalism and the Moral Life* (Cambridge, MA: Harvard University Press, 1989), pp. 21–38.

[376] As Jefferson wrote in the Declaration: "The history of the present King of Great Britain is a history of repeated injuries and usurpations, all having in direct object the establishment of an absolute Tyranny over these states. To prove this, let Facts be submitted to a candid world."

[377] On later-day tyrannies, see, for example, Michelle Alexander, *The New Jim Crow: Mass Incarceration in the Age of Colorblindness*, rev. ed. (New York: The New Press, 2010, 2012); Zachary Roth, *The Great Suppression: Voting Rights, Corporate Cash, and the Conservative Assault on Democracy* (New York: Crown, 2016); Carol Anderson, *One Person, No Vote: How Voter Suppression is Destroying our Democracy* (New York: Bloomsbury, 2018); and Shoshana Zuboff, *The Age of Surveillance Capitalism: the Fight for a Human Future at the New Frontier of Power* (New York: Simon & Schuster, 2019).

today. That mission is vital on its own, in which case – while Shklar did not say this word for word – the creation and maintenance of new and enduring Stories, however useful to society, is a puzzle to be solved, if at all, by people of good will but not necessarily by liberals.[378]

Philosophes and Philosophers

We can restate Shklar's thesis in historical perspective. Although she did not write about this directly, Shklar's recommendation reminds us that the Enlightenment was populated by *philosophes* and *philosophers*. The former – such as Voltaire and Paine – were involved in everyday life, were looking for solutions to urgent problems, and were acting on the basis of common sense rather than philosophy, while the latter (philosophers) were promoting ideas as complicated and abstract as the teachings of Kant and Hegel.[379]

For example, when Zeno said that an arrow shot into the air can never cover enough ground to reach its target tree, he was right, by the philosophical logic known as "deduction." Deduction says that, in principle, the arrow must first fly half of the distance to the tree, then it must travel half of the distance remaining, then half the distance from that point, and so on, therefore never getting through the last half, no matter how small, of the total distance.

But if real arrows are shot in real life, they *will* arrive. And someone must deal with them when they *do* arrive, regardless of how, in principle, and philosophically speaking, one need not worry about that happening because, theoretically, they *cannot* arrive.[380]

---

[378] Shklar did not discuss "neoliberalism" in "The Liberalism of Fear" (1989). That term was not yet being used frequently in scholarly work.

[379] A discussion of the distinction between *philosophes* and *philosophers* appears in Henry Steele Commager, *The Empire of Reason: How Europe Imagined and America Realized the Enlightenment* (New York: Anchor-Doubleday, 1977), pp. 236–245.

[380] Neil Postman, *Building a Bridge to the 18th Century: How the Past Can Improve Our Future* (New York: Vintage, 1999), pp. 62–63, explores Zeno's paradox. That arrows arrive in real life we know from *induction* rather than *deduction*, where induction entails repeated examples, from deliberate experiments, or from findings based on simply observing tangible arrows. In short, we know that shot arrows will arrive by induction, or science, rather than by philosophy. One can agree with David Hume, in his *Treatise on Human Nature* (1738), Bk. I, and in his *An Enquiry Concerning Human Understanding* (1748), Bk. IV, that even many instances tallied by induction cannot produce certainty, in

Therefore, long ago it was the *philosophes*, and recently it was Judith Shklar, who, in effect, worried about vulnerable oaks and oppressed people, rather than about imaginary trees and hypothetical trajectories.

---

this case that the arrows in real life will surely reach the tree. But in real life, as opposed to Hume's philosophical point, we usually act on the basis of a *sufficient*, and not a *complete*, stream of evidence, in which case the philosophical weakness of induction does not prevent scientists (such as those who fashioned the Covid-19 vaccine) from deciding what is what and acting accordingly. On this point see Caitlin O'Connor and James Owen Weatherall, *The Misinformation Age: How False Beliefs Spread* (New Haven: Yale University Press, 2019), pp. 27–31.

10 REFRAINING

Let us recall that political scientists talk about the "scope" of politics and the "methods" by which various aspects of that domain may be studied. Not every political scientist agrees on which methods – say, qualitative or quantitative, and their variations – are most feasible and/ or useful for exploring this or that aspect of politics. Nevertheless, discussion of them within the discipline – in books, articles, conferences, lectures, and conversations – is continuous and fruitful. Consequently, in this book, I am assuming that the matter of methods is fairly well understood and needs no elaboration here.

On the other hand, the scope of politics is less discussed. Yet there is a sense in which what I have called Stories surround and shape what we call politics. Therefore, I suggested that we regard Stories as falling within the domain of politics and deserving considerable scholarly attention.

Until now, political scholars have related to politics mainly as a set of complex contests between groups and interests within society; that is, as the process which Harold Lasswell had in mind when he defined politics as "who gets what, when, and how."[381] Now, however, especially when we are plagued with endless expressions of post-truth life – for example, Donald Trump's tweets, and seriously different views of American politics seen on Fox News as opposed to what appears on

---

[381] Harold Lasswell, *Politics: Who Gets What, When, and How* (New York: Whittlesey House, 1936).

CNN – we can see that not only are Lasswell's political factors there but so, too, are Stories which significantly influence how the usual give and take of politics is conducted and what it produces. I have suggested that "choosing" – as part of exercising an "ethics of responsibility" – is an appropriate response to some aspects of politics today, where Stories are very much in play and where some may be more dangerous than others. But choosing, as an intellectual feat, in complex political situations is not a simple matter. So let us note, in this chapter, that choosing should be accompanied by a measure of "refraining"; that is, of proceeding very cautiously, or not at all, with some sorts of scholarship that might undercut democratic principles and practices.

Refraining

In the circumstances, and following Shklar's advice, let us consider how investigating politics might proceed within the wider concept of scope that we are using here. Of course, in our nervous age, while an epistemological crisis makes it difficult even to know how to talk with one another, I hope that some scholars will take the role of *philosophe* seriously. I do, as when, in *A Political Science Manifesto for the Age of Populism* (2020), I criticized the downside consequences of neoliberalism.[382]

But it is not enough to decide, as modern *philosophes*, only that we will enter the fray. There is also the matter of how to do that and, on this point, we must take into account powerful impulses which dominate academic research.

Shklar said, in effect, that we should use common sense to see what is obviously cruel – tyranny, harassment, oppression, and discrimination – and then keep our eyes on that ball. See what is there, and then act accordingly. Without citing Shklar, many scholars since the Enlightenment are in the common-sense court, in that they are

---

[382] See David Ricci, *A Political Science Manifesto for the Age of Populism: Challenging Growth, Markets, Inequality, and Resentment* (New York: Cambridge University Press, 2020), esp. pp. 61–91. For recent political science scholarship on neoliberalism, see Jacob S. Hacker, Alexander Hertel-Fernandex, Paul Piersen, and Kathleen Thelen (eds.), *The American Political Economy: Politics, Markets, and Power* (New York: Cambridge University Press, 2022).

committed to searching deliberately and diligently for useful items of information. In Kant's term, they want "to know"; that is, they want to reach beyond old verities to fashion more accurate and, at least in some cases, more humane understandings of the world.[383] In Weber's terms, this impulse, to discover something not known or noticed previously, inspires both social and natural scientists, and it has fostered extraordinary achievements.[384]

Durability

The problem, with respect to Stories, is that this impulse can get out of hand, and that is where some kind of "restraint" might be called for. Remember that, come what may, people will tell, or will heed, Stories in order to make sense of their lives.[385] These Stories are, of course, false at least because they are incomplete. That is an awkward analytical reality. But even when they are false, some of them are effective. That is a crucial practical reality. In other words, some Stories actually *do* hold things together and make a decent life possible.

So far, so good. However, Stories must enjoy some durability in order to work well. That is, we cannot maintain social stability if we change Stories too frequently; we cannot know how to behave and how others will respond if we regard our Stories as only temporarily valid. In

---

[383] The common-sense court includes, among others, Michael Walzer, Alan Wolfe, and Michael Sandel. See Michael Walzer, *Spheres of Justice: A Defense of Pluralism and Equality* (New York: Basic Books, 1983), and *On Toleration* (New Haven: Yale University Press, 1997); Michael J. Sandel, *Justice: What's the Right Thing to Do?* (New York: Farrar, Straus and Giroux, 2009), and Alan Wolfe, *The Future of Liberalism* (New York: Vintage Books, 2010, 2011). These thinkers don't agree among themselves on all philosophical points, but they use common sense to arrive at those points.

[384] On this impulse, see Max Weber, "Science as a Vocation" (1919), in *The Vocation Lectures* (Indianapolis, IL: Hackett, 2004), esp. pp. 7–12.

[385] Analogously, ancient Greek and Roman myths may be regarded as narrative responses to large amounts of puzzling information which could not be explained in their era without the help of stories large and small. Jews, Christians, and Muslims eventually reduced all of this confusion when they offered single, but competing, Stories of monotheism. At that point, it is not the world that is puzzling but God. And the hopeful message of, say, the Book of Job, is that God, although incomprehensible to humans, will make, for deserving people, everything puzzling turn out well in the end.

short, we cannot maintain vital rights and operate crucial institutions if we move, again and again, from one Story paradigm to another.

The Scholarly Churn

Yet here we encounter an academic rub because, since the Enlightenment as an era, and while searching for enlightenment as learning more than was known previously, progressive scholars have repeatedly undermined small and even large Stories. In a way, that is typically how we operate, and constant churn is almost a hallmark of modern scholarship.[386]

This sort of undermining occurs for two reasons. First, small political stories are *often* false, and large political stories (Stories) are *always* false, therefore one can usually find in them, small or large, elements to legitimately criticize and reject. Second, the road to scholarly success is often, if not usually, paved with refuted stories and/or Stories, sometimes known as "hypotheses" or "theories," which were originally fashioned by senior scholars who made *their* reputations by contradicting *their* predecessors.[387]

For example, how many psychologists are now Freudians? Which sociologist today calls herself a Parsonian? How many historians extol Charles and Mary Beard? Or Richard Hofstadter?[388] What happened to Margaret Mead? Who cares now about Thomas Kuhn? Is John Rawls still at the cutting edge of philosophy?[389] Do economists

---

[386] See Chris Fleming, "The Tyranny of Trendy Ideas," *Chronicle of Higher Education* (July 1, 2019), at www.chronicle.com/article/the-tyranny-of-trendy-ideas/.

[387] That political scholars often aim at refuting stories and Stories may be discussed by philosophers of science, who analyze the sentiments which motivate scientists. Scientific work is admired in modern society, they say, and much of it is shaped by (hard and soft) scientists who are inspired by the philosophy of Karl Popper to believe that testing hypotheses, and refuting them repeatedly, is how science produces useful knowledge. On this point, see Michael Strevens, *The Knowledge Machine: How Irrationality Created Modern Science* (New York: Liveright, 2020), pp. 13–22, but esp. p. 20: "It is carnage, this mass extermination of hypotheses."

[388] Alan Wolfe admires Hofstadter. See Wolfe, *The Politics of Petulance: America in an Age of Immaturity* (Chicago: University of Chicago Press, 2018), *passim*. But on Hofstadter's mixed reputation today, see www.thenation.com/article/culture/richard-hofstadter-library-america-review/.

[389] Taking Rawls down a peg recently is Katrina Forrester, *In the Shadow of Justice: Postwar Liberalism and the Remaking of Political Philosophy* (Princeton: Princeton University Press, 2019). Rawls is, in effect, written off as obsolete by Daniel

rave over Nobelist James Buchanan or has he been relegated to conservative think tanks? Is Robert Dahl a key figure in recent discussions of democratic theory? Who still reads Clinton Rossiter's *Seedtime of the Republic* (1953), which described American exceptionalism and won the APSA's Woodrow Wilson Foundation Award for best (scholarly) political book of the year?[390]

The Perils of Change

Here is a matter of enormous importance. So let us be very clear about it. Concerning the perils of change, American conservatives are right, and not just Right. For example, Andrew Bacevich insists, in a useful anthology of conservative writings, that if great principles, practices, and institutions (he doesn't use the term Stories), or important parts of them, are continually challenged and rejected, essential elements of democracy may fall apart.[391] On that score, in recent years, many scholars and pundits have observed that, in some supremely important circumstances, vital pillars of democracy are crumbling for lack of conviction and trust.[392]

T. Rodgers, *Age of Fracture* (Cambridge, MA: Harvard University Press, 2011), pp. 184–185.

[390] Political scientists do not regard themselves as remiss for leaving behind once well-known and even celebrated works. (From respect for living Woodrow Wilson Foundation Award winners, I will not cite any of their forgotten works beyond that of Rossiter.) Thus the political science journal editors Daniel O'Neill and Michael Bernhard offer the following description of their Truth expectations in "Perspectival Political Theory," *Perspectives on Politics* (December, 2019), p. 954: "The goal of the research published here is to illuminate important problems in new ways, not to settle them once and for all (which we regard as an impossible and misbegotten enterprise in any event)." As gatekeepers for their discipline, the views of O'Neill and Bernhard should be regarded as typical and important.

[391] Andrew J. Bacevich (ed.), *American Conservatism: Reclaiming an Intellectual Tradition* (New York: The Library of America, 2020). The point of this collection of writings, as Bacevich explains in his "Introduction," p. xiii, is to illustrate why various writers on the Right have regarded modernity's penchant for constant change as dangerous and how that inclination might be tempered.

[392] From the Left, see Yasha Mounk, *The People Vs. Democracy: Why Our Freedom Is in Danger and How to Save It* (Cambridge, MA: Harvard University Press, 2018); David Runciman, *How Democracy Ends* (New York: Basic Books, 2018); and Steven Levitsky and Daniel Ziblatt, *How Democracies Die* (New York: Crown, 2018). From the Right, see Mitchell S. Muncy and Richard John Neuhaus (eds.), *The End of Democracy: The Celebrated First Things First Debate, with Arguments Pro and Con*

A Conservative Project

We should all – Right *and* Left – endorse this conservative caution, because wariness about change is not just a theoretical point. In fact, some aspects of recent American politics, well known to political scholars, add up to a short tale – which I would not call a full-fledged Story – that sheds light on the importance of stable concepts and tenacious commitment to them, in any society.

Thus, especially during the 1960s, as we noted already, people on the American Right felt that their principles and practices were being rejected by various thinkers and activists sometimes known as "the counterculture." One response to that rejection was to conclude that, while conservative ideas were true, the Right was losing out because those ideas were not being marketed well.

Senator Barry Goldwater made this point in *The Conscience of a Conservative* (1960):

> This book is not written with the idea of adding to or improving on the Conservative philosophy. Or of "bringing it up to date." The ancient and tested truths that guided our Republic through its early days will do equally well for us. The challenge to conservatives today is quite simply to demonstrate the bearing of a proven philosophy on the problems of our own time.[393]

The challenge identified by Goldwater in 1960 was taken up by very practical conservatives such as Lewis Powell, corporate lawyer and later Supreme Court Justice, and William Simon, Secretary of the Treasury and later head of the John Olin Foundation.[394] These men recommended using friendly institutions to promote conservative

---

and "The Anatomy of a Controversy" (Dallas, TX: Spence, 1997); Jonah Goldberg, *Liberal Fascism: The Secret History of the American Left, from Mussolini to the Politics of Change* (New York: Broadway, 2009); and Tucker Carlson, *Ship of Fools: How a Selfish Ruling Class is Bringing America to the Brink of Revolution* (New York: Free Press, 2018).

[393] Barry Goldwater, *The Conscience of a Conservative* (Shepherdsville, KY: Victor, 1960), p. 3.

[394] See Lewis Powell, "Confidential Memo: Attack on [the] American Free Enterprise System," address to the United States Chamber of Commerce, August 24, 1971, at https://scholarlycommons.law.wlu.edu/powellmemo/. See also William Simon, *A Time for Truth* (New York: Berkley, 1978).

ideas which they felt were being overwhelmed by liberal thinkers, scholars, journalists, and activists. The result was that conservatives reinforced existing right-wing outlets, and they sponsored new think tanks, newspapers, book publishers, fellowships, and talk-radio shows. The old and the new included, for example, the American Enterprise Institute, the Heritage Foundation, the Cato Institute, the Manhattan Institute, the *Washington Times*, the *Weekly Standard*, Regnery Publishing, Encounter Books, William Buckley's *Firing Line* television program, the Rush Limbaugh Show, the Federalist Society, the Bradley Foundation, the Coors Foundation, and the Charles Koch Foundation.

These agencies, charged with marketing long-term conservative traditions and private enterprise, came to be called the "counter-establishment."[395] Eventually, they found their ideal candidate for national office in Ronald Reagan, California's governor and later America's president, whose talent for fashioning persuasive and even folksy versions of ideas on the Right earned him the title of "The Great Communicator."[396]

Democrats Respond

In these circumstances, as the 1970s wore on, many Democratic politicians came to understand that they were engaged in a battle of ideas. However, some of them believed that, in the contest, their *old* ideas, such as those promoted during the presidential campaign of Senator George McGovern (D-SD) in 1972, could not overcome the growing popularity of some Republican candidates. Therefore, they concluded that they had to invent *new* ideas in order to win their fair share (or more) of elections.

---

[395] Sidney Blumenthal, *The Rise of the Counter-Establishment: The Conservative Ascent to Political Power* (New York: Union Square Press, 1986, 2008).
[396] His chief pollster and strategist went even further. See Dick Wirthlin, *The Greatest Communicator: What Ronald Reagan Taught Me About Politics, Leadership, and Life* (New York: John Wiley, 2004). In his "Farewell Address to the Nation," Ronald Reagan insisted that although he was often called "the Great Communicator," he was not expressing new ideas but old verities about an exceptional America. See the Farewell Address at www.reaganfoundation.org/media/128652/farewell.pdf.

The epitome of Democratic enthusiasm for new political ideas appeared in speeches and campaigning by Senator Gary Hart (D-CO), who sought the Democratic presidential nomination until he retired from the field after being photographed with a young woman (not his wife).[397] The challenge was then more broadly taken up by the Democratic Leadership Council (DLC), founded in 1985, whose members, such as Virginia Governor Chuck Robb, Missouri Congressman Dick Gephardt, Georgia Senator Sam Nunn, and Connecticut Senator Joe Lieberman, did not so much invent new campaign ideas as abandon old ones, choosing not to portray themselves as especially devoted to Franklin Roosevelt's New Deal, and shifting toward the political center.[398]

While DLC Democrats achieved some electoral gains, including consecutive presidential terms for Bill Clinton, they maintained their distance from New Deal enthusiasms. Therefore, as we have seen, they eventually moved to fashioning new ideas in the form of specific policy proposals for various groups, such as women and Black people. The result was that the current two-camp standoff continues under President Joe Biden, with the Right dedicated mainly to a fairly stable Story line, and the Left engaged mainly in proposing, sometimes consecutively and sometimes simultaneously, miscellaneous elements of what President Barack Obama called "Change we can believe in."[399]

---

[397] See Gary Hart, *A New Democracy: A Democratic Vision for the 1980s and Beyond* (New York: Quill, 1983), esp. pp. 7–15.

[398] A caustic description of this move to the center, written about the first Clinton presidential campaign, appeared in Joan Didion, "Eye on the Prize," *Political Fictions* (New York: Vintage, 2001), pp. 119–166. See the same shift described in Lily Geismer, "Reinventing Liberalism," *Left Behind: The Democrats' Failed Attempt to Solve Inequality* (New York: Public Affairs, 2022), pp. 106–139; and Gary Gerstle, *The Rise and Fall of the Neoliberal Order* (New York: Oxford University Press, 2022), pp. 137–140.

[399] When Bernie Sanders in 2016 promoted his One Percent update of New Dealism, Hillary Clinton, a former DLC member, barely responded. Instead of trying to unite the party's voters by offering her competitor Sanders the vice-presidential nomination like presidential nominee John F. Kennedy offered that nomination to Lyndon Johnson, who was his competitor in 1960, she passed over Sanders and lost the election narrowly to Donald Trump. In 2020, Joe Biden was deferential to his early competitor Bernie Sanders and, while campaigning already as the Democratic frontrunner, proposed New-Deal-like social and economic programs that would in November enthuse Sanders and his supporters, such as Senator Elizabeth Warren. On this point, see www.rev.com/blog/transcripts/joe-biden-speech-transcript-on-economic-recovery-plan-july-9.

Imperfect Scholarship

The moral of this tale – featuring two ambitious political parties – is that many Americans, including perhaps most in the Republican base but others as well, want their lives to proceed within a framework of familiar principles and performances. That is, they will not respond enthusiastically to leaders who, to some extent, propose to conduct public life under conditions of constant uncertainty due to ever-changing aspirations and expectations.[400]

But academics are often guided at work less by the wisdom of political tales than by the hope of succeeding professionally; that is, less by general visions for society than by what they and their colleagues expect of one another. Therefore, a respectable scholarly ethic which promotes constant criticism, constant amendment, constant falsification, and constant rejection, may produce troublesome research findings. If, for example, those will confirm considerable degrees of voter ignorance and institutional tyranny, they may weaken social solidarity and collective enthusiasm for democratic principles and practices.[401] Or, to rephrase the matter, they may undermine the Stories (which, of course, are not entirely true) that promote and legitimize democratic sentiments.

---

[400] For example, see John Guest, *In Search of Certainty: Answers to Doubt When Values are Eroding and Unbelief is Fashionable* (Ventra, CA: Regal Books, 1983). That people need stable traditions and commitments is the message of R. R. Reno, *Return of the Strong Gods: Nationalism, Populism, and the Future of the West* (Washington, DC: Regnery Gateway, 2019). Reno is the editor of *First Things*, a journal which endeavors to promote "a religiously informed public philosophy."

[401] See David Ricci, *The Tragedy of Political Science: Politics, Scholarship, and Democracy* (New Haven: Yale University Press, 1984), esp. pp. 291–318. Those pages describe two commendable goals, of empirical research and of faith in democracy, as sometimes clashing. For recent examples of this sort of empirical research, see Bryan Caplan, *The Myth of the Rational Voter: Why Democracies Choose Bad Policies* (Princeton: Princeton University Press, 2007); Kay Lehman Schlozman, Sidney Vera, and Henry E. Brady, *The Unheavenly Chorus: Unequal Political Voice and the Broken Promise of American Democracy* (Princeton: Princeton University Press, 2012); Kirby Goidel, *America's Failing Experiment* (Lanham, MD: Rowman & Littlefield, 2013); Jason Brennan, *Against Democracy* (Princeton: Princeton University Press, 2016); and Christopher H. Achen and Larry M. Bartels, *Democracy for Realists: Why Elections do not Produce Responsible Government* (Princeton: Princeton University Press, 2016).

Random Momentum

In short, teachings which are academically routine may be politically unhelpful. Criticism, amendment, falsification, and rejection are highly regarded for bringing us to postulate or discover new things, while working within a context of serious learning. And such acts – a modern academic routine, really – generate achievements in many academic fields of inquiry. In those fields, practitioners who merely repeat what is already known may be regarded as stodgy and falling short of vocational standards of excellence.

Therefore, scholars are admonished to seek what is new, new, new. The result is what may be called "random momentum," a series of accomplishments which go nowhere in particular. Across many disciplines, colleagues know the drill: "Most research [on this subject] addresses only *one* of these concerns"; "It is not only *what* the legislators say but *how* they say ..."; "We lack solid evidence regarding *whether* and *how*"; "Among the existing accounts of [X] ... none has properly accounted for ..."; "Casting the question more broadly"; "This literature has not considered the possibility that ..."; "We do so by exploring an aspect of [Z] ... that has received little systematic attention"; "[Our] new dataset ... promises to expand the frontiers of research on ..."; "Much has been written about [B] ... however, we have done little to document it"; "The use of [C] models ... continues to grow .... However, several common misconceptions about the models ... persist." And so forth.

These examples are not contrived. They are all adaptations or paraphrases, some with emphasis supplied, from passages which appeared in articles published recently in the *American Political Science Review*, *P.S.*, and *Perspectives on Politics*. In which case, for many practitioners, those formulations, and others like them, accurately reflect academic aspirations.

Holding Back

The problem here is a small-scale version of the large-scale dynamism that troubled Karl Polanyi, and later Andrew Bacevich, when they criticized liberal faith in change. The question is, where does all this scholarship go to? The answer is, nowhere in particular but, also, perhaps, into dangerous territory. Here, in fact, is where we might take into account Weber's call for scholarly responsibility.

Politics, Weber insisted, is a singular subject for study because of its potential impact on society. Politics, he said, is sometimes driven by an ethics of ultimate ends which some people believe are true and desirable in an absolute sense. Such ends, he said, may gratify and even inspire us. But they, or clashes between them, may produce bad outcomes. Accordingly, when relating to ultimate ends, and after updating Weber's terms a little, political scholars even today should consider what results various Stories might generate; that is, what consequences they might produce.[402]

Implications

One implication of this imperative is obvious. If it seems that a certain Story's consequences will be dangerous, said Weber – writing soon after the First World War devastated much of Europe[403] – then we are vocationally enjoined to criticize it.[404]

[402] Weber advocated a sort of Pragmatism without using that term, promoting a mission of relating sensibly to propositions according to what they are likely to produce. Scholars, or pundits, or advocates, or activists, or just ordinary citizens, who feel that Weber's guidelines are too secular or progressive, can still take his advice but check out Story propositions via the standards recommended by Paul, Philippians 4:8 (KJV): "Finally, brethren, whatsoever things are true, whatsoever things are honest, whatsoever things are just, whatsoever things are pure, whatsoever things are lovely, whatsoever things are of good report; if there be any virtue, and if there be any praise, think on these things."

[403] Perspectives change, therefore we may not fully sense today how terrible European losses in the First World War were. Various sources agree that approximately 2,500 American soldiers died in Afghanistan during twenty years, from 2001 to 2021. In the First World War Battle of the Somme, 20,000 British soldiers were killed *during the first day* of fighting, on July 1, 1916. See www.britannica.com/event/First-Battle-of-the-Somme.

[404] There are many ways of doing this. For example, see the French cultural critic Julien Benda, *The Betrayal of the Intellectuals* (orig., 1928; Boston: Beacon, 1955). Benda argued that the First World War was fueled by (in our terms) incompatible national Stories, in the sense that intellectuals in country after country endorsed the competing narratives promoted by their own governments and abandoned any shared sense of civilized standards, across political borders, which had formerly enabled *clercs* throughout the West – *clercs* were Christian professionals whose "kingdom is not of this world" (p. 31) – to honor good even in times when some humans were doing evil. Hence Benda's concept of the treason (*traison*) of modern intellectuals (*clercs*).

A second implication is less obvious but very relevant to what we know of the modern marketplace for ideas, where scholars report on what they have discovered. Here is where the dynamic of random momentum challenges us not just to avoid the worst but to bolster the best. Thus, in the case of Stories – even if Weber did not use that term – we are obliged, I think, as cautious members of our own society, to refrain from automatically, repeatedly, persistently, and across the board, in line with professional imperatives, undermining Stories which people need in order to bring order and, hopefully, progress to their societies.[405]

Yet that situation, paradoxically, justifies thinking that we should not just refrain from saying certain things but that, somewhere down the road, perhaps we should consciously say other things which we know are not true. And to infer as much brings us, unexpectedly, to the need for occasionally "dissembling," which is the third in our trio of vocational guidelines on the matter of Stories: "choosing," "refraining," and "dissembling."

So let us consider now the sometimes odd guideline of dissembling.

---

[405] The later-day Pragmatic philosopher Hillary Putnam made this point in academic terms, in his *Renewing Philosophy* (Cambridge, MA: Harvard University Press, 1995), p. 133: "deconstruction without reconstruction is irresponsibility."

11 DISSEMBLING

Shoshana Zuboff points the way:

> I approach political writing as public education, and I regard
> public education as the highest calling. My writing is the sign
> and signal of my devotion to my children's futures and all chil-
> dren's futures. Writing is for the world. Political writing is for
> healing the world. That is the crucible of my ambition, even
> when I fall short. (Shoshana Zuboff)[406]

Professor Zuboff's sentiments are admirable. However, it is not easy
to contribute to what she calls public education today. Here, our post-
truth context will not leave us alone. In an age of information overload
and epistemic confusion, citizens will look for inspiration to powerful
Stories, and they will not give up the comfort which Stories provide
just because someone will point out that those Stories are not true.[407]

---

[406] This passage is quoted in www.newstatesman.com/uncategorized/2020/06/political-writ-
ing-art-orwell-prize-bernardine-evaristo-colson-whitehead-charles-moore. On Zuboff's
wider views, see her *The Age of Surveillance Capitalism: The Fight for a Human Future
at the New Frontier of Power* (New York: Simon & Schuster, 2019).

[407] For example, see John F. Kennedy, "Commencement Address" at Yale University, 1962:
"[W]e must move on from the repetition of stale phrases to a new, difficult, but essential confrontation with reality. For the great enemy of the truth is very often not the

For example, in January 2020, Congressman Adam Schiff (D-CA) tried *fact-checking* his statements to the Senate during the first impeachment trial of Donald Trump. Specifically, Schiff insisted on hewing to what he regarded as (small) truths in this particular case.[408] After hearing him out, fifty-two out of fifty-three Republican senators, without taking testimony or interviewing witnesses, voted to acquit the President on charges of abuse of power.[409] What foiled Schiff (of course, he knew this would happen) was that all those Republicans had already endorsed a Story which, at least momentarily, was immune to evidence (facts) which they did not want to hear.[410]

The Trump impeachment "trial," about Trump's relations with Ukrainian president Volodymyr Zelensky, unintentionally generated a striking lesson, because it demonstrated that reason and rationality, at least nowadays, are not necessarily normal but sometimes even abnormal characteristics of political behavior.[411] That is, on public matters, but hopefully not on all matters, it now seems like

lie – deliberate, contrived, and dishonest – but the myth – persistent, persuasive, and unrealistic .... We enjoy the comfort of opinion without the discomfort of thought." See www.presidency.ucsb.edu/documents/commencement-address-yale-university.

[408] Read Schiff's statement at www.politico.com/news/2020/01/22/adam-schiff-opening-argument-trump-impeachment-trial-102202.

[409] On the Senate vote, see https://ballotpedia.org/Impeachment_of_Donald_Trump,_2019-2020. In an era less polarized than today, Senator Joseph McCarthy (R-WI) was censured in 1954 by Democratic *and* Republican Senators. That vote was 67–22. In *United States* v. *Nixon*, 418 U.S. (1974), the Supreme Court voted 8–0 to compel Nixon to submit to Congress various tapes of (possibly incriminating) White House conversations. Today's polarized Supreme Court would probably not decide such a political issue unanimously.

[410] The argument was that, even if Trump had tried to condition foreign aid to Ukraine on the Ukrainian president's investigating the Biden family, Trump's effort to that end would not qualify as an impeachable offense. So there was no need to call witnesses and hear testimony. See "Quick Acquittal: How Mitch McConnell Orchestrated the end to Trump's Impeachment trial in 15 days," at https://edition.cnn.com/2020/02/05/politics/acquittal-trump-impeachment-trial-mcconnell-15-days/index.html.

[411] Some pundits are always available to make this point. For example, in nineteenth-century England, Walter Bagehot insisted that "stupidity ... is nature's favorite resource for preserving steadiness of conduct and consistency of opinion." Fortunately, he noted, "in real sound stupidity, the English are unrivalled." (Bagehot is quoted in Jacques Barzun, *The House of Intellect* [New York: Torchbooks, 1959], p. 148.) Along similar lines, Benjamin Disraeli, in *Coningsby: or the New Generation* (orig., 1844; New York: Signet, 1962), pp. 110–111, wrote that the main thing in politics is to offer "a good cry."

merely recounting facts to modern Americans, or at least to a great many of them, will not work.[412]

But if that is the case, people who object to specific false Stories can only compete against them by telling other false Stories – remember, all Stories are false – which are more persuasive. And that is a paradoxical recipe for scholarly action when much of the scholarly world is designed not to tell stories (at least, not consciously), or Stories, at all.

Dissembling

What I just said warrants repetition, in six parts. If (1) your fellow citizens *must* have Stories, but if (2) *all* Stories are *false*, then (3) there *will be times* when, (4) in order to speak *to good effect*, (5) you must tell an *alternative* Story, (6) which will *also* be *false*.

Yes, you may condemn, and admirably so, elements of tyranny by pointing out small truths, based on pragmatic empiricism, which political scientists know very well how to do. For example, in my opinion, the consequences of permitting rich individuals, organizations, associations, corporations, committees, and more to contribute large amounts of money or expensive forms of other help to politicians of both major American parties can, and should, be illuminated again and again by empirical research.[413]

---

[412] Various commentators have remarked on this disconnect. For example, see Todd Gitlin, "The Enigma of Constancy: The Resilience of Trump's Base," at https://salmagundi.skidmore.edu/articles/229-the-enigma-of-constancy-the-resilience-of-trumps-base. See also Alex Evans, *The Myth Gap: What Happens When Evidence and Arguments Aren't Enough?* (London, UK: Eden Books, 2017), *passim*, whose central thesis is that "evidence and rational arguments" must be linked by stories, which Evans calls "myths," else the former will not sway public opinion.

[413] This point is related to the fact that stories constitute a form of political power. Political scholars should constantly explain that the phrase "money talks" is not just a popular expression but a description of how money is used to tell, display, and promote; that is, to exercise enormous framing power over the way voters will see the candidates and react to them. In that sense, money is a wherewithal for stories and Stories. On some of money's power in politics, see law professor Lawrence Lessig, *Republic Lost: How Money Corrupts Congress – and a Plan to Stop It* (New York: Twelve, 2012), esp. ch. 10, "*What So Damn Much Money Does*," pp. 125–171. For an anthropological analysis of money's power, see Janine R. Wedel, *Unaccountable: How Elite Power Brokers Corrupt our Finances, Freedom, and Security* (New York: Pegasus, 2014), esp.

But occasionally, to make your teachings as persuasive as possible to people who are not already in your camp – or to convince young people, not already sorted, to join your camp – you should tell alternative Stories. And you should do that even though, in the light of learned insights, you know that your own Stories, in some respects, will be at least partly false.

Historians

We can amplify that last point. Until the 1960s, roughly speaking, American historians such as Allen Nevins, Arthur Link, Richard Hofstadter, Oscar Handlin, John Higham, Arthur Schlesinger, Jr., and David Potter wrote about, but did not always agree on, the nature of American life. Then, starting approximately in the 1970s, younger historians produced and promoted mostly small, specialized research findings which say little about the big, national picture.[414]

Jill Lepore

Even as their colleagues focused on smaller subjects, however, some historians continued to appreciate the importance of large narratives.

ch. 1, "New World, New Corruption," pp. 3–29. For a political science approach, see Larry M. Bartels, *Unequal Democracy: The Political Economy of the New Gilded Age* (Princeton: Princeton University Press, 2008), esp. pp. 29–63, which shows that, more than their Democratic counterparts, elected Republicans promote public policies leading to economic inequality. For another political science approach, see Benjamin I. Page, Jason Seawright, and Matthew J. Lacombe, *Billionaires and Stealth Politics* (Chicago: University of Chicago Press, 2019), pp. 127–138, which explains why, even when large sums of money are given, it is difficult to measure how much influence the money generates for wealthy contributors.

[414] This shift in focus is described in Joyce Appleby, Lynn Hunt, and Margaret Jacob, *Telling the Truth about History* (New York: Norton, 1994), pp. 129–159, esp. pp. 146–159. See pp. 158–159, 198–200, which explain that: (a) a great many social history projects and publications after 1970 were difficult to assimilate into long-standing academic understandings of the nature of American society. Consequently, (b) postmodern philosophical notions – which suggested that researchers could not be objective – drove large-scale, all-encompassing, American-exceptionalism narratives almost entirely out of the profession of history. Nevertheless, historians still argue that their training enables them to provide useful predictions about where the country has been and where it can go now. On that score, see Jo Guldi and David Armitage, *The History Manifesto* (New York: Cambridge University Press, 2014).

Therefore, we can learn from, say, Harvard's Jill Lepore, who warned that, "when scholars stopped writing national history, other, less scrupulous people, stepped in."[415] Or, to identify the specific danger, "when scholars stop trying to write a common history for a people, nationalism doesn't die. Instead, it eats liberalism."[416]

In fact, a bottom line for Lepore is that if you leave the field of Stories, not everyone else will. And that worried her, as it worries me.[417] Therefore – in the terms I am using – what Lepore said, somewhat anxiously, is that those whom she called "less scrupulous people" tend to create or promote Stories (she did not use that term) which, in her opinion, are bad for the country.[418]

In other words, according to Lepore, in the marketplace of ideas America needs what she called a "New Americanism," which will encourage patriotism toward a country dedicated to "human equality and dignity," where scholars will promote, about that country, "a history that tells the truth, as best it can."[419]

[415] Jill Lepore, *This America: The Case for the Nation* (New York: Liveright, 2019), p. 19. In the category of "less scrupulous people," Lepore apparently had in mind (pp. 132–133) Bill O'Reilly (Fox News) and Steve Bannon (Breitbart News).

[416] *Ibid.*, p. 20. By "liberalism" here, Lepore meant post-Enlightenment democracy and republicanism broadly defined, not one half of the contemporary contest between "liberal" and "conservative" ideas within America.

[417] As an obvious case of how much depends on which story one tells about the national experience, there were two Stories which, for generations, and with vastly different implications, explained the Civil War as either the War of the Rebellion (against the Union) or the War Between the States (a matter, for some, of equal sovereignties between the North and the South). Among other sources, see David W. Blight, *Race and Reunion: The Civil War in American Memory* (Cambridge, MA: Harvard University Press, 2001). See also Richard Cohen, *Making History: The Storytellers Who Shaped the Past* (New York: Simon & Schuster, 2022), ch. 11, "America against Itself – Versions of the Civil War," 292–324.

[418] Beyond those who Lepore deplored as "less scrupulous people," we should consider that Stories are so important to public life that activists and partisans will occasionally conclude that history, as a basis for some of those Stories, is too important to be left to historians. That is the case, for example, with the current campaign to evoke belief in the thesis that America as a society began to take shape when the first enslaved people landed on the coast of Virginia in 1619. The advocates of that thesis clearly agree with Neil Postman on the importance of "large stories." See especially Nikole Hannah-Jones, Caitlin Roper, Ilena Silverman, and Jake Silverstein (eds.), *The 1619 Project: A New Origin Story* (New York: One World, 2021), p. 452: "Origin stories function, to a degree, as myths designed to create a shared sense of history and purpose. Nations simplify those narratives in order to unify and glorify, and these origin stories serve to illuminate how a society wants to see itself – and how it doesn't."

[419] Lepore, *This America*, p. 137.

That last phrase – "as best it can" – resonates here because, when Lepore used it, it was as if she acknowledged that Stories are always incomplete, that they sometimes clash, that they are at least somewhat subjective, and that they are, at bottom, false (well, not true). But also, in our terms, it was as if she observed that, even when Stories are persuasive, they are not all equal. In which case, in Lepore's professional opinion, the existence of Stories whose consequences seem harmful obliges scholars to offer *better*, alternative Stories.

Actually, because she believed that what people espouse together is cardinally important – as I have said all along – Lepore had already proceeded to tell an alternative Story in *These Truths: A History of the United States* (2018).[420] All this, of course, while knowing that in America's modern marketplace for ideas, she would have to defend her ideas against conservative views of the same subject, in a long-term face-off characterized by passionate and well-funded opponents.

Wilfred McClay

In these circumstances, it is worth noting, among Lepore's adversaries on the Right, the historian Wilfred McClay and his *Land of Hope: An Invitation to the Great American Story* (2019).[421] For McClay, a meticulous scholar at the University of Oklahoma, the competition with liberals like Lepore is clear, starting on his book's front cover where, in McClay's title, the word "the," rather than "a," serves to demote any other Story.

A contest like this is enormously complicated, and these two books are long, with McClay's covering 429 pages and Lepore's filling a truly hefty 792 pages. Therefore, I cannot fully describe here how their Stories stand against each other.

Both insist that America is a great country and that Americans are a magnificent people. To that end, both review, positively, many classic events and outstanding characters in America's past. Consequently, it would be unfair to say that, while one lists this or that important incident or person, the other is delinquent for ignoring the same things.

---

420 Lepore, *These Truths: A History of the United States* (New York: Norton, 2018).
421 Wilfred McClay, *Land of Hope* (New York: Encounter Books, 2019).

However, with regard to those things, Lepore and McClay sometimes assess them differently, to the point where Lepore has her heroes and villains (in the eyes of the Left) while McClay has his heroes and villains (in the eyes of the Right). Furthermore, Lepore focuses strongly on American downsides, on what remains to be done about this or that group or problem in American life, whereas McClay tends more to highlight American upsides, to tell readers mainly about inspiring American events, trends, and personalities.[422]

For our purposes, we should note that the contest between Stories promoted by scholars like Lepore and McClay is certain to continue, because both sides are sustained by friendly publishers. McClay, for example, was on this occasion published in the marketplace for ideas by Encounter Books, which is a conservative publisher that was created in 1997 to be part of a "counter-establishment" against the impact of liberal ideas in American society. Another entity in that counter-establishment is Washington's Heritage Foundation (created in 1973), which sponsors *The Daily Signal* (founded in 2014), whose columnist Jarrett Stepman, in his *The War on History: The Conspiracy to Rewrite America's Past* (2019), very plainly promotes rightist interpretations of famous people, such as Christopher Columbus, Robert E. Lee, Henry Ford, and Franklin D. Roosevelt, and familiar events, such as slavery, the Civil War, and the Second World War, in American history.[423]

---

[422] The conservative tenor of McClay's tale, when it opposes that told by Lepore, is often expressed in nuances, subtleties, inflections, and gradations. For example, about *people*, McClay notes, *Land of Hope*, p. 4, that everyone in America is either an immigrant or descended from immigrants, because even American Indians came to the New World from Siberia. One implication there is that Native Americans don't have any special rights and were not particularly wronged because they were not, in fact, "native," being only old-time newcomers. On the other hand, McClay also describes many *events* in American history from a conservative point of view. Thus, his treatment of President Franklin D. Roosevelt and the New Deal, pp. 302–315, uses the format of (in paraphrase): "Yes, this particular New Deal measure was somewhat useful. But it was not entirely successful and it had the following drawbacks."

[423] Jarrett Stepman, *The War on History* (Washington, DC: Regnery Gateway, 2019). For another clash between American history books, see, on the left, Howard Zinn, *A People's History of the United States, 1942 – Present* (orig., 1979; New York: Harper Perennial, 2005), versus, on the right, Larry Schweikart and Michael Allen, *A Patriot's History of the United States: From Columbus's Great Discovery to the War on Terror* (New York: Sentinel, 2004).

Political Thought

Lepore's commitment to a contest between large narratives is not typical even of historians.[424] Therefore, assuming that most academicians are not in the Storytelling business, I will conclude this book with some propositions which illuminate our situation and describe what politically minded scholars might do to improve it.[425]

* * * * *

We are professionally encouraged not to *endorse* stories, of any size, as if stories promote clashing interests in society while scholars should be neutral rather than partisan.[426] Nevertheless, because all Stories are false, it is (often) not difficult to *disprove* them, and we are tempted to do that frequently, to get ahead where we work.

The sticking point here is that Stories, if not stories, are needed by societies in a very general sense, in order to infuse individual and

---

[424] But some historians do discuss how their specific research topics may fit into competing, general versions of the nature of American life. For example, David Waldstreicher, "The Changing Same of U.S. History," *Boston Review* (November 10, 2021), which contrasts Gordon S. Wood, *Power and Liberty: Constitutionalism in the American Revolution* (New York: Oxford University Press, 2021), and Carol Anderson, *The Second: Race and Guns in a Fatally Unequal America* (New York: Bloomsbury, 2021). See Waldstreicher at https://bostonreview.net/articles/the-changing-same-of-u-s-history/.

[425] If we consider that modern politics is conducted via television (or even smaller screens), and that the world of screens demands stories and Stories, Lepore's views are familiar, even if she is not, to scholars who write about communications. For example, James Poniewozik, *Audience of One: Donald Trump, Television, and the Fracturing of America* (New York: Liveright, 2019), see p. 276: "Our culture, like any culture, has its set of myths and archetypes that our leaders borrow material from that the rest of us use to frame and make sense of our lives. 'All in the Family' and 'Breaking Bad' are as much a part of that corpus now as Shakespeare and the Bible. Speaking the language of metaphor and story shouldn't be considered a frivolity beneath serious civic discussion. Just the opposite. Unless we engage with it to find the narratives that appeal to the best in people, someone else will gladly use it to appeal to the worst."

[426] This injunction – that political scholars should usually not take sides – and its origins are discussed in David Ricci, *The Tragedy of Political Science: Politics, Scholarship, and Democracy* (New Haven: Yale University Press, 1984), esp. pp. 144–169. For a more philosophical account of the concept of objectivity, see J. M. Sprenger and J. Reiss, "Scientific Objectivity," in E. Zalta (ed.), *Stanford Encyclopedia of Philosophy* (Fall, 2014), at https://stanford.library.sydney.edu.au/archives/win2018/entries/scientific-objectivity/.

collective life with meaning. Especially in politics, Stories are needed in order to unite our affections and facilitate joint action.[427]

Nevertheless, following our professional instincts, we tend to reject Stories, more or less across the board. The problem there is like babies and bathwater, in that, by doing one good thing (seek veracity), we may unwittingly lose another (maintain efficacy).

* * * * *

Here, then, is the setting. Some Stories, both attractive and persuasive, are bad for people's collective health. But some Stories are wholesome, at least relatively speaking. And that last reality suggests, as a matter of principle, that we should not leave this field entirely, as if to say, a pox on all your houses. Rather, in the matter of Stories, there is an element of scholarly responsibility which suggests *not* that we must tell *no* Stories but that we should tell at least *some* tales which are *better* than harmful Stories now being told.[428]

William James

William James placed this axiom of practical wisdom front and center in his Pragmatic philosophy when he observed that, although

---

[427] See this point explained via social choice (or collective action) theory in Frederick W. Mayer, *Narrative Politics: Stories and Collective Action* (New York: Oxford University Press, 2014), pp. 1–49.

[428] I do *not* recommend that scholars *always* refrain from demolishing Stories when doing so seems justified to them. For example, I admire the writings of conservative historian Andrew Bacevich, who has repeatedly attacked the Story which, he says (but not using the word Story), has encouraged politicians to militarize modern American foreign policy and start endless wars. Among other works of his, see Bacevich, *Washington Rules: America's Path to Permanent War* (New York: Metropolitan, 2010); *The New American Militarism: How Americans are Seduced by War* (New York: Oxford University Press, 2013); and *The Age of Illusions: How America Squandered its Cold War Victory* (New York: Metropolitan, 2020). In *The Age of Illusions*, Bacevich does not use the terms that I do. But he does come close to describing faith in American exceptionalism as an American history Story, unfortunately mistaken, which is today seriously untrue and urgently in need of adjustment and revision. Specifically, he wants Americans to pay more attention to the realistic, ironic, and even tragic vision of Protestant minister Reinhold Niebuhr and less attention to the recent, inspiring, and dangerous tale of America as leader of both "the West" and "the Free World." For Bacevich, in *The Age of Illusions*, pp. 166–171, keeping Niebuhr in mind would lead to "responsible statecraft."

war evokes commendable virtues of solidarity and self-sacrifice, we should, obviously (that is, by common sense), condemn war because of its attendant horrors. The lesson there, according to James, is that, if scholars will want to foster warlike virtues anyway, they should do so by promoting what in 1910 he called "the moral equivalent of war,"[429] whereupon new (anti-war) stories or Stories (he did not use those terms) and practices would promote virtue without pain and destruction.[430]

As we have seen, Judith Shklar cast her net beyond war to additional outrages. She suggested what liberal scholars should investigate and teach about, when she recommended that they take a stand against various kinds of tyranny.[431]

To that Shklarian end, as I noted earlier, we should anxiously note two large and obvious cases of tyranny that threaten America today. The first is political imbalance, which flows from long-standing institutional arrangements, permits a national minority to thwart a national majority's preferences, amounts to minority rule, and denies the principle of government by consent.

The second is neoliberalism, which perpetuates economic growth, generates large economic inequalities, such as the One

[429] William James, *The Moral Equivalent of War, and Other Essays* (orig., 1910; New York: Harper Torchbooks, 1971). The title essay of that book is available at www.uky .edu/~eushe2/Pajares/moral.html. James earlier described some of the virtues he had in mind, such as "lonely courage," in his Dedication Speech on the occasion of unveiling in Boston, on May 1, 1887, a monument to Robert Shaw, the White commander of the Union's all-Black 54th Massachusetts Regiment. See the speech at https://college .holycross.edu/faculty/sluria/william_james_speech.html.

[430] See also Christopher Hedges, "The Myth of War," *War is a Force that Gives Us Meaning* (New York: Anchor, 2003), pp. 19–42. As Hedges says: "The enduring attraction of war is this: Even with its destruction and carnage it can give us what we long for in life. It can give us purpose, meaning, a reason for living .... And war is an enticing elixir. It gives us resolve, a cause. It allows us to be noble" (p. 3).

[431] Shklar was writing about liberals. As a matter of principle, her call to combat tyranny can also motivate conservatives. Of course, they will not always agree with liberals on exactly what constitutes tyranny. For example, Dinesh D'Souza condemns what he regards as a kind of tyranny practiced by liberals in his *Death of a Nation: Plantation Politics and the Making of the Democratic Party* (New York: All Points Books, 2018). See also Tammy Bruce, *The New American Revolution: How You Can Fight the Tyranny of the Left's Cultural and Moral Decay* (New York: Harper, 2005), and James Kalb, *The Tyranny of Liberalism: Understanding and Overcoming Administered Freedom, Inquisitorial Tolerance, and Equality by Command* (Wilmington, DE: Intercollegiate Studies Institute Books, 2008).

Percent syndrome, leaves many people behind and desperate, and therefore provokes among many voters resentment, which can generate populism.

The Conservative Way Forward

As for how to tell Stories about such situations, today's conservative spokespeople, who are now America's leading Storytellers, have pointed the way. Yes, conservatives tell Stories.[432] And those Stories appeal strongly to many people. But what conservatives actually do is offer attractive Stories leavened with *qualifications*. And that strategy of conceding qualifications may work in the marketplace for ideas by making it difficult there to decisively "refute" such "conjectures" – that is, Stories – just because they are, in some respects, false.[433]

That is the case, for example, with the Story spun by political commentator Ben Shapiro about how "reason" and "Judeo-Christianity" made "Western civilization," to which America belongs, "great."[434] Shapiro's Story, in *The Right Side of History* (2019), is not exactly true, because some acts of the West – say silencing Galileo, maintaining New World slavery, enforcing colonial rule, using children for factory labor, strip-mining coal in the Appalachians, perpetuating the

---

[432] This Storytelling may be implicit or explicit. Trump's is often *implicit*, as in the slogan "Make America Great Again!" The word "again" implies that America was once greater than it is now, and that, for this, someone must be culpable. For an *explicit* Story, see George W. Bush's First Inaugural Address: "We have a place, all of us, in a long story – a story we continue, but whose end we will not see. It is the story of a new world that became a friend and liberator of the old, a story of a slave-holding society that became a servant of freedom, the story of a power that went into the world to protect but not possess, to defend but not to conquer. It is the American story – a story of flawed and fallible people, united across the generations by grand and enduring ideals. The grandest of these ideals is an unfolding promise that everyone belongs, that everyone deserves a chance, that no insignificant person was ever born. Americans are called to enact this promise in our lives and in our laws. And though our nation has sometimes halted, and sometimes delayed, we must follow no other course." (At https://abcnews.go.com/Politics/story?id=122003&page=1.)
[433] Karl Popper, *Conjectures and Refutations*, 2nd ed. (orig., 1963; New York: Routledge, 2003).
[434] See Ben Shapiro, *The Right Side of History: How Reason and Moral Purpose Made the West Great* (New York: Broadside, 2019).

Holocaust, dropping atomic bombs on Hiroshima (instead of out to sea as demonstrations), and failing to adequately address global warming – were, or are, more dreadful than great.[435] And the list is very long.[436]

But Shapiro casts such acts (if he mentions them) as unfortunate blemishes, as temporary aberrations, as personal failures, and so forth. Therefore, they are simply mistakes that should be disavowed and that many people have already decided to correct. In which case, Shapiro's central thesis, the Story itself, about "Western civilization," remains powerful and attractive.[437]

Once Again

The points I have proposed here challenge what we usually expect of scholarship. They suggest, in fact, that *some* professors, in *some* fields, for *some* of the time, should knowingly promote *some* Stories, which are inspiring and politically useful even though they are *not entirely true*.

This is not to say that, in order to oppose an old Story, we must invent a new Story from scratch. Shklar observed that scholars (well, actually, liberal scholars) do not compose Stories, and then she argued that we are not to blame for that fact. And Weber simply

---

[435] Soon after the Holocaust, some Christian thinkers fashioned the concept of "Judeo-Christianity" as a commendable expression of religious tolerance. But it is also internally problematic, in the sense that Judaism and Christianity, as theological Stories, are really very different. Which is why devout Jews are not Christians and vice versa. For example, see Jacob Neusner, *Jews and Christians: The Myth of a Common Tradition* (London: SCM Press, 1991), and Harold Bloom, *Jesus and Yahweh: the Names Divine* (New York: Riverhead, 2005).

[436] Some readers might want to add to the list predators like Facebook (now hidden behind the name Meta), which have, for the sake of profit, deliberately addicted children to their products. Other readers might want to add internet looters, like Amazon, who undersold their competitors (brick-and-mortar stores), some to the point of bankruptcy, by refusing to collect state sales taxes. Still others might want to note the free-rider legislators and lobbyists, say in Delaware and South Dakota, who conspired to enact laws which leave wealthy individuals and corporations with tax rates lower than those imposed on their chauffeurs and maids.

[437] There is a paradox here, because a liberal might regard Ben Shapiro's Story as a case of Richard Rorty's Pragmatism, in that Shapiro, in his own way, is keeping his eye on a "dream country" (more attractive than reality) rather than on exactly the one he "wakes up to every morning." For liberal criticism of conservative historian Niall Ferguson for making "the West" look more attractive than it really is, see David Bromwich, "What is the West?" *Moral Imagination* (Princeton: Princeton University Press, 2014), pp. 273–286.

charged scholars to choose (between "causes"). If we follow his advice
we will find, I think, that at least some ethically responsible Stories –
for example, like the Stories of Reinhold Niebuhr – are available for
updating, on the shelf, so to speak.

When all is said and done, we can promote those Stories even
though academic criticism of error will inevitably arise. For example,
Lepore's Story, in *These Truths* (2018), is said by some to be overly
enthusiastic about government regulation of the economy,[438] and the
Story told by Louis Hartz, in *The Liberal Tradition in America* (1955),
about early Americans bravely fleeing European oppressions then creating and maintaining a constitutional order, has been faulted for not
sufficiently condemning American racism and misogyny.[439]

In Short

In short, we must choose between Stories. At the penultimate moment,
criticism of what we chose can be acknowledged: Yes, I can admit
that something is not true in the Story which I promote. But I can also
discount that criticism, along the lines of Ben Shapiro, as if my ethically responsible Story's main thesis is satisfactory but needs only to be
realized more fully.

---

[438] Against Lepore, *These Truths*, see www.hoover.org/research/jill-lepores-slanted-truths/.
[439] In *The Liberal Tradition in America: An Interpretation of American Political Thought
since the Revolution* (New York: Harcourt, Brace, and World, 1955), p. 3, Hartz said
that he would talk about "the storybook truth about American history: that America
was settled by men who fled from the feudal and clerical oppressions of the Old World."
For criticism of Hartz from political scholars, see James L. Kloppenberg, "In Retrospect,
Louis Hartz and 'The Liberal Tradition in America,'" *Reviews in American History* (September, 2001), pp. 460–478, and Rogers M. Smith, "Beyond Tocqueville, Myrdal and
Hartz: The Multiple Traditions in America," *American Political Science Review* (September, 1993), pp. 549–566.

12 WHAT NOW?

This book does not propose a "theory" about stories, but I have used instead various "terms" to frame the matter at hand.[440] Those terms include, among others, a post-truth context, the epistemological crisis, the Enlightenment, humanism, disenchantment, popular sovereignty, political and economic imbalances, Stories which perpetuate both imbalances, majority rule, minority rule, innovation, disruption, the marketplace of ideas, tyranny, "causes," the ethics of responsibility, choosing, refraining, dissembling, and more.

So here is the essence of the matter. We live in a world of post-truth. We cannot get around it. We are trapped in that reality for the foreseeable future; it weighs upon every sort of human relationship, from the public to the personal. It is anyone's guess where all this is going. Some of us will invite children for Thanksgiving dinner and they will sit at the table thumbing their phones. What does that mean? And will their children come to Thanksgiving dinners at all?

In the circumstances, I considered some aspects of politics in this muddled world, where untruth infects the Stories which shape our lives. To that end, I explored something of where political scholars are,

---

[440] This point is further explained in the "Afterword," pp. 194–205.

how they got there, and how they might go forward. Now, then, is the time for summary remarks.

On the Left

Before I offer those, however, a disclaimer is in order concerning what some readers may regard as bias in this book. Earlier, I described two cases – of political and economic imbalances – in order to show that academic talk about political Stories is not merely an academic matter. I will admit, however, that those two cases are mostly related to, or maintained by, factions and Stories on the Right. And some readers may feel that I was too hard on the Right because I am somewhere on the Left.

Well, yes, I am not on the Right. But I warned about two particular imbalances not because I am on the Left but because I believe those cases are *exceptionally dangerous*. That is, I thought that having a look at those imbalances, which may eventually explode, might be particularly likely to bring readers to decide that some scholars, as Weber said, should track the possibly harmful impact of Stories (causes) on public life.

However, I want to emphasize that for me to highlight Stories on the Right does not mean that I assume there are no Stories worth challenging on the contemporary Left. My point of principle is that political scholars should check and assess all "big stories" in Postman's phrase, or all "causes" in Weber's term, or all "Stories" in mine. All as in every sort, as in "What's sauce for the goose is sauce for the gander."

For example, on the Left, there is some enthusiasm for a Story about America as a society based on the principle of equality which, presumably, underlies the Declaration of Independence. This narrative is promoted by, among others, Harvard's Danielle Allen, *Our Declaration: A Reading of the Declaration of Independence in Defense of Equality* (2014).[441]

It is an inspiring tale. Nevertheless, I could argue (although not here, for lack of space) that individual equality, while very important to many Americans today – think of Black Lives Matter or #MeToo – is not really what the Founders had in mind when they opted out of

[441] (Cambridge, MA: Harvard University Press).

the British Empire. In other words, the proposed Story, that the Declaration is about equality, may serve the felt needs of some factions in America today, and therefore telling that Story is an unsurprising partisan ploy. But, in my view, the Story is simply not true.[442]

Another potential Story, related to the preceding one, proposes that, while leading the North, the West, and several Border states during the Civil War, Abraham Lincoln revised constitutional law so as to reject a Union based on long-standing but unethical compromises, which included support and protection for slavery. Instead, according to Harvard's Noah Feldman, *The Broken Constitution: Lincoln, Slavery, and the Refounding of America* (2021),[443] Lincoln and his Republican majorities in the national government enacted the 13th, 14th, and 15th Amendments (1865, 1868, and 1870) which, by abolishing slavery and granting citizenship to formerly enslaved people, overrode the original Constitution and bequeathed to America a new Union framework which would serve as a moral beacon for future generations.

Again, it is clear that this potential Story, if widely espoused, might be politically useful for validating claims promoted by some current American factions. But saying that the new Constitution is a moral beacon does not make it so, because competing factions in the nation are constantly lobbying Congress and litigating in the federal courts precisely because they do *not agree* on which moral principles the Constitution might embody. In fact, the Constitution, while usually revered, is interpreted differently by Americans who have developed polarized visions of right and wrong on matters such as race, gender, education, abortion, welfare, energy, and environmental protection.

A third narrative along these lines appears in Nikole Hannah-Jones, Caitlin Roper, Ilena Silverman, and Jake Silverstein (eds.), *The 1619 Project: An Origin Story* (2021).[444] This narrative, sponsored by

---

[442] A different approach to promoting equality is offered by Walter Benn Michaels, *The Trouble with Diversity: How We Learned to Love Identity and Ignore Inequality* (New York: Picador, 2006, 2016). Michaels does not claim that equality is enshrined in the Declaration but that, from wherever it beckons, the principle of economic equality is ignored by many on the American Right and Left who, generally speaking, prefer respect for identity (immediately gratifying) rather than a concern for redistribution (very hard to achieve) of tangible resources.

[443] (Cambridge, MA: Harvard University Press).

[444] (New York: One World).

the *New York Times*, declares that enslaved people were first brought to Virginia in 1619, before the White Pilgrims came to Massachusetts in 1620; that their work and cultural achievements were essential to the pursuit of American happiness; and that Black Americans, while insisting that "all men are created equal" (as written in the Declaration of Independence), have for generations, while suffering from discrimination and oppression, served America "prominently" as "democracy's defenders and perfecters."

In which case, says Hannah-Jones, "It is time, it is long past time, for reparations." Hannah-Jones and her co-authors are especially relevant to our discussion of Stories, because they are explicit about their Storytelling. As they put it in *The 1619 Project*,[445] the current "origin story" of the United States centers upon White Americans, as if "they won" independence, "they tamed" the West, "they fought" the Civil War to "end slavery," and "they" were "the architects and champions of democracy." The country, Hannah-Jones says, needs "a truer origin story" which more accurately portrays the crucial role of Black people in America's history.

In other words, Hannah-Jones proposes to replace the current, White-centered Story (or "cause" in Weber's term) in (some of) America's affections with a new, Black-centered Story (or "cause"). Without taking sides in the intense controversy between leftist and rightist partisans on this issue – with fierce face-offs over "systematic racism," "critical race theory," and "identity politics" – I can suggest, in a preliminary way, that the Black-centered tale framed by Hannah-Jones and her colleagues is not entirely true. This is because it does not manage to explain, although it tries to do so, how a sector ranging, over the years, from 12 to 16 percent of all Americans, can account for the central importance within America which the 1619 Project attributes to it.[446]

Of course, that the proposed Black-centered Story is somewhat false does not make the White-centered Story entirely true. An extreme

---

[445] *The 1619 Project*, ch. 18, "Justice," pp. 452–476.

[446] These numbers, from 12% to 16%, I compiled from decennial census counts made for several generations after the Civil War. They should be regarded as approximate because deciding who is Black or not depends on how citizens describe themselves to census-takers who go door to door registering inhabitants. The official racial categories for the 2020 American census are explained in www.census.gov/programs-surveys/decennial-census/decade/2020/planning-management/release/faqs-race-ethnicity.html.

version of the latter appeared in The President's Advisory 1776 Commission, *The 1776 Report* (January, 2021). This *Report* insists that the United States did not get started in 1619 but was founded "on July 4, 1776," and that "The facts of our founding are not partisan. They are a matter of history." Which means that they are true, in some permanent way.[447]

Furthermore, says the *Report*, "the American people have ever pursued freedom and justice." Accordingly, while offering qualifications like those postulated in Ben Shapiro's *The Right Side of History*, the *Report* concedes that "the American story has its share of missteps, errors, contradictions, and wrong." However, these wrongs, such as slavery and segregation, "have always met resistance from the clear principles of the nation."[448]

I could argue more completely, but not here, that this potential Story, commissioned by then-President Trump, is at least partly false. A wide range of leading American historians, some White and some Black, agree that it is simply not true that only a few deplorable political "compromises" enabled slavery to continue after 1789 in America, or that only foot-dragging by some White Americans, during the era of Jim Crow and later, obstructed the full realization of their country's great ideals of freedom *and* equality.[449]

More to Say

But enough of disclaimers. From what I did *not* analyze, let us turn to summing up what I *did*.

First, there is more to say about everything I have discussed. On the one hand, that is because the matters I addressed are very important. They are not fleeting concerns, they will not go away, and

---

[447] Commission Members included Hoover Institute Fellow Victor Davis Hanson and *Claremont Review of Books* editor Charles Kesler, and Ex-Officio Members included Secretary of State Mike Pompeo, Secretary of Housing and Urban Development Ben Carson, and Assistant to the President for Domestic Policy Brooke Rollins.

[448] These quoted phrases are from the *Report*, p. 1, available at https://trumpwhitehouse .archives.gov/wp-content/uploads/2021/01/The-Presidents-Advisory-1776-Commission-Final-Report.pdf.

[449] For historians opposing the 1776 Report, see www.historians.org/news-and-advocacy/aha-advocacy/aha-statement-condemning-report-of-advisory-1776-commission-(january-2021).

their partisans will not flag and desist. So political tales, like the poor, will always be with us.[450]

On the other hand, there is more to say because even though stories, and Stories, are cardinally important in politics and therefore deserve our attention, there is a sense in which, as I explained earlier, we do not really know what it is we are trying to understand. After all, given their nature – that stories large or small are not entities which can be scientifically defined, like lions or moons – we do not know exactly where most of them begin and where they end, we do not know exactly which ones are more or less powerful, and we do not know, in an overall analysis, exactly who is inspired by, or indifferent to, or offended by, many of them.

In which case, at least some political scholars should look at, and teach about, political tales. That is not because we believe that, in the end, we can explicate them precisely and understand them conclusively. It is because, now and into the future, we know that they are, and will be, so politically potent that we should not risk leaving them alone, for fear of dangerous results. So let us learn more about them.

Puzzles and Problems

In these circumstances, without forecasting specific outcomes, I will suggest a logical dichotomy that I posited in earlier writings.[451] There are conditions in life which constitute "puzzles" and there are those which constitute "problems." Puzzles (such as how to build a bridge,

---

[450] For example, an early version of the MAGA story, before Trump gave it that name, appeared during America's Cold War confrontation with international Leftists. See James Burnham, *Suicide of the West: An Essay on the Meaning and Destiny of Liberalism* (New York: John Day, 1964). A later-day version of the MAGA story is told, from within the "great books" tradition, by Hillsdale College's historian Paul Rahe, *Soft Despotism, Democracy's Drift: Montesquieu, Rousseau, Tocqueville, and the Modern Prospect* (New Haven: Yale, 2009), *passim*, but esp. p. 280: "tyrannical ambition and servile temptation will always be with us, as they are most emphatically now. The choice is, nevertheless, ours. We can be *what once we were* [emphasis added], or we can settle for a gradual, gentle descent into servitude. It is high time that we reclaim what is, after all, our legacy as Americans, for the genuine self-government that we once enjoyed in plenitude .... And let our virtue be individual responsibility."

[451] For example, in Ricci, *Politics without Stories: The Liberal Predicament* (Cambridge, UK: Cambridge University Press, 2016), pp. 5, 189.

or how to facilitate online shopping) have solutions which are sometimes hard to find but, when worked out, permit us to move on. Problems (such as how to make dating [courting] 100 percent safe, or how to fairly draw Congressional district lines) have no solutions; they are intractable; and we must live with them, for better or worse.[452]

In our circumstances, the current situation, where persuasive Stories are false yet embraced nevertheless, is a problem. It has no solution. Stories cannot be made true, therefore they will continue to be false. Which means that we must live with false Stories and even promote some of them.

The challenge, then, is to pursue what is better in those Stories and criticize what is worse. To meet this challenge, cautious scholars, in the name of common sense, should avoid professional overkill, should be wary of "random momentum," and should resist some aspects of their professional "churn."

I am projecting this warning in somewhat academic terms. Expressed in other terms and circumstances, however, it is a point of principle which sages have long recognized even if they have not always framed it with precise injunctions. For example, the Hippocratic Oath admonishes medical doctors, generally speaking, to "do no harm." And Ecclesiastes cautions us, also generally speaking, but right on target, that "in much wisdom is much grief: and he that increaseth knowledge increaseth sorrow."[453] Scholars (and everyone else) should keep both warnings in mind.

Not Always Telling the Truth

Ergo, let us resist some of our professional routine, at least sometimes. To do so is not our *only* scholarly mission. But it is, I believe, *one* mission among others. It is, unfortunately, difficult to serve. And that is an understatement.

In fact, the challenge of not always telling the truth, in any realm, on the grounds of what Weber had in mind when he spoke of

---

[452] I earlier suggested that gerrymandering has favored the Republican Party. It is also true that, when conditions permit, Democrats may tilt the system on their own behalf. See www.vox.com/22961590/redistricting-gerrymandering-house-2022-midterms.
[453] Ecclesiastes 1:18 (KJV).

the ethics of responsibility, is one of the great moral tests in civilized life. It posits no clear standards of performance, like athletes used to aim for a four-minute mile or a seven-foot high jump. Therefore, when Weber called on scholars to act responsibly, he could not say, in advance, exactly what teaching according to the ethics of responsibility would require in various circumstances. He could not say, and neither can I.[454]

Aha!

Which brings me almost to the end of what I have to say. In support of my propositions, I have written more about interpreting things already known than about promoting any new item like, say, a scientific discovery – such as a new frog in the Amazon rainforest – based on empirical research and fresh data.

I hope, though, that some readers will have experienced an "Aha!" moment. That is, actually, my ultimate goal. It would be a moment of suddenly feeling – perhaps unexpectedly – that we should occasionally embrace the proposition that telling something not true can be virtuous.[455]

This does not mean that, regardless of what we know to be the case, scholars should feel free to lie about it. To lie often, as a matter

---

[454] Using a common-sense approach, Michael Walzer explored some aspects of this problem in his *Spheres of Justice: A Defense of Pluralism and Equality* (New York: Basic Books, 1983). There, Walzer showed how, if we aspire to act responsibly in different realms of life – from war to religion, from art to education, and more – we should apply alternative, and sometimes conflicting, standards of moral conduct. The point is that, until you categorize a given situation, you may not know what standards to apply to it.

[455] For almost a century now, scholars have noted that totalitarian societies suppress some aspects of knowledge and memory. In which case, the matter of occasionally dissembling, in liberal societies, on behalf of politically desirable ends, has been treated gingerly (or not at all) by democratic thinkers such as Steven Levitsky and Daniel Ziblatt (*How Democracies Die* [New York: Crown, 2018]); Timothy Snyder (*The Road to Unfreedom: Russia, Europe, America* [New York: Tim Duggan Books, 2018]); David Runciman (*How Democracy Ends* [New York: Basic Books, 2018]); John Campbell (*American Discontent: The Rise of Donald Trump and the Decline of the Golden Age* [New York: Oxford University Press, 2018]); and Philip N. Howard (*Lie Machines: How to Save Democracy from Troll Armies, Deceitful Robots, Junk News Operations, and Political Operatives* [New Haven: Yale University Press, 2020]). For a complex analysis, see Hannah Arendt, "Truth and Lying" (1967), in Arendt, *Between Past and Future* (New York: Penguin, 1993), pp. 227–264.

of normal practice, as if accuracy and reliability are irrelevant to how we work, would be to betray academic standards in modern society. But to experience an "Aha!" moment in this case is only to feel that we should *occasionally* offer understandings which we believe will be useful even though we know – like it or not – that, at some level of detail and accuracy, they are *not entirely true*.

We should, I think, accept the invitation to occasionally perform an act of "unconventional virtue" because, as time passes, like fish swimming in water which they overlook, it is in the nature of our living together in complex societies that there are always some realities which we slight, some things "that we know but do not know." That is, there are things which our predecessors have already discovered, but which we sometimes forget to take into account when we focus, momentarily, on other important matters.[456]

We can rephrase that. There are things which, from time to time, we must sort out, which we must consider to remind ourselves of how not just to live in this world but how to live in it *well*. And one of the surprising requirements for doing that, oddly enough, is to dissemble, if only occasionally.

We Are Not Alone

Fortunately, we are not alone. We are not the first people who are challenged by how to deal with truth and we will not be the last. One folktale, for example, asks, in everyday terms, whether the guest at a wedding party should declare that the bride is pretty, to make her feel good on this special day, even if she is not. In other words, when is a wedding guest permitted, or even morally obliged, to disregard promoting the truth, which is itself a moral imperative, and to tell a well-intentioned but useful lie in order to accommodate the commendable pursuit of happiness?[457]

Historians remind us of famous cases. For example, Plato, who more or less invented political philosophy, proposed telling "noble

---

[456] Some thoughts along these lines, including the quoted phrase, appear in Justin E. H. Smith, *Irrationality: A History of the Dark Side of Reason* (Princeton: Princeton University Press, 2019), *passim*, but esp. 287–289.

[457] This ethical puzzle appears in the Babylonian Talmud, *Ketubot* 16b–17a.

lies," not in order to recommend the practice of dissembling but to achieve desirable political results. Thus, on behalf of good ends, one may tell a few whoppers or, just as well, tales like the Myth of Er, the dead soldier in Plato's *Republic* (*c*.375 BC) who came back from the underworld to tell humans of rewards there to the just and punishments to the wicked.

Later, Niccolò Machiavelli, who was an experienced Renaissance courtier, knew that an occasional fib – the ruler behaving like a fox – could promote the safety and welfare of a prince's city. To say as much, of course, in his famous Chapter XVIII of *The Prince* (1532), was to set aside familiar principles of truth and integrity. Nevertheless, said Machiavelli, in effect, the ends really *can* justify the means, but only *sometimes*.[458]

After which, Otto von Bismarck, the Prussian prince who unified modern Germany in 1871, is said to have advised us not to look too closely at the give and take of politics, even though it is an essential activity in any society. As Bismarck is reputed to have said, making laws is like making sausages. You want it to get done successfully, but you don't want to know exactly what goes into the product.

The case for setting exactitude aside to good effect can also come from men and women who deal in avowed fiction. Such writers know they are not reciting scientific facts but personal opinions. Therefore they feel comfortable writing plays, poetry, novels, and more, according to whether or not those might help people live well together (which is, for fiction writers, a kind of truth). Thus Salman Rushdie, accused of blasphemy in 1989 by Iran's Ayatollah Khomeini, insists that "We must work to overturn the false narratives of tyrants, populists, and fools by telling better stories than they do – stories within which people might actually want to live."[459]

Evoking the same sentiment, Friedrich Durrenmatt, in *The Physicists* (1962), told a tale starkly fit for our times.[460] In a psychiatric hospital after the Second World War, a brilliant physicist fears

---

[458] Machiavelli, *The Prince* (1532), ch. XVIII.

[459] Rushdie's remarks, at the 2022 Emergency World Voices Congress of Writers, are excerpted in www.nytimes.com/2022/05/15/arts/pen-conference.html.

[460] (New York: Grove Press, 2010).

that his government will exploit his discoveries to make horrendously destructive weapons. Therefore he pretends, while living in the hospital together with two patients who claim to be Isaac Newton and Albert Einstein, that he has lost his mind and that he now believes he is Johann Wilhelm Mobius. To dissemble as a madman is preferable, "Mobius" thinks, to openly telling the world, via scientific papers, what he has discovered.

The Ultimate Mission

Even the wisest of mentors, of course, cannot tell us for sure, before the event, under which circumstances, precisely, we should dissemble. So a final word on the subject reminds us of our duty. Knowing when to pursue Truth, and when to maximize other values, are delicate and difficult matters.[461] That they are both, however, does not mean that we are excused from trying to do the right thing. As Tarfon insisted in *Ethics of the Fathers* (c. AD 200), 2:21 – "It is not incumbent upon you to complete the work, but neither are you at liberty to desist from it."

---

[461] For example, see Martin Jay, *The Virtues of Mendacity: On Lying in Politics* (Charleston: University of Virginia Press, 2010); David Runciman, *Political Hypocrisy: The Mask of Power, from Hobbes to Orwell and Beyond*, rev. ed. (Princeton: Princeton University Press, 2018); and Sophia Rosenfeld, *Democracy and Truth: A Short History* (Philadelphia: University of Pennsylvania Press, 2019).

AFTERWORD

It is difficult to write a scholarly book during an epistemological crisis. That is because writing today, about any important subject – such as politics, finance, literature, the media, education, the rural–urban divide, immigration, climate change, feminism, drugs, guns, abortion, pets, and more – is challenged by our increasing inability to trust one another, to agree on basic facts, to talk considerately to adversaries, and, not least of all, to maintain the democratic principles and practices which sustain us together.[462] It is a situation in which no matter what we write, we do not know whom it will reach and how it will be received.

Formats

In these circumstances, some afterthoughts are warranted about how, in my mind, I framed some public aspects of our post-truth age.

---

[462] For example, in this essay (see n. 82) I assumed that American polarization has been driven mainly by the Republican Party. On that point, in his *The Deconstructionists: The Twenty-Five-Year Crack-Up of the Republican Party* (New York: Doubleday, 2022), liberal journalist Dana Milbank agrees. But conservative pundit David Horowitz, in his *The Enemy Within: How a Totalitarian Movement is Destroying America* (Washington, DC: Regnery, 2021), disagrees. I therefore sidestepped both of those sources and chose to cite instead think tankers Thomas Mann, from the Brookings Institution, and Norman Ornstein, from the American Enterprise Institute. Their book, *It's Even Worse than*

The first relates to a procedural, or methodological, matter which may be particularly important to political science colleagues.

Theories

When facts fade away, stories step up. As we have seen, that is how modern political talk discourse works. Therefore, in the age of post-truth I especially addressed certain kinds of political Story (which are false) and two current crises (political and economic) which some of those Stories perpetuate.

There is, however, no "theory" in what I have written. And its absence is worth noting here because many books written by political scientists explain that research about some aspect of public life – say, about legislative coalitions, voting behavior, the market for political ideas, the evolution of parties, the maintenance of civil rights, or the attachment to sentiments of Right or Left – can best be understood via a theory of the matter which the author will propose and confirm with statistical data and/or other information about relevant people and events.

This book did *not* expound such a theory. First, because the Stories it examined and discussed are impossible to define precisely and therefore cannot, in my opinion, be inserted usefully into a theoretical context. After all, exactly what is a Story? Second, because political stories are so numerous in the post-truth age that I was unable to frame them within any set of terms which a theory might propose. Once you start looking for Stories, you see that they are present in almost every important political situation.

Essays

By commenting on this format issue, I intend no criticism of other books which expound scholarly theories. I am saying only that I chose to do something different in this book, which was to write an "essay." In this case, an essay is a professional project which takes for

It Looks: How the American Constitutional System Collided with the New Politics of Extremism (New York: Basic Books, 2016), I regard as more objective.

its subject an important matter which is so complex, and perhaps even so convoluted, that it must be approached from many different angles of analysis, one after another and sometimes doubling back to earlier angles.[463]

Put this another way. Aristotle famously said that one should be as scientific as the subject permits.[464] His insight suggested for my project the following lesson. When even literary people cannot say exactly what a Story is, or where one begins and where it ends, or whether a particular Story stands alone or is intricately linked to other Stories, and so forth, it seemed to me that we can think constructively about political Stories. But we cannot, as Aristotle pointed out, do that scientifically. Therefore I addressed political Stories only in a general and common-sense way.

So *Post-Truth American Politics: False Stories and Current Crises* did not offer a theory about political Stories in post-truth America. Instead, via terms such as false stories, the epistemological crisis, progressivism, conservatism, humanism, disenchantment, polarization, gridlock, neoliberalism, the liberalism of fear, tyranny, and the ethics of responsibility, I discussed how we might think constructively about those Stories which, definable or not, are crucial to the country today.

Our Melting Iceberg

I believe those thoughts are sensible. But they may seem especially so if we will think of them together with icebergs. Mental images of enormous icebergs breaking up can remind us of catastrophic global warming today. However, they can also project a useful metaphor

[463] Writing an essay resembles research as performed by historian William McNeill, who described his "method" as follows: "I get curious about a problem and start reading up on it. What I read causes me to redefine the problem. Redefining the problem causes me to shift the direction of what I'm reading. That in turn further reshapes the problem, which further redirects the reading. I go back and forth like this until it feels right, then I write it up and ship it off to the publisher." McNeill is quoted in John Lewis Gaddis, *The Landscape of History: How Historians Map the Past* (New York: Oxford University Press, 2002), p. 48.

[464] Aristotle, *Nichomachean Ethics*, Book 1, 3: "Our discussion will be adequate if it has as much clearness as the subject-matter admits of, for precision is not to be sought for alike in all discussions, any more than in all the products of the crafts" (in Richard McKeon [ed.], *Introduction to Aristotle* [New York: Modern Library, 1947], p. 301).

of intellectual stress, such as when, while the Second World War raged, George Orwell declared that he felt like he was sitting on a melting iceberg of formerly reputable understandings. These, he thought, had for many years assumed that democracy was the best political regime available, and that modern thinkers and doers, leaders and followers, activists and ordinary voters, were capable – via science, reason, common sense, and useful traditions – of creating and maintaining it.[465]

To recall Orwell in recent years is to sense that we are perched on a comparable iceberg, where what we have long believed about democracy seems less and less tenable because it is being challenged, undermined, and/or rejected in favor of a jumble of truths and untruths, a mass of steadily financed contradictions and oppositions, a relentless campaign to entertain rather than to educate, an overwhelming flood of information and misinformation, sent to us especially via radio, television, computers, and smartphones, designed to distract rather than to edify.[466]

In this post-truth era, when even plain facts are contested, we saw, in this essay, that clashing political Stories take up the slack.[467] They increasingly compete for our attention and affections, to a point

---

[465] "Inside the Whale" (1940), in George Orwell, *Inside the Whale and Other Essays* (London: Penguin, 1962), p. 48: "The literature of liberalism is coming to an end .... As for the writer, he is sitting on a melting iceberg; he is merely an anachronism, a hangover from the bourgeois age, as surely doomed as the hippopotamus."

[466] Distraction is no small problem in modern society. See Adam Gazzaley and Larry D. Rosen, *The Distracted Mind: Ancient Brains in a High-Tech World* (Cambridge, MA: MIT Press, 2016). The book reviews research findings from academic psychology and neuroscience. It especially highlights (pp. 76–79, 178–179) the failures of "multitasking," which many (distracted) people believe they can do effectively.

[467] The problem of contested facts has reached Americans in every walk of life. For example, Supreme Court judges have begun to differ on the facts of cases brought before the Court. Thus Justice Neil Gorsuch and Justice Sonia Sotomayer did not agree on what actually happened in the case of *Kennedy* v. *Bremerton* (2022) and therefore disagreed on what legal conclusions should be drawn from what they differentially stipulated that Kennedy, a high school football coach, had done. See https://slate.com/news-and-politics/2022/06/coach-kennedy-gorsuch-prayer-public-schools.html. We expect (or, we used to expect) experts such as Gorsuch and Sotomayer to project the same set of facts. If they don't, cognitive dissonance sets in and the post-truth society deteriorates into what Matthew D'Ancona, in *Post Truth: The New War on Truth and How to Fight Back* (London: Ebury, 2017), p. 56, describes as: "You choose your own reality, as if from a buffet."

where we are painfully polarized and massively gridlocked, unable to resolve dangerous situations which are rooted in large political and economic inequalities. These generate glaring disagreements, which may lead to widespread violence. Or perhaps even to civil war.

Donald Trump

All these things I discussed during twelve chapters of this book. Here, I want to note further that, while I wrote all that, a figurative elephant named Donald Trump crowded into the room where I was working.

Between January 20, 2017 and January 20, 2021, Donald Trump served as America's 45th president. During those years in the White House, he followed in office men such as George Washington, Thomas Jefferson, Andrew Jackson, Abraham Lincoln, Woodrow Wilson, Franklin Roosevelt, and Dwight Eisenhower.

Compared to such exemplars, Trump was the epitome of post-truth politics. He cared little or not at all about truth.[468] He was an elephant whose rhetoric was outrageous, who scorned accuracy, who had no administrative talent, who projected disdain, distortions, exaggerations, fabrications, and conspiracies, and who got elected as a barker for the lethal story of MAGA; that is, that we must make America great *again*, as if it is in terrible shape now because someone (wink, wink) ruined it (at some unstated moment).[469]

How, I thought, could a democratic society get a grip on its immense problems if Trump was, at that moment, the available national leader?[470]

---

[468] During the four years of his presidency, the *Washington Post* catalogued more than 30,000 instances of what it called "President Donald Trump's false or misleading claims." See this explained in www.washingtonpost.com/politics/2021/01/24/trumps-false-or-misleading-claims-total-30573-over-four-years/.

[469] A clear version of the MAGA story appeared in Trump's Inaugural Address. See www.politico.com/story/2017/01/full-text-donald-trump-inauguration-speech-transcript-233907.

[470] In those years, I thought of Trump as a symptom of post-truth politics, as if to him the truth was less important than the impact of his narrative. However, Trump sometimes simply sidestepped post-truth behavior, to the extent that he produced distracting "spectacles" rather than misleading "statements." On this point, see David Bromwich, *American Breakdown: The Trump Years and How They Befell Us* (New York: Verso, 2019), p. 51.

The Main Point

Regardless of how I felt about Donald Trump, in the 2016 federal election 62,984,828 Americans voted for him and, roughly speaking, the MAGA story. We can say that, in those days, his supporters did not know exactly what they would get when he took office. No one did. Yet in 2020, after four years of seeing Trump serve in the White House, 11,231,326 *more* Americans, for a total of 74,216,154, voted for him and the same – again, roughly speaking – MAGA story.

With this elephant figuratively in the room, I started to write. I did not think that President Trump would be reelected in 2020. I did believe, however, that, as time passed, the real lesson of Americans voting in 2016 and 2020 was that, on the Right and on the Left, and maybe especially on the Right, tens of millions of decent, hardworking, generous, responsible, neighborly, and patriotic men and women had, and probably still have, painful grievances which are not being adequately addressed by their political system.

That being the case, where a post-truth environment turns "facts" into an intellectual minefield of contested "opinions," and where the marketplace for ideas lends persistent weight to a wide range of partisan Stories such as those which empowered candidates such as Donald Trump, Hillary Clinton, and Joe Biden, I concluded that we should pay attention to whichever Stories inspire or shock, encourage or infuriate, praise or scorn, soothe or stagger, various voters. Specifically, we should look at what those Stories say, at who tells them, at what they promise, at who they convince, at who they offend, and at what results, if any, they are likely to produce.[471] And we should do this, when it will be sensible, via what I called choosing, reframing, and dissembling.

---

[471] This mission will seem more or less sensible depending on who reads these lines. For example, James Poniewozik, the chief television critic of the *New York Times*, feels comfortable declaring, in his *Audience of One: Donald Trump, Television, and the Fracturing of America* (New York: Liveright, 2019), p. 276, that "You could argue that the division in American politics isn't so much between parties or even ideologies but between narratives. One sees diverse groups as adding to the country's strength and talent; another sees them as competitors for limited resources .... One sees life like *Friday Night Lights*, where the team can only be as strong as the larger community; another sees it as *The Walking Dead*, where you hang tight with your own kind against teeming hordes of the Other." See also Alex Evans, *The Myth Gap: What Happens When Evidence and Arguments Aren't Enough?* (London: Transworld Publishers, 2017). Evans,

A Test Case

Yes, but none of this will be easy. For example, some of the difficulties of choosing, refraining, and dissembling appear in Christopher H. Achen and Larry M. Bartels, *Democracy for Realists: Why Elections do not Produce Responsive Government* (2016). The book was published by an outstanding university press (Princeton) and, according to its blurbs, is "a major contribution to modern social science" (Donald Kinder), "must-reading for anyone interested in democratic theory and American politics" (Robert Putnam), and "will become an instant classic, shaping our thinking on democracy for decades to come" (Thomas Mann).

The Folk Theory

Achen and Bartels open by declaring that, "in the conventional view," ordinary people have definite preferences; they express these in their voting; and government officials respond by serving those preferences. "That way of thinking about democracy," the book continues, "has passed into everyday wisdom …. It constitutes a kind of 'folk theory' of democracy, a set of accessible, appealing ideas assuring people that they live under an ethically defensible form of government that has their interests at heart."[472]

Achen and Bartels say that this way of thinking "has been severely undercut by a growing body of scientific evidence," by which they mean a set of research findings produced mainly by political scientists. That evidence shows that most people vote on the basis of how they *feel* rather than what they actually *know* about government policy and practices.

In the light of such evidence, Achen and Bartels propose that most Americans live, mistakenly, among unfounded beliefs which do

who describes himself as a "government advisor," says that *The Myth Gap* "is a book about stories" (p. xiii) because, to make our world livable, "we need powerfully resonant stories, and they need to be stories that unite rather than divide us. Not so long ago, our society was rich in these kinds of stories, and we called them myths. Today, though, we have a myth gap. And to fill it, we need new myths that speak about who we are and the world we inhabit" (p. xx).

472 Christopher H. Achen and Larry M. Bartels, *Democracy for Realists: Why Elections do not Produce Responsible Government* (Princeton: Princeton University Press, 2016), p. 1.

not match the facts of life. All American political thinkers are largely unrealistic, they say, because "both liberals and conservatives" believe that government is more responsive to "popular sovereignty" than it really is.[473] Or, in another formulation of the same charge, "American thinking, both popular and scholarly," is, regrettably, "dominated" by "the folk theory of democracy."[474]

This, says *Democracy for Realists*, is what explains why Abraham Lincoln at Gettysburg praised government "of the people, by the people, and for the people," and it is why Fourth of July speeches promote naive notions about what America actually was in the past and is today. Or, as Achen and Bartels scoff, "The history of democratic thought – including much contemporary political science – is marked by an addiction to romantic theories."[475]

Refuting the Folk Theory

Using political science research findings, Achen and Bartels explain in chapter after chapter of their book that the folk theory is mistaken, that elections don't *really* produce "mandates" (reflecting voters' preferences), that "reforms" and "referendums" don't *really* facilitate "popular control," that "retrospective voting" (punishing those who hold office and have ruled unsatisfactorily) is not *really* rational but based on ignorance in the short term and neglect of the long run, that people don't *really* vote on the basis of coherent policy inclinations but to express group memberships (via what is now called identity politics), etc., etc., etc.

After which *Democracy for Realists* offers its bottom line: "[We] are not prepared," say Achen and Bartels, "to supply, in this concluding chapter, a well-worked out, new theory of democracy." However, "[we can] summarize our findings," prepare the "intellectual ground on which a more realistic theory might be built, and highlight some of the key concepts and concerns" that may become parts of a new theory.[476]

---

473 *Ibid.*, p. 2.
474 *Ibid.*, p. 297.
475 *Ibid.*, p. 19.
476 *Ibid.*, p. 298.

Missing Stories

Democracy for Realists lays out a wide array of research findings and offers a challenging political analysis. The problem is that the book falls short of weighing in on political stories.

First, as I have noted in *Post-Truth American Politics*, most political scientists don't talk about or investigate matters as vague and nebulous as political stories (the *genus*), or political Stories (the *species*). Therefore, Achen and Bartels write about what they call a "theory." It is as if, for them, "theories," but not "stories," are to be studied by scientists, in the post-Enlightenment era which Max Weber described as "disenchanted."

Second, the theory that Achen and Bartels dismiss out of hand is actually a political story and even a political Story. Wherefore, and especially if it is a Story, its purpose is not to compute facts, like an equation, but to express sentiments, via rhetoric, which may help people to coexist and fit in to the place where they live. That is, Stories are for inspiration, for making the world meaningful, for showing us – not necessarily by counting what we can count – how our lives make sense, if at all, even unto the Story of Job.

In this context, the Declaration of Independence, Lincoln's great speeches, Franklin D. Roosevelt's Annual Message on "Four Freedoms," Martin Luther King, Jr.'s "I have a dream" call across the Reflecting Pool for civil rights, thousands of Memorial Day eulogies across the land, and academic treatises about "retrospective voting," are not there in order to convey laboratory or survey proofs about exactly how Washington and its components work or do not work at any particular time. They are parts of a Story, or a large narrative, which (a) portrays us all as players (citizens) in a democratic game, rather than (b) as subordinate people (subjects) who are excluded from that game, and which (c) makes us members of a community which may need fixing but which (d) in some deep, mysterious, and often optimistic way, tells us something of where we used to be, where we are now, and where we might go in the future.

Back to Postman

Democracy for Realists relates to what it calls the folk theory mainly to dismiss it as mistaken. On this score, we should recall the insight of Neil

Postman. It is the nature of large Stories, he said (although he did not use that term), "that people cannot live without them." What he meant was that members of a society *must* have Stories in order to think of themselves as a society, in order to enable themselves to live together as citizens (relatively) peacefully and (relatively) prosperously.

In other words, like taxes, Stories are the stuff of civilization. *Democracy for Realists*, however, is somewhere else. The book proposes that the folk theory (1) is believed by all Americans but (2) is not true. In which case, (3) those who believe in it should disown the theory.[477] Yet if what Achen and Bartels call a "theory" is actually a "Story," then their project (4) aims at disposing of something which Postman said – and on this I agree with him – Americans cannot live (well) without.

In other words, Achen and Bartels, as meticulous and scientific scholars, are so committed to "the facts" that they promulgate a great many of them unreservedly. In the process, however, they recommend throwing away what is, in effect, a national Story (they don't use that term) even though, as they put it, "unfortunately," we are "not prepared to supply, in this concluding chapter, a well-worked out, new theory of democracy."

Choosing, Refraining, and Dissembling

Here we arrive at brass tacks. In *Post-Truth American Politics*, I have discussed how challenging a particular Story might be accompanied by suggesting that people should switch to some safer Story which is available to them, such as Reinhold Niebuhr's notions about prudence and moral limits in American history.[478]

---

[477] As Achen and Bartels put it: "Just as a critical step toward democracy occurred when people lost faith [during the Enlightenment] in the notion that the king had been anointed by God, we believe that abandoning the folk theory of democracy is a prerequisite to both greater intellectual clarity and real political change" (p. 328). As we saw in this essay, however, conservative thinkers such as Karl Polanyi and Andrew Bacevich warned against such confidence, holding that changes do not always produce "progress" but might instead reduce "the welfare of the community." Philosopher William MacAskill, in *What We Owe the Future* (New York: Basic Books, 2022), *passim*, adds that, ethically speaking, any changes of principle and/or practice that we make today should be justified by how we believe they might affect the welfare of future communities.

[478] See Reinhold Niebuhr, *The Children of Light and the Children of Darkness: A Vindication of Democracy and a Critique of its Traditional Defense*, 2nd ed. (New York: Charles

Instead, in effect, Achen and Bartels lob a hand grenade into what they describe as how Americans traditionally think about the society which they live in and how its democratic character warrants devotion, support, and sometimes even sacrifice. But they do not ask if throwing hand grenades into public life is what social scientists should be doing.

Step sideways for a moment. Queen Elizabeth II's funeral took place in London in September 2022. During those several days, thousands of spectators watched her cortège pass, its flags snapping, its cavalry prancing, its bagpipes skirling, while impassive Grenadier Guards and somber Royal Family members slow-marched down historic avenues, and while additional thousands of people lined up for kilometers to pay their last respects at the Queen's coffin, which was topped by more than 2,900 gem stones in the glittering Imperial State Crown.

Let us note that these people were, for the most part, committed to a vision of themselves and their Queen where the vision – about Britain's one-time Empire, the great Commonwealth, parliamentary democracy, national unity, enduring grandeur, courage, duty, service, fortitude, devotion, loyalty, and more – (a) helps the United Kingdom hold together as a functioning and prosperous community but (b) is not entirely true according to available empirical evidence.[479] Should the numerous anchors, experts, and pundits who commented on the funeral spectacle for several days have told

---

Scribner's Sons, 1944, 1960), "Foreword to the First Edition," p. xiii: "Man's capacity for justice makes democracy possible; but man's inclination to injustice makes democracy necessary."

[479] For example, the vision surely downplayed how much damage the Empire inflicted on its colonial subjects during more than two centuries. See Harvard University's Caroline Elkins, *Legacy of Violence: A History of the British Empire* (New York: Knopf, 2022), pp. 13, 16: "Violence was not just the British Empire's midwife, it was endemic to the structures and systems of British rule. It was not just an occasional means to ... imperialism's end; it was a means and an end for as long as the British Empire remained alive. Without it, Britain could not have maintained its sovereign claims to its colonies .... Such violence included corporal punishments, deportations, detentions without trial, forced migrations, killings, sexual assaults, tortures, and accompanying psychological terror, humiliation and loss." Oxford University's Nigel Biggar, *Colonialism: A Moral Reckoning* (London: William Collins, 2023) is less critical of the British Empire. He concedes much of the Empire's violence but also praises Britain for ending the slave trade, establishing the rule of law, reducing tribal vendettas, and more.

those people, and others in the television-viewing audience, how unrealistic that Story is?

Put that another way. Most Americans want to live in a democracy, even if it is imperfect, rather than in any other sort of society. If, among them, a shared faith in democratic politics exists, even though it is somewhat mistaken, is that faith something which scholars and teachers should challenge without limit? Is handing out information (based on what we consider to be "the facts"), no matter what that information adds up to, the right thing to do?

Back to Weber

To recall a point from earlier chapters, what are we to make here of Weber's ethics of responsibility?[480] With regard to existing Stories, are we not obliged, somehow, to consider the likely consequences of our research and reporting? Or are only doctors, by the Hippocratic Oath, enjoined to "do no harm"?

In *Post-Truth American Politics*, I have said that I know of no simple answers to such questions. I therefore argued for always choosing, sometimes refraining, and occasionally dissembling, as rules of thumb for analyzing Stories. Such rules are not precise. But neither are the ways in which Stories intersect with politics.

---

[480] Weber said we should rank Stories (he called them "causes") as more or less dangerous. Let me note, then, as an Israeli, that, at the time of this writing, some very powerful Israeli politicians – such as Bezalel Smotrich, Itamar Ben-Gvir, and Orit Strook – have persuaded Israel's Prime Minister Benjamin Netanyahu to promote, against the Palestinians, an extremely dangerous interpretation of the Covenant (a Story) which they believe God made with Abraham. In that interpretation, God gave to Abraham and his descendants all of the Holy Land, thus theologically condemning negotiations to make a Palestinian state in any part of that Land. An alternative Story, which is less dangerous I think, and which is endorsed by many but not a majority of Israeli voters, is that Israel must end the military occupation of the West Bank and the Gaza Strip to enable Israelis and Palestinians to separate into two independent states – this is the so-called "two-state solution" – so that each nation will prosper by itself and avoid going to war against the other, rather than living together in the same state as they do now.

INDEX

Milton Keynes UK
Ingram Content Group UK Ltd.
UKHW040334041023
429911UK00002B/21

9 781009 396455